Levels of Socio-economic Development Theory

Levels of Socio-economic Development Theory

David Jaffee

PRAEGER

New York
Westport, Connecticut
London

Library of Congress Cataloging-in-Publication Data

Jaffee, David.
    Levels of socio-economic development theory / David Jaffee.
        p.   cm.
    ISBN 0-275-93285-0 (alk. paper).—ISBN 0-275-93286-9 (pbk. :
alk. paper)
      1. Economic development.   2. Economic development—Social aspects.
3. Organizational change.   4. Dependency.   5. Developing countries—
Economic policy.   I. Title.
HD75.J33   1990
338.9—dc20   89-48749

Library of Congress Catalog Card Number: 89-48749
ISBN: 0-275-93285-0 (cloth)
     0-275-93286-9 (paper)

First published in 1990

Praeger Publishers, One Madison Avenue, New York, NY 10010
An imprint of Greenwood Publishing Group, Inc.

Printed in the United States of America

∞

The paper used in this book complies with the
Permanent Paper Standard issued by the National
Information Standards Organization (Z39.48-1984).

10 9 8 7 6 5 4 3 2 1

For Marianne,
Katy,
and
Anna

CONTENTS

CONTENTS

PREFACE

The aim of this book is to acquaint readers with contemporary theories of development. Most theories of development attempt to explain international disparities in income, wealth, standard of living, and economic growth. The complexity of this task has given rise to a vast assortment of competing explanations. A basic challenge for students sifting through the literature is to organize the theories in a way that illuminates the differences and similarities among the various theories. With this purpose in mind, the theories of development in this book are organized by "levels of analysis"—individual, organizational, societal, and international. Some theories focus on the characteristics of individuals within a nation; others, on the structure of work organization; others, on the existing social, economic, and political institutions; and still others, on a nation's position in the international system. These levels of theory identify a particular set of factors as the cause of development or underdevelopment. Organizing theories of development in this way serves to emphasize the important role of theory, and of the levels of theory in shaping one's description, explanation, and interpretation of the development process. It also points to one of the leading sources of debate and controversy among development theorists: What is the appropriate level of analysis for understanding socio-economic change?

The material presented in this book is geared for advanced undergraduate and graduate courses in development, social change, and comparative sociology, as well as those dealing with topics in political economy and socio-economics. The scope is inevitably interdisciplinary. The study of development touches the subject matter of sociology, economics, political science, and psychology. The book discusses theories associated with each of these fields. Further, the focus of theoretical concern extends beyond the problems of less-developed nations to the advanced industrial societies. No nation is immune to the continuous struggle for economic growth and accumulation. Recent and chronic economic crises plaguing advanced capitalist economies indicate the precarious nature of each and every development strategy.

I wish to express my sincere thanks to the following friends and colleagues who read sections of the manuscript and offered many valuable suggestions: Alan Neustadtl, Harland Prechel, Sally Simpson, Randall Stokes, and Rhys Williams.

Special thanks are due Marilyn Glass, who typed the manuscript with skill, patience, and a good measure of tolerance.

1

INTRODUCTION: THE MEANING OF DEVELOPMENT AND THE LEVELS OF THEORY

In any area of scholarly inquiry, there are always several ways in which the phenomena under study may be sorted and arranged . . . the observer may choose to focus upon the parts or upon the whole, upon the components or upon the system. . . . Whether he selects the micro- or macro-level of analysis is ostensibly a mere matter of methodological or conceptual convenience. Yet the choice often turns out to be quite difficult, and may well become a central issue within the discipline concerned. . . . The responsible scholar must be prepared to evaluate the relative utility—conceptual and methodological—of the various alternatives open to him, and to appraise the manifold implications of the level of analysis finally selected (Singer 1961:77).

The study of socio-economic development is a truly interdisciplinary venture. Analyzing the causes and consequences of social change requires crossing the conventional boundaries of academic social science. Each field of social science—anthropology, economics, history, political science, psychology, sociology—has some insight to contribute. Socio-economic change shapes, and is shaped by, individual perceptions and beliefs, cultural patterns, economic organizations, methods of production and distribution, socio-political arrangements, and the international economy. The process of development is broad and all-encompassing. It is difficult to discount the importance of any social pattern or institution.

Explaining development is further complicated by the fact that each discipline is composed of subdisciplines, subareas, and subfields that tend to emphasize one particular slice of social reality. Social scientists tend to focus upon one or a small number of factors as the key to understanding socio-economic development. The purpose of this book is to review some of the most prominent contemporary theories of development.

It is important to understand the way theory shapes our interpretation of all social events, including socio-economic development. Theories provide a framework for making sense of the world. Most things we observe, experience, and study are extremely complex and are caused by a variety of different factors. Each and every factor responsible for some event or process cannot be taken into account. We therefore, often unconsciously, rely on a theoretical framework that directs our attention to a very small part of the larger reality. In this way theories serve to simplify complex processes by offering a set of concepts that allows us to select, categorize, and label various forms of action and change, and to make inferences about cause and effect.

The process of socio-economic development, which is complex and wide-ranging, has given rise to a multitude of theories, explanations, arguments, and assertions. Students of development are often perplexed by the vast assortment of explanatory models. There are so many theories, perspectives, and approaches, all claiming to explain development; yet they conflict with and contradict one another. How is one to choose among competing explanations? Are there correct and incorrect theories? What evidence can be used to determine the empirical validity of the various models of development?

These questions hound all areas of scientific inquiry, but they are especially problematic for the social sciences. Explanatory precision is a difficult task, given the subject matter of social science. Humans and their social organizations defy the regularity and predictability of the natural and physical sciences. There are no iron laws of social behavior and social change. Therefore, the field of social science is open to a variety of equally compelling explanations and interpretations.

The political content of the subject matter in the social sciences is an equally important reason for divergent and contradictory theoretical claims. All social theories contain certain political assumptions and policy implications. There are conservative, mainstream, orthodox, liberal, radical, and Marxist social theories. The development and selection of a theoretical model is, therefore, heavily influenced by one's political predilection rather than by an objective assessment of the available data and evidence. Even when social scientists consult the available evidence, questions can be raised about the validity of data or the methods of analysis employed, or empirical results can simply be ignored. A theoretical conversion is an unlikely outcome.[1]

This book makes no claim or attempt to rise above this theoretical and methodological fray. The theories of development reviewed in it are not subjected to any rigorous systematic empirical assessment. Rather, the fundamental purpose here is twofold. First, the book seeks to illuminate the diversity of theoretical perspectives, the assumptions and logic underlying them, and their political implications. Second, it is important to recognize that a large part of the debate among development theorists hinges on the level of analysis at which the various theories operate. The "level-of-analysis" question is particularly critical and serves as the organizing theme for the chapters in this book. We turn to that question after a discussion of the meaning of development and social change.

THE MEANING OF SOCIO-ECONOMIC DEVELOPMENT

There is considerable disagreement over the meaning and measurement of socio-economic development and what actually constitutes "true development" (see Baster 1972). This debate will not occupy us here. Most of the theories reviewed in this book attempt to explain international disparities in economic wealth and social welfare. *Socio-economic development*, in this sense, refers to the ability to produce an adequate and growing supply of goods and services productively and efficiently, to accumulate capital, and to distribute the fruits of production in a relatively equitable manner. The gap between rich and poor, developed and underdeveloped, or First and Third World nations reflects variations in these socio-economic capacities. While there is widespread agreement that socio-economic development involves production, accumulation, and distribution processes, the study of development has been heavily influenced by particular sociological concepts and economic measures. Sociological studies have emphasized the traditional-to-modern transition as part of the larger process of social change. Economists, on the other hand, tend to view development in terms of economic growth. Each of these perspectives has shaped the contemporary definition of socio-economic development.

The Concept of Social Change

In sociology, the terms "social change" and "development" are frequently used interchangeably. A closer examination of the development literature, however, indicates that the two terms differ in their level of generality. Social change is usually regarded as a constant, ongoing process affecting many areas of life, whereas development is used to denote more specific, empirically measurable, forms of change.

According to Kornblum (1988:566), *social change* refers to "variations over time in the ecological ordering of populations and communities, in patterns of roles and social interactions, in the structure and functioning of institutions, and in the cultures of societies." Social change, as this definition implies, is a broad, multidimensional process affecting numerous aspects of social life. It operates at a variety of socio-economic levels. At the individual level there are the changes in cultural beliefs and attitudes; at the organizational level there are changes in roles and patterns of interaction; at the societal level there are changes in the functioning of major institutions and the demographic processes of rural-to-urban migration.

The classical study of social change has been dominated by the assumption that each of these patterns of change—ecological, cultural, interactional, and institutional—is an inevitable subcomponent of a broader logic moving societies from the traditional to the modern form. This *modernization perspective*, along with the associated *traditional-modern dichotomy*, has a long legacy in classical sociological thought, and it is deeply entrenched as the leading conceptual apparatus employed for the purpose of understanding the most significant features of social change and development.

The traditional-modern dichotomy owes a great debt to the classical sociological thought of Emile Durkheim (1858–1917) and Ferdinand Tönnies (1855–1936). Durkheim's primary concern was with the mechanisms holding societies together and promoting social order. He believed that the bases of social order differ in traditional rural and modern industrial societies. Durkheim used the term *mechanical solidarity* to describe the form of cohesion and solidarity in traditional society. Under mechanical solidarity, social order is derived from the similar experiences and shared sentiments of members of the rural preindustrial community. Common values serve to promote order and harmony, and to regulate social behavior.

Mechanical solidarity is undermined in the transition to the modern industrial society. In place of similar sentiments and experiences, the increasingly complex division of labor in modern society subjects members to different roles and experiences. There is a shift from a "collective conscience" to an emphasis on individualism. Members of the society assume specialized roles and occupations. Differentiation, rather than similarity, is the defining characteristic of the modern society.

In Durkheim's scheme the changing organization of society is problematic because members no longer share common experiences and sentiments—there is no value consensus. Durkheim used the term *anomie* to describe the destabilizing effect of the breakdown of mechanical solidarity on individuals and the larger society. Anomic society is characterized by normlessness. Norms regulating and controlling behavior are absent or poorly defined, and the society is threatened with conflict and collapse.

In Durkheim's model, however, a new form of solidarity emerges that stems from the division of labor in the modern society. This is called *organic solidarity*. Cohesion in modern systems is based on the functional interdependence of members of society. With the complex division of labor each and every member of society depends on other members for the provision of goods, services, and needs. Like the biological organism, the parts are interdependent and complement one another. This results in a different but equally effective form of social unity and a new normative system that regulates the occupational responsibilities and forms of exchange and interaction among members.

Ferdinand Tönnies presented a similar scheme that described the most significant features of the traditional-to-modern transition. Tönnies used the term *gemeinschaft* to refer to the rural traditional society, in which personal relationships are close and informal and there is a general sense of community among members. This is contrasted with the *gesellschaft*, the modern urban society characterized by formal organizational and impersonal relationships among members. In the transition from *gemeinschaft* to *gesellschaft*, close-knit communal bonds are severed and replaced by relationships in the modern urban mileu that are transient, short-term, and shallow. Under *gesellschaft* individuals are said to be isolated, atomized, and poorly integrated components of a larger mass.

The theories of Tönnies and Durkheim are precursors of contemporary models of development that use the traditional-modern distinction. These contemporary models assume that the labels "traditional" and "modern" are empirically applicable and that the transition from the traditional to the modern is inevitable and desirable. Tönnies and Durkheim emphasized the roles and interaction patterns in traditional and modern societies. Contemporary modernization theorists, following this model, believe that the role and interaction patterns of the modern society—differentiated, specialized, and impersonal—are requirements for development.

Another element of the traditional-modern scheme that has been accepted by certain contemporary development theorists is the assumption that the traditional-to-modern transition creates social-psychological strains on the population. Durkheim's concept of anomie and Tönnies' argument about the negative consequences of broken communal ties raise the specter of potential instability in the modern urban mileu. These reservations have been incorporated in the theory of the *mass society*. This theory assumes that rapid social change will have negative psychological effects, increasing the likelihood of unconventional, radical, and violent political behavior. Such instability is regarded as a negative by-product of the traditional-to-modern transition and has resulted in development theories that prescribe institutional mechanisms aimed at preventing potential insurrection.

The classical sociological theory of Max Weber also plays a prominent role in the traditional-modern image of social change. The most notable feature of modern society for Weber was the emergence of bureaucratic organization. Bureaucratic operating principles, applied to organizations and institutions, were regarded by Weber as the superior and most efficient means for the accomplishment of goals. Because the characteristics of bureaucratic organization—clearly defined goals and duties, universal rules and regulations, specialization, meritocracy, accountability, rational legal authority—are associated with modern society and its central institutions, many theories of development prescribe these institutional characteristics and operating procedures as requirements for socio-economic development.

The traditional-modern comparison, with its long legacy in the sociological discourse on social change, has evolved from a pair of descriptive, polar-opposite, ideal-type concepts into an explanatory model of development. The application of the traditional-modern model to contemporary theories of development is discussed in Chapters 2 and 4.

The Meaning of Development

While the concept of social change tends to be used as a catchall term for any and all forms of change over time within a society, the concept of development usually refers to some measurable form of progress. The most common measure of development, by far, is gross national product (GNP). GNP measures the total value of goods and services produced by a nation during a single year. For purposes of comparability GNP is expressed in a common currency, usually dollars, and reported in per capita terms to take into account the size of a nation. Thus, GNP per capita is interpreted as the value of output in a given year per person.

Using this measure, development is said to take place when GNP per capita increases over time. The change in GNP per capita between two points in time is referred to as the *economic growth rate*. The growth rate is calculated as the percentage change in GNP per capita. GNP and growth rate data are reported on an annual basis for most nations in the world.

A study by David Morawetz (1977) examined changes in GNP from 1950 to 1975 for "rich" and "poor" nations. The rich nations are those members of the Organization for Economic Cooperation and Development (OECD).[2] The poor nations are those not included in the OECD that make up the regions of South Asia, East Asia, Africa, Latin America, and the Middle East. Morawetz was interested in whether the gap between rich and poor countries, as measured by GNP, was growing, shrinking, or remaining stable.

Morawetz calculated two different measures of the gap between rich and poor nations—the absolute and the relative gaps. The *absolute gap* is the difference between the average GNP per capita of the rich and poor countries. In 1950 the gap was $2,218; in 1975 it had grown to $4,863. Thus, the absolute gap between rich and poor nations more than doubled over the 25-year period.

The *relative gap* is measured as the GNP per capita of poor nations as a percent of the GNP per capita of rich nations. Such a measure is often used to indicate that even though the average GNP per capita of the poor nations (or a single nation) increases, it may still make up a smaller percent of the average GNP per capita of the rich nations. This is because the rich nations may have experienced even higher rates of growth. Thus, the relative position of nations remains unchanged.

The relative gap decreased from 1950 to 1975. In 1950 the average GNP per capita of poor nations amounted to 6.7 percent of the average GNP per capita of the rich nations. In 1975 it increased to 7.2 percent of the average GNP per capita of rich nations. However, it should be pointed out that the closing of the relative gap indicated by these figures is primarily the result of the inclusion of Middle East oil-exporting nations. Extreme disparity still exists. If we examine the change in the relative gap for different regions, the data indicate that the average GNP per capita of South Asia, Africa, and Latin America was a smaller percentage of the average GNP per capita of the rich nations in 1975 than in 1950.

The data analyzed by Morawetz paint a rather pessimistic picture about the future prospects for less-developed nations. At least collectively they seem to be falling farther and farther behind advanced industrialized nations on the GNP measure. Much of this book is devoted to examining explanations for why this gap is so large and why it continues to grow.

A more general issue concerns the adequacy of GNP as a measure of development. Suppose the data indicated—which they do for certain nations—a rapidly growing GNP and a closing gap. Would this economic performance signal development, modernization, and progress? There is considerable debate over this question. It was once believed that a growing and expanding GNP was the ultimate goal of development because a growing economy brought an improvement in all spheres of life. The economy would be richer, jobs would be created, people would have more money, the quality of life would improve, poverty would disappear, industry would expand, and life as we know it in the advanced industrial economies would be reproduced in the less-developed nations.

This optimistic scenario has not come to pass. More important, even for nations that have been lucky enough to experience rapid rates of economic growth, many of the assumed positive by-products have not materialized. This fact calls into question the validity of GNP as an adequate indicator of development. Rapid growth has not necessarily resulted in higher incomes for workers, better health care, more housing, a reduction in poverty, or a more democratic or egalitarian society. On the contrary, there are numerous examples of rapid growth accompanied by a decline in the standard of living, increasing poverty, rising inequality, and political repression. In fact, these are frequently regarded as necessary, though hopefully temporary, conditions for growth.

These problems with GNP measures have led to an increasing emphasis on alternative measures of development. Development is more than a purely quantitative economic process; it should also involve a qualitative improvement in the life of a nation's population. Much of the contemporary theoretical and empirical literature is concerned with the provision of basic needs and the physical quality of life as alternative means of assessing the developmental performance of nations (Chapter 4). This typically involves focusing upon the poverty rate, infant mortality, literacy, educational enrollment, caloric intake, access to medical care and the availability of housing and sanitation facilities. While the provision of these basic needs is related to a nation's level of economic development, economic growth is an insufficient condition for ensuring the availability of these services. These components of the quality of life are potential, but not inevitable, products of an expanding economy. An important question for development researchers is the conditions under which economic growth translates into an improvement in the quality of human life or, conversely, is achieved at the expense of the population.

The overemphasis on GNP also tends to obscure the structural obstacles to development that pervade many less-developed economies. The concept of *underdevelopment*, also widely used in the contemporary development literature, denotes a socio-economic structure characterized by a reliance on the export of raw materials and primary products, regional disparities in economic growth, poorly integrated economic sectors, domination by external forces, a poorly developed class structure, and a chronic balance-of-payments crisis fueling the accumulation of debt. The historical and contemporary forces responsible for these structural impediments are a major focus of the international-level models of dependency and world-system theory (Chapter 6).

LEVELS OF ANALYSIS AND SOCIAL SCIENTIFIC EXPLANATION

Levels of Analysis and Socio-economic Development

This chapter began by noting the vast number of theories designed to explain socio-economic development. In this book theories of development are distinguished by their level of analysis. In the scheme proposed here, a theory's *level of analysis* is based on the "units of analysis" selected to explain socio-economic development.[3] Different theories draw attention to particular sets of causal factors. In the study of development these might be the attitudes and values of individuals, or the system of industrial relations, or the rules and logic governing the economic system, or the policies of the state, or the forces of the world economy. These independent variables, or predictors of development, are observed at different levels of analysis. Attitudes and values are observed at the *individual level*, industrial relations at the *organizational level*, the logic of the economic system and policies of the state at the *societal* (or national) *level*, and the forces of the world economy at the *international level*.

This book examines these four distinct levels of theory guiding the explanation of socio-economic development. The general framework is summarized in Table 1.

At the level closest to individuals and their beliefs and actions are individual-level theories. These theories of development focus on the values, motives, attributes, and characteristics of individuals as the source of socio-economic development. Theories of this type emphasize individual traits such as the level of achievement motivation, the degree of entrepreneurial talent, the attachment to modern ideas, or the possession of human capital. These perspectives share the assumption that individual characteristics translate into national social development.

Theories at the organizational level of analysis examine the structures and practices of work organizations and enterprises in order to determine how they influence human behavior and contribute to social, economic, and political development. Organizations are structures with characteristics distinct from those at the individual level. The structural properties of organizations cannot be reduced to the individual attributes of their

Table 1
Levels of Analysis in the Study of Socio-economic Development

Level of Analysis	Causal Mechanism	Example of Theoretical Proposition	Effect
International	World Economic Forces and International Interactions	The greater the dependence on direct foreign investment, the slower the rate of economic growth	N A T I O N A L
Societal	National, Political, Economic, and Social Institutions	The greater the reliance on capitalist principles, the greater the rate of economic growth	D E V E L O P M E N T
Organizational	Structure of Work Organizations Producing Goods and Services	The greater the use of Japanese management principles, the higher the rate of productivity and economic growth	N T OR U N D E R
Individual	Individual Beliefs, Attitudes, Motives, and Characteristics	The greater the "need for achievement" among a nation's population, the greater the rate of economic growth	D E V E L O P M E N T

members. An organizational level theory might argue, for example, that successful agricultural development requires a particular land tenure arrangement, or that economic growth depends on the use of certain industrial organizational techniques, such as a Japanese management system. In both cases the organizational arrangement used for producing goods is assumed to be a (or the) leading causal factor in explaining development.

The societal level of analysis directs attention to the causal role of broader social institutions in the process of development—how social institutions are organized, the economic system used to produce and distribute goods, the type of political system, and the role of government policies. This level of analysis links societal characteristics—institutional,

political, and economic—to the level and rate of socio-economic development. The societal level is distinct from, and often determines, organiza-
tional- and individual-level attributes, and its properties cannot be reduced
to some combination of organizational or individual components. One
might argue, from the societal perspective, that rational bureaucratic
principles must govern a society's institutions if the society is to develop
in a smooth and efficient manner, or that free-market capitalism is the most
effective economic system of production and distribution.

Furthest from individuals, the international level of analysis focuses on
political and economic forces that operate at the global level. In the
international system nations interact with one another, commodities are
traded and exchanged, capital investment flows across national borders,
and nations are subjected to interdependence, domination, and exploitation. These global dynamics are seen as significant factors for socio-
economic development. Existing at the highest level of analysis, the
international system subsumes all those levels below it, and is not
reducible to the properties of the lower levels of analysis. International-
level theories of development, such as dependency and world-systems
theory, are powerful models that have gained considerable prominence
since the mid 1970s. These theories focus on the role of colonialism,
imperialism, foreign capital investment, and trade patterns in shaping the
course of social change in less-developed nations.

The organization of development theories by levels of analysis serves
four important purposes. First, this organizing framework introduces
readers, in a sequential and systematic way, to a subject matter that grows
increasingly complex as broader levels of analysis are considered. Second,
the presentation of topics follows a logical hierarchy of analytic schemes
that are fundamental to social scientific theory and explanation. Third, this
organizing framework reveals one of the major sources of debate and
controversy in the field of development—the appropriate level of analysis.
And fourth, this method provides an analytic framework for the study of
national and international development that cannot be gained from a strict
case study approach.

Two final points about the levels of analysis framework deserve mention. First, many theories of development cannot be pigeonholed into a
single level of analysis. While most theories tend to focus on a particular
level as the site of the primary causal factor, the best theories integrate and
account for different levels of analysis in an interconnected causal chain.
Second, while we distinguish among explanatory levels of analysis, all the
theories of development discussed in this book seek to explain social
change and development at the national level. For this reason theories of

socio-economic development can be regarded as systemic or macro because they are concerned with change in whole societies or social systems over time. The primary theoretical variation, therefore, lies in the accounts and causal factors used to explain societal-level changes.

Levels of Analysis and Social Theory

The level-of-analysis issue extends far beyond the field of socio-economic development. The debate among development theorists over the appropriate level of analysis is just one component of a more fundamental theoretical debate in social science (see Edel 1979). One of these theoretical divisions involves the distinction between *individualistic* and *structural/holistic* explanations of human behavior. Individualistic explanations view human behavior as largely the product of individual characteristics and personality traits. Structural/holistic explanations, in contrast, interpret human behavior in a broader social context, as the result of external social forces, structures, and institutional arrangements.

In the study of development these two positions are often counterposed when we seek to explain human behavior in the economic sphere. Agricultural producers or peasants, for example, have often been described as behaving in traditional and irrational ways because they do not attempt to maximize agricultural output or invest in methods that would enhance agricultural productivity. This behavior, in turn, is said to hamper the development of the agricultural sector. This individualistic explanation locates the problem in the attitudes and values of peasants and, therefore, suggests the need for modern rational values to be internalized by these agricultural producers. The structural/holistic approach, on the other hand, examines peasant behavior in the context of the incentive systems of broader institutional structures. From this perspective peasant and tenant systems of agricultural organization, and the associated lack of control over the agricultural surplus by producers, serve as disincentives for extra investment of labor and capital.

These divergent theoretical interpretations have different policy implications. For the individualistic approach the solution is to change the mind-set of the peasants; for the structural/holistic model the solution is to change the organizational system under which goods are being produced. Many of the major disputes in social science stem from the individualistic versus structural/holistic theoretical cleavage (see Campbell 1981 for some other dividing lines).

Some additional examples from the contemporary social science literature illustrate the broad scope of this level-of-analysis debate. One question is whether it is appropriate to use individual-level attributes to explain structural and societal-level phenomena. Unlike the study of peasant behavior, this question involves explaining a nonindividual-level outcome using individual-level variables. One might argue, for example, that national development depends upon a certain set of individual beliefs about the value of work. This is an individual-level explanation of development. The use of individual characteristics as explanatory variables is a hotly contested issue. A common position on this question argues that:

> individual interests, motivation, and perceptions, can never adequately explain individual behavior. Both organizational and societal factors must be taken into account in explaining variations in rates of individual behavior occurring in different types of situations. *But the reverse is not possible—one cannot explain organizational or societal processes by theories of individual behavior or social interaction.* [emphasis added]. (Alford and Friedland 1985:15)

When the level of analysis of the dependent variable is nonindividual, the individual-level factors lose their explanatory utility. Organizational and structural factors take precedence. This is a significant issue for the study of development, given the propositions advanced by theorists employing the individual level of analysis.

A second, related problem emerges when connecting the individual and nonindividual levels of analysis. A common tendency is to infer, from organizational and societal characteristics, the psychological attributes of the individuals within these organizations and societies. Individual attributes are then used as the explanation for organizational and societal characteristics. A recent study of working-class consciousness directly addresses the logic of this argument, and views it as:

> an example of the fallacy of *psychological reductionism*—the assumption that the structure of any society can be reduced to the wishes and motivations of its members. Society is much more than a straightforward embodiment of the wills of the people within that society. . . . The attempt to explain structural phenomena solely in terms of psychological attributes has been justifiably derided in social science as psychological reductionism. (Vanneman and Cannon 1987:15, 19).

Examining the causal role of different levels of analysis also raises the distinction between "voluntarism" and "determinism." The *voluntarist* perspective assumes that social actors—individuals, organizations, and nations—can easily convert desires into actions; that actors exercise free will to do as they please and shape their own destiny. The *determinist* view tends to emphasize the obstacles, structural impediments, institutional arrangements, and power relations that prevent actors from freely realizing their subjective desires. There is considerable overlap between the individualistic and voluntaristic, as well as the structural/holistic and deterministic, modes of social explanation.

The competing levels of analysis and associated theories of development reviewed in this book reflect these general theoretical debates. The levels-of-analysis scheme can be viewed as a "nested hierarchy" of progressively broader levels of analysis where behavior and change at each level is constrained by forces operating at higher level(s) of analysis. The freedom of individuals to act upon their values, beliefs, and convictions is often constrained by the organizational context in which they work, the distribution of power in the society, the forces of the international system. As we move to higher reaches of the hierarchy, away from the individual level, international factors may seem remote and distant, yet they affect individuals through their impact on the intermediate societal and organizational levels. In a similar fashion, productive enterprises (organizations) are constrained by societal-level arrangements and international forces. Last, the freedom of nations to act as they please and pursue particular policies is constrained by a global system of inequality and world market forces. Situating the relationship between levels of analysis in this way points to the structural constraints on social action and socio-economic processes.

THE PLAN OF THE BOOK

The chapters in this book are organized around the levels-of-analysis scheme outlined above. Chapter 2 reviews some of the leading individual-level theories of development. These include theories that focus upon psychological attributes and cultural practices as well as those which emphasize the human capital characteristics of the population. In addition, this chapter elaborates the unique human contribution to the production process, and the philosophical and sociological sources of the individual-level theses. The claims and logic of the individual-level model of development are subjected to a critical assessment. The purpose of this chapter is to introduce students to the individual-level arguments about development and to point to the significant shortcomings of such models.

Chapter 3 is devoted to the organizational level of analysis. The organization of work and production at the enterprise level is a largely overlooked area of development theory, yet if one peruses the development literature, there are many models and case studies that point to the importance of organizational arrangements and structures. The chapter begins by pointing out the role of organizations in shaping the motives and behavior of individuals. The purpose is to provide a corrective to the purely individual-level formulations. Both agricultural and industrial organizational arrangements influence the pace of development, political dynamics, and the geographic distribution of populations. These features of the development process are discussed for both developed and less-developed nations. Some of the contemporary arguments of organizational theorists regarding the most appropriate organizational form for dynamic economic production are reviewed.

Chapters 4 and 5 address theories of development that operate at the societal level. These are the national forms of social, political, and economic organization that are said to influence development. In Chapter 4 some of the classic arguments of structural functionalism and the modernization school are critically examined. Included as well are economic theories of development, GNP models, and basic needs approaches. Chapter 5 takes up issues of comparative socio-economics and the claims about the relative efficacy of capitalism and socialism. The contrast between theory and practice is emphasized. The chapter concludes with a review of some contemporary prescriptions for developed and less-developed nations involving corporatist and export-oriented development strategies.

Chapter 6 moves the analysis of development to the highest plane—the international system. In this chapter the highly popular dependency/world economy approach is presented. This includes an outline of the basic propositions of this perspective and some of the modern theorists associated with this framework. The international mechanisms affecting development—the capitalist world system, the exchange of commodities, the flows of capital and investment, and the interaction among nations—are examined. The chapter concludes with a discussion of the "new international division of labor."

Chapter 7, the conclusion, summarizes the main points and arguments advanced throughout the book and encourages efforts to integrate the different levels of analysis.

NOTES

1. On the subjective and political nature of theory construction and selection, see Gouldner (1970:chs. 1 and 2). The problems of "imperfect empiricism" in the social sciences are neatly reviewed in Spencer (1987).

2. Members of the OECD are Australia, Austria, Belgium, Canada, Denmark, Finland, France, Federal Republic of Germany, Greece, Iceland, Ireland, Italy, Japan, Luxembourg, the Netherlands, New Zealand, Norway, Portugal, Spain, Sweden, Switzerland, Turkey, the United Kingdom, and the United States.

3. The term "level of analysis" is widely used in discussions of social theory and explanation and in the analysis of different social scientific topics. The definition tends to vary depending on the context. Perrow (1986:142) uses the term to denote the "levels of environment" that progress upward toward the world level and regress downward toward individuals and their biological makeup. Scott (1981), in sharp contrast with the usage here, determines the theoretical level of analysis by the nature of the dependent variable. Alford and Friedland (1985) use levels of analysis to construct a metatheoretical model, and attempt to link each level of analysis to major theoretical perspectives on the state.

2

INDIVIDUAL-LEVEL THEORIES OF SOCIO-ECONOMIC DEVELOPMENT

At the most basic level, all forms of economic accumulation involve human energy and effort. For this reason a great deal of development theory is aimed at the micro level and considers psychological and cultural attitudes, dispositions, values, and needs related to human motivation and effort. Without the expenditure of human energy, there is no production, no surplus, and no growth. Where individual differences correlate with variations in the size or growth of output, it is common for these individual differences to be held accountable for the developmental performance. Such a logic has produced myriad explanations directed toward discovering the key motivating psychology conducive to high rates of output. This chapter explores the origins of the link between individual characteristics and socio-economic development, and reviews the literature isolating the individual characteristics required for development. Prior to this task we briefly consider the distinct contribution of the human resource to the production process.

INDIVIDUAL DIFFERENCES AND THE UNIQUE NATURE OF LABOR

As already noted, one of the great theoretical divides in social science is between individual and structural explanations of behavior and social change. Increasingly, social scientists are attempting to develop theoretical models that bridge the micro and macro levels (see Coleman 1986). The general position advanced in this chapter is that individual or micro-level theories of development are inadequate. This does not mean, however, that properties operating at the individual level are irrelevant for socio-economic development; only that they must be linked to other structural characteristics of a society. In this section we consider the unique nature of humans as a factor in the production process.

The phrase "everyone is different" is both trite and asociological. However, it reflects a fundamental truth: individuals can be distinguished from other elements of the production process, such as land and capital, in that humans cannot be standardized. Individuals enter organizations and institutions with different experiences, thoughts, and orientations. In addition, because humans have the capacity to reflect upon and change their environment, their control and coordination are forever problematic. People may objectively possess skills and capacities, but in order for these to be of any value in the process of production, they must desire to use these abilities. For the same reason that "all people are different," humans are also the most unpredictable and uncontrollable elements of the production process.

This fundamental point on the unique nature of humans is a central element in managerial theories of work behavior and Marxist theories of production. The unique properties of humans, or labor, lie at the foundation of the two fields of study. The entire field of organizational behavior is based on the generally implicit assumption that managing the human resource for the purpose of production is the most challenging of all tasks. Other elements of the production process, such as machines and raw materials can be molded and shaped with the appropriate technology. There is no analogous solution for humans. Thus, great effort is spent studying and manipulating the values and attitudes of individual workers. The time devoted to the study of organizational behavior belies the assumption of neoclassical economics that land, labor, and capital are equivalent commodities, and suggests that there are, in fact, significant differences between these factors of production. Organizational structure and design, the primary topics of Chapter 3, provide the most common strategies for the predictable control of human motivation and behavior.

Marxian political economy also distinguishes labor from other factors of production. A distinction is made between "true commodities," such as machines, products, and natural resources, and the "pseudo-commodity" of labor (Storper and Walker 1982). Though labor takes a commodity form in the sense that people "sell" their mental and physical energy for a wage in a labor market, and are subjected to the laws of supply and demand, labor differs from true commodities in a number of important ways.

The distinction is best illustrated in the production process where an employer brings together the factors of production—land, labor, and capital—and must confront the fact that human labor is conscious and alive; labor can collectively and/or individually react to its environment. Thus, labor can make demands on employers that increase its cost. Workers can decide, after they have been hired, that they should be paid more money, that working conditions are unsafe, that fringe benefits are necessary. Through strikes, work stoppages, and union organization people are able to "up the ante" after an employment relationship has been established. Other commodities, once purchased, do not possess this capacity.

Further, as organizational behavior specialists are equally aware, there is no guarantee that the employer will get what is paid for with the "pseudo-commodity" of labor. Workers can consciously reduce or increase their work effort. Managerial strategies are specifically designed to control this fluctuation. Organizational techniques and ideologies designed to shape the behavior of workers are an often overlooked but integral part of the development process.

Last, labor leaves the work place at the end of the day to engage in leisure and sustenance, to reflect and develop new ideas, to involve itself in communities and cultures, and to consume material goods. All of these processes further influence the work orientation and world view of the individual.

The distinctions between human labor and other commodities have many political-economic implications that are taken up in subsequent chapters. They are all based on the very simple micro-level observation that we began with—humans cannot be standardized; unlike "true commodities" they are conscious, reflective, and indivisible.[1] This basic axiom is important for the study of socio-economic development. One of the key ingredients required for the production of goods and services is labor power, and a large part of the process of economic development involves social relations and ideologies aimed at controlling this uncertain and unstandardizable element. In this sense, production is never simply a technical matter but always a social process. In the remainder of this chapter we review critically a number of approaches to socio-economic development that focus on the question of individual differences.

INDIVIDUALISM AND DEVELOPMENT

It is not surprising that individual-level explanations for development look to ideologies and values that prevailed alongside the rise of industrial capitalism. The Industrial Revolution brought forth the most rapid development of the productive forces and accumulation of wealth. It is logical, therefore, to examine not only the material but also the subjective forces that may have been responsible for this monumental economic expansion. This question—the causal role of subjective versus objective factors as explanations of social change—has generated an intense and ongoing debate among social scientists. It has been taken up as part of the broader conflict between Weberian and Marxist social theory.

Max Weber and the Protestant Ethic

A major theoretical impetus for individual-level models is provided by the classical sociological theory of Max Weber, most notably in *The Protestant Ethic and the Spirit of Capitalism* (1930). Weber is closely associated with the argument that ideas foster the emergence of socio-economic systems. This *primacy of ideas* position—that individual and collective beliefs are causally prior to the development of social structures, institutions, and systems—was presumably motivated by Weber's desire to challenge the Marxian contention that the dominant beliefs and ideas of a society are merely a reflection of the material interests of the ruling class. In the Marxist model, the ruling ideas of any period are seen as ideological beliefs that legitimate and justify the existing socio-economic system. Thus, in contrast with the "primacy of ideas" logic, socio-economic systems emerge first and are followed by the development of a belief system that supports the existing arrangements and the interests of the dominant class. Weber's response to this position should be seen, more precisely, as an attempt to demonstrate the mutually reinforcing nature of, or "elective affinity" between, the socio-economic organization and prevailing value system of a society (see Lowy 1989).

For our purposes, however, the key question is what kinds of ideas are said to have an elective affinity with capitalist social organization, and thus contribute to rapid economic growth. For Weber, Protestantism contained certain beliefs that supported and promoted the rise of capitalism. There are two basic elements of Protestantism that tend to be linked to capitalism in Weber's work. The first, associated with Lutheranism and the Reformation, is the break from the Catholic tradition of the church as the sole intermediary between God and the believer, and the establishment of a more individualized system of belief. Under Protestantism, believers have a direct relationship with God that goes beyond the church. The Protestant concept of the "calling" implies that one's duty to God extends to all spheres of life, including work. This represents a departure from the traditional, collective, and institutional forms of social control of the Catholic church, a rejection of the distinction between monastic and worldly pursuits, and the promotion of greater individualism and autonomy. These developments are viewed as consistent with the demands of a capitalist market economy.

The second and more important component of Protestantism said to support the institutions of capitalism is derived from the Calvinist sect. Calvinism associated hard work and job commitment with godly duty and virtue, and ultimate salvation. The association of work, and the worldly pursuit of material gain, with religious sanctity represented a sharp break from traditional Roman Catholic ethics and provided religious justification for forms of economic behavior and motivation demanded by an emerging capitalist economy. This Calvinist version of Protestantism, emphasizing individual effort devoted to hard work and worldly success, is the foundation of the Protestant ethic. A crude and vulgarized version of the Weberian perspective might, therefore, argue that attachment to the ideals of the Protestant ethic is a necessary condition for dynamic capitalist expansion.[2]

In fact, Weber's analysis did not posit such a causal ordering. Prior to the emergence of a Protestant belief system, capitalist socio-economic forces were already operating. Weber's point was to show how the material interests and behaviors of the emerging bourgeoisie were supported by a particular religious ideology. The "elective affinity" between material interests and beliefs suggests that each facilitates the advancement of the other. The mutually reinforcing nature of ideas and interests has largely been obscured in the more recent individual-level models of development that instead assert the causal priority of ideas and culture.

Eisenstadt's (1968a) treatment of the Protestant ethic thesis represents a more balanced approach in its elaboration of the institutional and structural factors facilitating and reinforcing Protestant religious beliefs. This distinguishes Eisenstadt from some of the modernization theorists to be considered shortly. As he points out, many of the new social roles, such as entrepreneur, existed prior to the rise of Protestantism. Protestantism was absorbed and institutionalized, and eventually flourished, because it complemented many preexisting forms of social and political organization. For example, the individualism and autonomy often associated with Protestant doctrine were, in Western Europe, already established to some degree in social and political organizations. The regional and political autonomy of urban areas, and the politically decentralized structure of Western towns, are often cited as major explanations for the rise of the West (Chirot 1986:ch. 2). More generally, the strength of Eisenstadt's analysis is its recognition of the contingent nature of religious beliefs. The extent to which Protestantism, or any other belief system, will generate modernization or economic expansion hinges on the presence or absence of a variety of other economic, social, and political structures.

Liberalism and Individualism

The philosophy of classical liberalism has had a major influence on individual-level theories of development in two important ways. First, the philosophy of liberalism has contributed to the Western bias for explanations that emphasize the causal role of individual beliefs and actions. Second, liberalism advances a number of assumptions about essential human motives and behavior that are assumed to promote development.

Methodological individualism refers to the view that individual beliefs and actions are the primary causal forces explaining social change. This perspective can be linked to classical liberal theory and its development alongside the emergence of capitalism. The rise of institutions unique to capitalism—free and mobile labor and free markets—shaped the basic assumptions of classical liberal theory concerning the latitude of human freedom and the role of human action. The deterioration of feudal bonds of servitude and lifelong ties to the land led to the development of a free labor force that was able to move voluntarily to employment opportunities and determine the conditions of its employment. Free labor is regarded as a necessary condition for the development of capitalism. Free markets involve the voluntary association of buyers and sellers of goods and services, and free choice over what to buy and what to sell. In the classical liberal world view, individual freedom is embodied in the operation of markets. Since market exchange requires no institutional intervention or coercion, and is based on free and voluntary association, individuals are viewed as sovereign and autonomous agents able to shape their lives and futures.[3]

With the emergence of market institutional arrangements, liberal philosophy apportions significant weight to the actions of individuals in the explanation of social phenomena. No longer do caste, craft, and feudal distinctions determine one's life chances and the shape of society. Individual freedom and choice in a capitalist society elevate the causal role of human behavior and characteristics. Liberal philosophy's individualist bias permeates Western social science and is evident in the widespread tendency to explain human action with psychological models, social problems as the product of individual cultural deficiencies, and development as the result of individual beliefs. Often overlooked are the institutional, structural, and environmental forces shaping human behavior, generating social problems, and influencing development.

A second key element of classical liberalism is the assumption that human action is motivated by selfish, greedy, or material desires. In this view, human choices are driven by utilitarian principles of self-interest. Macpherson (1973) uses the term "possessive individualism" to describe this strand of liberal thought. According to Macpherson, liberal philosophy defines human freedom as the ability of humans to use their individual capacities to maximize satisfaction. One's level of satisfaction, in turn, is based on domination over things and objects—the ownership, consumption, and possession of material goods. It is assumed that individuals have an inherent and insatiable desire for material goods, and therefore the liberal notion of freedom involves the right of individuals to pursue these strivings.

These assumptions about the human essence have worked their way into theories of development at two different levels. At the individual level, self-interest and the desire to maximize material gain are regarded as rational sentiments that promote aggregate socio-economic development. At the societal level, the argument for the superiority of capitalism as a development strategy is based on the assumptions that humans are by their very nature selfish and greedy and, thus, development requires adopting institutions that are consistent with these inherent human motivations.

The Work Ethic

Elements of the Protestant ethic and classical liberal theory have been combined to produce the contemporary notion of the "work ethic."[4] The work ethic refers to "beliefs about the moral superiority of hard work over leisure or idleness, craft pride over carelessness, sacrifice over profligacy, earned over unearned income, and positive over negative attitudes toward work" (Andrisani and Parnes 1983:104). This overworked concept has been incorporated into countless theoretical explanations that amount to little more than simplistic tautologies. The typical argument runs something like this: Individual adherence to the work ethic is the key to successful collective performance. Economically effective organizations and societies must (now, by definition) contain members with a strong attachment to the work ethic; less successful enterprises must (also by definition) possess members who have not internalized or developed the work ethic. The existence of the work ethic is assumed, rather than empirically established, when other organizational or individual characteristics are present. Following this logic, the decline of the work ethic is the universal culprit responsible for any socio-economic ill—the decline of the U.S. economy, the loss of U.S. international competitive advantage, the rise in poverty, and on and on.

The problems with the work-ethic logic as an explanation for socio-economic development will be dealt with shortly. As an ideology, however, it is an important force motivating and controlling labor. The essential message of the work-ethic ideology is directed toward labor, not capital. A poorly developed work ethic is rarely cited when we observe the rich at leisure, accumulating unearned income through inherited wealth and property. Instead, it is evoked in the case of the unemployed, under-employed, or destitute laborer. The work ethic is a virtue reserved for the working classes. As a labor official once remarked, "If hard work were really such a great thing, the rich would have kept it all for themselves" (cited in Barbash et al. 1983:55).

A more limited application of the work ethic thesis concerns its relation-ship to individual rather than collective outcomes. Does one's attachment to the work ethic predict one's labor market status and/or economic success? The standard logic posits that those with a well-developed work ethic will be more successful economically than those who lack this trait. This view of economic success reinforces the belief that individuals are ultimately responsible for their status and position in society. The empirical literature attempting to determine the effects of the work ethic on labor market success is full of contradictory but statistically significant findings. There are also a large number of statistically insignificant "non-findings." The evidence is mixed. One can show a broad set of results that conform to the expected association between the work ethic (measured empirically in about as many ways as it is used stylistically) and labor market outcomes, such as occupational status and income.

However, concurrent association does not establish causality. One can argue that the causal direction should be reversed, with the work ethic malleable and subject to modification based on one's labor market status and experience. There is strong evidence suggesting this pattern. Longitudinal studies, for example, indicate that those with the highest rates of unemployment and fewest weeks worked experience the greatest weakening of the work ethic; low-paying jobs with little room for career advancement are related to increasing anti-work attitudes; youths in low-status jobs at the start of a period, and those who move into low-status jobs, are more likely than comparable youth in high-status jobs to lower their labor market ambitions and decrease their commitment to the work ethic (see Andrisani and Parnes 1983). In short, the studies suggest that initial labor market status has a greater influence on the work ethic than vice versa.

Given this ordering of the relevant variables, and the fact that labor market status is to a large extent determined by social class background, there will be a substantial portion of the population who, due to their lower position in the stratification system, have a loose attachment to the work ethic as measured attitudinally. Behaviorally, on the other hand, this same population generally chooses work over nonwork, knowing that getting paid is better than starving, and is realistically aware that economic success requires more than positive attitudes about the goodness of hard work.

Finally, even if everyone were to start out with a solid work ethic, it is difficult to imagine how this state of affairs could be maintained in stratified societies and organizations that base their ability to accumulate wealth on the very inequalities that seem to undermine the work ethic. Capitalist market economies are based on and maintain an unequal distribution of income and productive resources. Work organizations in most societies are built upon hierarchical structures of unequal authority and power. In this sense, the structural reality of economies and work organizations mediates the attitudinal disposition of individual workers. Again, the causal primacy of individual-level subjective beliefs in the explanation of individual success or national development is difficult to sustain.

MODERN INDIVIDUALS AND NATIONAL DEVELOPMENT

The logic that leads theorists to examine the values and attitudes prevalent during the rise of industrial capitalism informs the *individual modernization approach* to development. This perspective argues that Third World development depends upon the diffusion and adaptation of modern Western values. It combines a classic dose of ethnocentrism with the comparative logic that turns the association between modern values and wealthy societies into a proposition about the causal prerequisites for socio-economic development. Again, the causal logic assumes that values and attitudes precede forms of social organization and economic growth; that values and attitudes prevalent in the industrial societies are responsible for the aggregate level of social wealth. It then follows that the aggregate poverty of less-developed nations is the result of the inappropriate values held by people living in these nations. This model condemns the values held by those in poor countries to guilt by association.

The individual modernization arguments represent only one component of the broad modernization paradigm. Broadly, the process of modernization involves the proliferation of modern ideas and institutions in "traditional," "backward," or "stagnant" regions and nations. The diffusion of modern culture and social structure is said to facilitate development, growth, and industrial progress. In this optimistic scenario all nations are seen as potential recipients of the modern recipe for development. As modern ideas, behaviors, and organizational systems are inevitably adopted, nations will follow the path and eventually achieve the status of the advanced industrial nations of the West. Development, in this model, is viewed as an evolutionary and unilinear process whereby all nations evolve from traditional to modern forms and follow a single trajectory of socio-economic progress.

Modernization theorists have tended to emphasize the modernizing impact of ideas and/or institutions. In this chapter we focus on the arguments at the individual level that identify the cultural beliefs and behavior patterns required for development. What follows is a sampling of some of the leading works in this area. The reader will note that there is a tendency to cite the most ideal and romantic elements of Western capitalist culture as the necessary conditions for the socio-economic development of Third World nations.

The literature emphasizing the dynamic role of the individual entrepreneur fits squarely into this tradition. The social economist Joseph Schumpeter (1949) considered the entrepreneur to be the harbinger of economic growth. Entrepreneurs are innovators who take the factors of production, combine them in new ways, and apply these novel amalgamations to the production process. The introduction of innovative techniques by entrepreneurs restructures the production process and moves it to a qualitatively higher level. This is the essence of innovation and the key to socio-economic development.

Less clear, in this formulation, is the motivation for entrepreneurial activity. Schumpeter suggests that the profit motive is an insignificant factor, and this is echoed in subsequent theories emphasizing the individual agent. For Schumpeter, the profit motive is incidental because the entrepreneur is not the bearer of risk and, therefore, is less concerned with the extent to which expenses are compensated by returns in profit. It is capitalists and shareholders who put up the capital and who, ultimately, are seen as the beneficiaries of entrepreneurial innovation.

Other writers have attempted to specify the conditions generating the entrepreneurial spirit and the factors facilitating the translation of this spirit into dynamic economic activity. This effort involves, inevitably, a consideration of other levels of analysis. Rostow (1956), for example, suggests that the emergence of an entrepreneurial elite requires more than simply an appropriate value system. It also requires an emerging elite that is denied access to the conventional sources of power and prestige—an oppositional elite. Additionally, the society in which this entrepreneurial class emerges must be flexible enough to allow this incipient elite opportunities for economic advancement, even if these may be unconventional. Finally, Rostow suggests that, despite all the emphasis placed on the "entrepreneurial precondition," there are a number of broader structural changes that precede or accompany most economic "take-offs" (see Chapter 4). Among those he cites are changes in agricultural techniques and the development of a market system of exchange.

Hoselitz (1957) also places entrepreneurship at the center of his explanation of development and, like Rostow, believes that there are a number of broader structural conditions that contribute to the institutionalization of this belief and behavioral system. Hoselitz maintains that many forms of social and cultural change begin with behaviorally deviant actions among certain members of the population; the actions of certain groups violate the norms of appropriate behavior. Merchants and businessmen, for instance, are deviants in the context of Western feudal society. Logically, deviant behavior is likely to be pursued by those culturally and socially marginal segments of society who, given their marginal status, must locate a niche in the social structure from which income can be derived. Jewish and foreign moneylenders in medieval Europe are examples.[5] A final condition for the institutionalization of entrepreneurialism is the redefinition of societal objectives by existing elites. However, "as long as an elite is interested primarily in maintaining its own position of power and privilege, this may mean that the masses are degraded, that economic progress is slow, and that general poverty prevails" (Hoselitz 1957:40). Ironically, this is a common description of the behavior of the capitalist elite in Third World nations today.

In spite of these theoretical attempts by Rostow and Hoselitz to broaden the framework for analyzing the emergence of value-cultural systems and associated forms of economic behavior, the fundamental question remains: If entrepreneurs are required for dynamic socio-economic development, what prevents their emergence in the less-developed societies? This question is troubling since, in the individual-level models, backward and less-developed nations by definition lack the particular personalities and individuals necessary for economic growth. The basic concern of individual-level modernization theorists is to identify the cultural variations between traditional and modern societies that are responsible for their divergent economic statuses.

One of the strongest and most influential statements on this issue is offered by Everett Hagen in his *On the Theory of Social Change* (1962). For Hagen, personality types and their behavioral manifestations are the source of social change. "The interrelationships between personality and social structure are such as to make it clear that social change will not occur without changes in personalities" (p. 86). As it happens, modern societies possess *innovational personalities,* a psychological complex that should breed some version of the Schumpeterian entrepreneur. Traditional societies, on the other hand, are the recipients of a less flattering portraiture—the *authoritarian personality.*

The "innovative personality," according to Hagen, is the mirror image of the "authoritarian" type. Innovative individuals respond to new experiences and stimuli not with frustration but with a sense of understanding and imagination; they do not evade problems but are attracted to the challenge of dealing with new situations; they do not rely on fantasy or magic solutions because for them the world is orderly and understandable. If any anxiety exists among this personality type, it is the "gnawing feeling that they are not doing enough, or not well enough" (1962:99). Anxiety is reduced through creative achievement. Members of traditional society, on the other hand, are uncreative:

> He perceives the world as an arbitrary place rather than an orderly one amenable to analysis and responsive to his initiative. His unconscious processes are both inaccessible and uncreative. He resolves his relationships with his fellows primarily on the basis of ascriptive authority. He avoids the anxiety caused by facing unresolved situations in the physical world by reliance on the judgment of authority. (1962:98)

The psychology of development, expressed in Hagen's personality types, is also found in the work of Daniel Lerner (1958), whose study of Middle Eastern societies had an enormous impact on modernization theory. Lerner also identifies an ideal personality type, one he claims emerges from the experience of physical mobility in Western industrial society:

> People in the Western culture have become habituated to the sense of change and attuned to its various rhythms. . . . We are interested in empathy as the inner mechanism which enables newly mobile persons to operate efficiently in a changing world. Empathy, to simplify the matter, is the capacity to see oneself in the other fellow's situation. This is an indispensable skill for people moving out of traditional settings. . . . It is a major hypothesis of this study that high empathetic capacity is the predominant personal style only in modern society,

which is distinctively industrial, urban, literate, and participant. . . .
To wit: social change operates through persons and places. . . . If new
institutions of political, economic, cultural behavior are to change in
compatible ways, then inner coherence must be provided by the
personality matrix which governs individual behavior. We conceive
modernity as a participant style of life; we identify its distinctive
personality mechanisms as empathy. (1958:47, 49–50, 78)

This empathetic style of life can be contrasted with Lerner's description
of traditional society and people. Traditional societies, in his account, are
nonparticipant and characterized by a poorly developed division of labor.
Traditional people are constrained by kinship ties and lack bonds of
interdependence, their horizons are limited and parochial, their decisions
involve only "known quantities" and familiar situations (Lerner 1958:50).

It should be noted here that Lerner's comparative descriptive analysis
is also a well-known and familiar quantity because it conforms directly to
the earlier observations of Durkheim (1966) on the bases of social
solidarity in traditional and modern societies and Tönnies (1963)
gemeinschaft (traditional community) and *gesellschaft* (modern society)
typology (see Chapter 1). The only difference is that Lerner employs these
heuristic typologies as explanatory variables. Traditional patterns of life,
interaction, and decision making are responsible for the traditional and
backward state of the society. As with many of these kinds of models, cause
and effect are muddled and it is difficult to establish whether beliefs and
personalities are the cause or the consequence of traditionalism and
modernity. Finally, in further differentiating "participant" from "nonparticipant" society, Lerner argues that in the modern participant society
people are educated, well informed, able to change jobs freely, and
expected to hold opinions on important public matters. Traditional
societies are characterized by just the opposite.

The influential work of David McClelland (1961) represents a further
variant of the individual modernization approach. Instead of a work ethic,
an innovative personality, or an empathetic-participant orientation, Mc-
Clelland argues that the central ingredient for economic progress is the
presence in the population of a "need for achievement." According to
McClelland, the motivational drive to overcome challenges, take risks,
advance one's interests, and succeed for the sake of an inner feeling of
accomplishment is derived from a national cultural context. His analysis
indicates that this need for achievement is statistically associated with the
socio-economic development level of nations. McClelland believes the

need to achieve must be instilled in Third World populations if their nations are to develop economically.

This theory is not without empirical support, though methods and conclusions have been the subject of a great deal of controversy. McClelland examined the content of popular documents, such as folk tales, children's stories, and textbooks from preliterate as well as modern societies, in an effort to gauge the cultural message disseminated and the extent to which it reflected the need for achievement. He then investigated the relationship between the level of the need for achievement displayed in the documents and socio-economic development. He found that the high-need-for-achievement nations had higher levels of economic development. In spite of this innovative and interesting theory-testing strategy, little additional cross-national support has been garnered for the achievement formulation.

Inkeles and Smith (1974) provide yet another version of the individual modernization perspective. The classic sociological dichotomy differentiating traditional and modern societies is applied to individuals such that we find two kinds of people, those who are traditional in character and personality structure and those who are modern. Like McClelland, the authors construct an elaborate research methodology involving cross-national interviews and an overall modernization scale. The methodological sophistication and rigor of the research is impressive indeed, and the authors place a great deal of confidence in their findings. They define the "modern man" as follows:

> He is an informed participant citizen; he has a marked sense of personal efficacy; he is highly independent and autonomous in his relations to traditional sources of influence, especially when he is making basic decisions about how to conduct his personal affairs; and he is ready for new experiences and ideas, that is, he is relatively open-minded and cognitively flexible. (1974:290)

Inkeles and Smith believe that these basic attitudes and values support modern institutions and thus facilitate the modernization of society. They go on to note that modern institutions require people who can "discharge responsibility without constant close supervision"; who operate with trust, confidence and sympathy toward co-workers and subordinates; who are "flexible and imaginative in the interpretation of roles" (1974:314–15). In sum, there is an identifiable modern personality type possessing a special set of traits that facilitate, and are compatible with, the process of modernization and economic development. A modern social structure requires modern individuals.

Two basic problems with the conclusions of Inkeles and Smith's study are also applicable to the parallel formulations of Hagen, Lerner, and McClelland. These concern some of the character traits that are labeled "modern" (rather than traditional). Inkeles and Smith believe that the modern person is characterized by participatory political tendencies, a developed sense of efficacy, the ability to arrive at decisions autonomously and independently, and an open and flexible approach to new experiences and world views. Since this psycho-cultural mind-set is closely related to the level of modernization, we should find this empirically grounded version of the Renaissance human in ample supply in modern industrial societies. However, in the United States, which is often held up as the embodiment of all that is modern, the most recent and best available evidence (Hamilton and Wright 1986) indicates that for the vast majority of citizens the major focus of life is the family, and the major concern is providing for the family and "making ends meet." Though typically associated with traditional societies, it appears that communal-kinship ties and basic economic concerns structure and shape the lives and routines of the world's most modern citizens.

Further, the characterization of the modern society and population as necessarily participant is refuted by the evidence for at least the U.S. polity: over half of the eligible population in the United States does not even engage in the simplest of political acts—voting; most Americans are ill informed about most issues and exhibit low levels of political sophistication (Converse 1964; Verba and Nie 1972); most prefer the "simple, concrete or close to home" to the "remote, general, and abstract" (Converse 1964); and large proportions of the U.S. population express feelings of political inefficacy, powerlessness and distrust toward politicians and the political system (Wright 1976). All of this suggests that the modern participant society described by Inkeles and Smith, and Lerner, is a fictional account or a utopian vision of a future democratic citizenry and society. At minimum, this evidence casts doubt on the idea that participant personality traits are causally related to the level of socio-economic development. The modern person, as defined by these accounts, is a rare species indeed.

None of this is meant as an indictment of the U.S. mass character structure, nor as a declaration of the traditional nature of U.S. society. Rather, it is a statement about individuals that can be only understood within the broader context of the socio-economic organization of the society in which they operate. There is abundant evidence indicating that levels of participation and perceived efficacy and autonomy (the "modern" traits) are related to one's social class position. This suggests that the modern person is not a spontaneous creation but a product of circumstance; that the opportunity for individuals to become modern in the sense described by Inkeles and Smith is not equally distributed within modern societies. Many of the praiseworthy modern traits identified by these theorists require resources of power, authority, and wealth. As these are unequally distributed and/or entirely absent for the vast majority of citizens, so, too, are many of the consequent personality traits. The same sort of stratification system that produces the differential socio-cultural experience across classes within a nation is mirrored at the cross-national level in such a way that variations in national-aggregate wealth and power are translated into personal experiences and attitudes that may appear either traditional or modern. The critical issues are the origin of these experiences and attitudes, how they relate to broader systems of power and inequality, and whether they determine socio-economic development.

This raises a second problem involving the values and attitudes that supposedly buttress modern institutions. Among these, again using Inkeles and Smith, are the ability to accept and discharge responsibility without close supervision, to manifest mutual trust and confidence in co-workers, to subordinate special interests to the goals of the larger organization, and to be flexible in the interpretation of rules. These alleged features of industrial organization are, in fact, rarely found even in the modern capitalist societies. In contrast, the organizational forms contributing to the development of modern capitalism involve hierarchy, inequality, supervision, and the rigid control of workers. In producing for profit and a world capitalist economy there has historically been little incentive to institute the participatory forms of industrial organization implied by Inkeles and Smith. In fact, they run counter to the interests of the international and national economic elites. While these elites may contain those modern persons who possess participatory skills, are aware of their influence, and maneuver without traditional constraints, they are at the same time constrained by a logic that eschews economic democracy and equality for those occupying lower socio-economic positions. In each of these examples we find a definition of the "modern" that is driven by an abstract, romantic, and empirically nonexistent image of the modern citizen and society.

A third and final rendition of the modern individual model is found in the work of Clark Kerr et al. (1964). In their theory of industrialism they emphasize the particular value structure of industrial society:

In the industrial society science and technical knowledge have high values, and scientists and technologists enjoy high prestige and rewards. . . . Education also has a high value. . . . The industrial society is an open community encouraging occupational and geographic mobility and social mobility. Industrialization calls for flexibility and competition; it is against tradition based upon family, class, religion, race or caste . . . the work force is dedicated to hard work, a high pace of work, and a keen sense of individual responsibility for performance of assigned norms and tasks . . . industrialization requires an ideology and an ethic which motivate individual workers. (1964:25–26)

Unlike the previous formulations, there is greater ambiguity over whether these highly valued traits are the cause or the consequence of the industrialization process. In some sections of the work the standard causal order is reversed in dramatic fashion. Industrialism is viewed as an almost teleological force, having a purpose and logic all its own that is largely independent of social forces or forms of economic organization. Once industrialization takes hold, other aspects of the society and polity conform to its imperatives. It is a package deal that includes only positive features. These are typically characteristics derived from advanced Western capitalist societies and seen as the inevitable by-product of the industrialization process.

This aspect of the theory of industrialism has given rise to *convergence theory*, the view that all industrial societies, regardless of political-economic philosophy, require certain values and modes of social organization. The ideologies that motivate and legitimate forms of authority and control, as well as the structure of control itself, are seen as imperatives of industrialism rather than as the product of particular forms of social organization such as capitalism, socialism, or fascism. As societies industrialize, they become more and more alike, and eventually converge, in their essential social, political, and economic features.

Many of the issues related to the industrialism theory are addressed in subsequent chapters on work organization and larger society-wide political-economic arrangements. One component of the industrialism theory relevant to the individual level emphasizes the role of labor training, skills, and education. This "human capital" approach is considered after a more systematic critique of the individual modernization model.

A CRITICAL ASSESSMENT OF INDIVIDUAL-LEVEL FORMULATIONS

There are many criticisms of the individual-level modernization theories presented above. Some of these involve the logic used and assumptions made by the theorists, while others point to the clear limits of these models as explanations for socio-economic growth. Portes (1976) presents a general critique that addresses many of the main problems with these theories. It is worth summarizing and elaborating some of his arguments.

Portes contends that there has been too much emphasis on beliefs and values in modernization theory because of the influence of structural functionalism. Structural-functionalist theory, which dominated sociology in the 1950s and 1960s, viewed the cultural system—the value-normative features of society—as a leading source of social order, social structure, and social change. In this theory values and beliefs assumed a major explanatory role in understanding macro social phenomena. In turn, this led to a relative neglect of other factors, such as the organization of the economy, the material interests of different groups, and the use of ideology to legitimate the system. Subjective factors, operating at the individual level but shared by members of society, took precedence over objective structural factors in the explanatory model of development. The claim that this represents a modern application of Weber's arguments in *The Protestant Ethic and the Spirit of Capitalism* is equally problematic. According to Portes (and as noted above), Weber situated the emergence of ideas squarely within the context of historical-structural forces, and thus these theorists are mistaken in evoking Weber for the purpose of positing the primacy of ideas.

A second difficulty concerns the "additive" model of social development, in which the transition to a modern industrial society is seen as a function of the number of people imbued with a particular set of Western values. Portes attributes this logic to the voluntarist position. In this formulation individuals exercise free will and are therefore able to translate their modern sentiments and desires into purposive action, unencumbered by structural obstacles and impediments. In reality, the ability to develop the "work ethic" and/or become a "modern man" is mediated by the socio-economic position of individuals. Opportunities for the acquisition of material goods are unequally distributed, as are those which permit the acquisition of a particular value orientation. Furthermore, even if we were to assume that all the members of society could suddenly raise their "need for achievement" or some other praiseworthy level of consciousness, it is difficult to imagine that this would create a necessary and sufficient condition for the modernization or industrialization of society. More likely, we would then begin listing all the other societal features that would have to be adjusted for such a transformation to take place. This, in itself, is testimony to the limits of such a model.

Portes goes on to list three often neglected factors that must be considered in a sociological model of development. The first—*structural constraints*—is probably the most important, serving as a fundamental corrective to individual-level formulations. In contrast with the view of voluntarism, one must recognize the existence of structural constraints in the form of social organizations and the distribution of material resources. These place limits and obstacles on both the emergence of certain value orientations and forms of behavior and the development of the larger society. Economic and political structures must be considered, and possibly overthrown, if particular values are to be advanced in the transformation of society. For example, the set of values found in Inkeles' modern man—participant, independent, and autonomous—could be realized, for a significant portion of the population in many nations, only through political, and probably violent, struggle with entrenched elites. The normative models of modernization theory tend to highlight stability and harmony rather than conflict and struggle.

A second aspect of the sociology of development, according to Portes, concerns those *Western values whose impact might retard rather than promote economic development*. Specifically, Portes cites "consumption-oriented" values. While these are an integral part of Western industrial culture, they may serve to stimulate excessive demands by the population that cannot be satisfied, or place a strain on existing resources more wisely directed toward other forms of investment. If we consider the behavior of those Third World individuals who have had the greatest exposure to Western values of entrepreneurship and consumption, we often find a legacy of elite behavior bordering on fraud, corruption, co-optation, and conspicuous consumption. The historical record is replete with documentation of the "comprador elite" who served, first and foremost, foreign multinational interests, and the wealthy landowning elite who squandered valuable foreign exchange for the importation of Western luxury products. The point is that the internalization of Western values in non-Western less-developed nations can prove as much an obstacle to as a harbinger of economic development.

The *evolutionary character* of the individual modernization model is the final point raised by Portes. This common criticism of the modernization model notes the historical and developmental path that is imposed on less-developed nations. In a typical scenario traditional nations presumably follow the path of industrial societies as modern cultural values are diffused and internalized. This scheme does not recognize the historical legacy that has created the "traditional" societies as well as the national and world economic structural constraints that make universal industrialization along Western lines highly unlikely. The qualitatively different nature of less-developed nations, a product of historical world economic forces, suggests a very different future and developmental trajectory.

The evolutionary element in modernization theory stems from the time-space fallacy common to many models of social change. At any one point in time we will notice that significant differences exist between nations in gross national product, percent of the population living in urban areas, infant mortality, and so on. These are variations between spatial or geographic units. There is a tendency to impose a temporal causal logic on this kind of cross-sectional data. It is then assumed that the richer, more urbanized nations have been developing longer and that the poorer, less urbanized nations see, in the modern industrial nations, their inevitable future. Modernity becomes a function of time, and the historical roots of contemporary Third World problems are disregarded. It is as if the process of development begins at some arbitrary moment when, according to modernization theory, less-developed nations are touched by modern values.

There are a number of additional points that address the general limitations of the individual-level models. First, many of these theories are plagued by a tautological or circular logic. This leads to the following type of proposition: Nations that industrialize possess the appropriate culture, and those which fail to develop along Western lines lack this culture. When nations decline, the culture is eroding; when they "take off," it is expanding. The presence or absence of the requisite value structure is determined a priori by the degree of industrial and economic growth—the effect creates the cause. This problem was noted above in the application of the "work ethic," and, as we shall see, crops up with structural modernization theories as well.

A second causal fallacy is the assumption that values and attitudes precede economic development. It is equally plausible that the psychological mind-sets of populations are the consequence rather than the cause of certain forms of development. It is the nature and course of socio-economic development that influences objective economic forces, material interests, and the proliferation of values and ideas. This point is related to the Weberian/Marxist question concerning the primacy of ideas and/or objective material conditions. In the individual modernization models there has been a one-sided preference for the former.

Third, subjective beliefs that are regarded as the key to economic progress must be assessed critically, for they often serve to legitimate existing inequalities. In many cases these ideologies are designed to motivate human energy and to lay responsibility for failure at the feet of the individual. The great emphasis placed on the "work ethic" and the "need for achievement" in Western society is consistent with this purpose. Poor societies and individuals are assumed to lack these positive traits, and this lack is regarded as the source of their economic failure. This simplistic logic does not grasp the multi-level complexity of the development process.

Fourth, it is imperative that the level-of-analysis limits of the individual-level theoretical ventures be emphasized and clearly understood. Individual-level theories are most useful when explaining differences between individuals. Can models based on the individual level of analysis explain variations across broader units of analysis such as organizations and nations? Apparently individual modernization theorists believe they can. The "additive" image of development suggests that the progress of the social whole is little more than a function of the sum of the individual subjective parts. This is base reductionism. While this kind of formulation crosses levels of analysis, it fails to adequately incorporate the structural properties of groups, organizations, societies, and world economic forces. The properties emerging from these larger units must be taken into account. This is the fundamental basis for the rejection of the individual-level model. In Andre Gunder Frank's (1969:67) critique of the individual modernization model, he states that it is:

> inadequate precisely because the scale of their theory and hypotheses is already too small to treat adequately the dimension and structure of the social system which gives rise both to development and underdevelopment.

Or, as Valenzuela and Valenzuela (1984:112, 114) conclude:

> Though there are variations in the literature, the *level of analysis* of a substantial tradition in the modernization perspective, and the one which informs most reflections on Latin America, is behavioral or microsociological. The primary focus is on individuals or aggregates of individuals, their values, attitudes, and beliefs. . . . And yet, precisely because modernization theory relies on a simple conceptual

framework and a reductionist approach, it is far less useful for the study of a complex phenomenon such as development or under-development.

Models that incorporate the logic of broader socio-economic structures are the subject of the chapters to follow.

There is one final point worth mentioning, given the current state of the world economy. This involves the argument that Western-based values emphasizing individualism and self-interest are somehow the necessary condition for economic, or at least capitalist, expansion. The contemporary case of Japan represents the most obvious challenge to this assertion, and there is no shortage of literature on the subject (Abercrombie et al. 1986:ch. 5; Morishima 1983; Lehmann 1982; Cochran 1985; Dore 1973). The values of nationalism, paternalism, and anti-individualism are said to characterize modern Japan (Morishima 1983), and stand in dramatic contrast with Western value systems. Rather than obstacles to growth, these cultural sentiments have generated a most dynamic form of capitalism. Much of this success has been contingent on the interplay between the paternalistic and collectivist sentiments and the broader organizational structures that define Japanese industry. It is important to emphasize in the Japanese case the point that has been made for the Western experience—the cultural values that are linked to economic success are not independent or autonomous but are reinforced and chan-neled in the context of objective organizational and societal structures and practices.

THE HUMAN CAPITAL APPROACH

Human capital is defined as an individual's productive skills, talents, and knowledge (Thurow 1970). Consistent with the individual-level mod-ernization approach, this theory explains growth and development by focusing on the characteristics of individuals. On the other hand, human capital theory recognizes that these traits are developed and nurtured in a broader organizational context. Human capital theory has been used to explain wage differences between individuals (Becker 1964), but our interest is in the way investment in human resources promotes national growth and welfare. Like physical capital, human capital can be improved, expanded, and made more productive through investment. Quite often this investment is undertaken by the government, for there are society-wide benefits in expanding the educational, training, and health capacities of the population. In this view the key to promoting productivity and economic growth is government investment in human capital (Denison 1965). For example, Harbison contends that

> The goals of development are the maximum possible utilization of human beings in productive activity and the fullest possible development of skills, knowledge and capacities of the labor force. If these goals are pursued, then others such as economic growth, higher levels of living, and more equitable distribution of income are thought to be likely consequences. (cited in Adelman and Morris 1973:101)

This basic idea is translated into the commonly held view that poverty in the Third World could be alleviated if people in these nations possessed modern technical skills. It should also be noted that the emphasis on education has links to the individual modernization models presented above. That is, through educational institutions individuals can be exposed to modern beliefs and values, which, in turn, presumably affect their orientation toward work and achievement. We have already discussed the limitations of this explanation for growth, and therefore concentrate on the more direct economic role played by educational expansion.

Studies by the World Bank (1980:ch. 5) suggest that there may be some payoff from investing in the expansion of primary education. Comparing farmers having four years of primary education with those who had none indicated that farm output was greater for the educated farmers. According to the authors of the report, "primary schooling is a training in how to learn, an experience in self-discipline and in working for longer-term goals" (1980:257). Apparently this experience can be applied to the actual operation and management of agricultural production with measurable consequences. In spite of the strong and consistent support for their hypothesis linking primary education and agricultural productivity, the relevance of these findings for the broader population and economy is quite limited. This particular study was of self-employed farmers who owned and controlled their own productive resources. For the vast majority of the population, who own no productive property, the educational payoff is contingent, first, on employment, that is, finding a job; and, second, on the capital technology applied to the labor process. Neither of these conditions should be taken for granted. In short, the central question is whether and how the expansion of education and skills will actually yield aggregate economic benefits.

The economic significance of skilled and educated labor lies in the potential "multiplier effects" of human capital investment. The conventional economic logic suggests the following: Skilled labor is more productive; productive labor produces goods more efficiently; efficient production results in higher profits and wages; higher wages stimulate demand; production to meet demand stimulates economic growth.

As applied to less-developed nations, there are a number of problems with this simple human capital chain of causation. First, one must consider what incentives exist for expanding educational opportunities. For many poor nations that continue to specialize in the export of primary products, there is no rational reason to expand mass educational facilities in any significant way, since job opportunities for the newly educated are quite scarce. It is important to take the structure of the economy into consideration when assessing what role education might play in the development process. If the economy cannot absorb educated labor, the educated are likely either to emigrate or to create political difficulties for the existing regime. If the economy is unable to meet basic family subsistence needs, then it is unlikely that the young will have the luxury of investing in human capital, since they must spend all or the majority of their time working in order to support family members.

Further, education cannot by itself create productivity gains; it must be joined with appropriate machinery, technology, and material inputs. It is here that a number of problems and contradictions emerge. Many forms of productive technology reduce the skill requirements of the applied labor and thus counteract the demand for skilled and highly trained workers. There is also a tendency for modern technology to reduce the amount of labor required for production. This means the typical labor surplus in less-developed nations goes unabsorbed and underutilized.

All of these comments suggest that human capital expansion is as much the consequence as the cause of certain forms of development. The positive association between aggregate educational attainment and level of development is suggestive, but the causal direction of this relationship is open to question. Does a supply of human capital create its own demand, or is supply stimulated and effectively utilized under particular economic conditions? As with the individual modernization models, it is useful to consider what might happen if a poor nation suddenly possessed a highly educated technically trained population. Would the economy automatically begin to grow rapidly? What countless adjustments would have to be made? Would the leaders of these countries be rejoicing or fleeing? While we can only speculate on the possible consequences, it is probably safe to say that many political, economic, and social structures would require modification and transformation. These changes would likely be opposed by privileged elites who have an interest in preserving the existing arrangements. In short, a simple change of individual capacities from uneducated to highly skilled is hardly a sufficient condition for development. Some may even argue that such a change will generate social regression and "political decay" (e.g., Huntington 1968).

The enthusiasm that originally accompanied the idea of educational expansion in less-developed nations has turned to frustration as the limits to such strategies have been realized. In spite of increasing educational enrollments and spending, poverty has not been reduced and equitable growth has not been achieved. There are many reasons, in addition to those above, for the failure of education to serve as the motor of development (see Simmons 1979). Much of the skepticism already expressed about the efficacy of educational expansion is echoed in some observations by John Simmons, who has studied international education policy extensively:

> The experience of the past 30 years indicated that most education strategies have failed to promote development, if development is conceived primarily as a process of improving the lives of the deprived majority of the world's population . . . . That the poor are becoming discouraged is revealed by falling primary-school enrollment rates in countries like Egypt, Nigeria and Pakistan . . . . In a few countries that got an early start, the nightmare of rioting students demanding jobs and a new government, or of a third of the school budgets being spent on children who drop out of primary school before reaching the third grade has become reality. (1983:263)

Simmons' illustrations from the Pakistan experience are equally sobering:

> Unemployment rates appear to be significantly higher among the educated than among the uneducated; forty percent of vocational school graduates are unemployed for 2–4 years after graduation; nine out of 10 pharmacy graduates leave the country. (1983:265)

His basic conclusion is that one cannot understand the consequences of individual exposure to education and training without a consideration of the broader levels of analysis that include the political, social, and economic systems of a nation. Studies confirming this position indicate that the translation of human capital expansion into economic growth requires, at minimum, the active intervention of the state in coupling the educational system to the needs of the economy (Hage et al. 1988).

A CONCLUDING COMMENT ON THE ROLE OF
SUBJECTIVE FACTORS

While this chapter has been critical of the individual-level models that stress the cultural/subjective determinants of socio-economic development, it is not the purpose to downplay the importance of the subjective orientation of individuals. The issue is whether this is the adequate level of analysis for explaining social change, and whether these subjective orientations are the prerequisites for objective economic structures and success. A much different issue, and one that maintains the critical necessity of considering subjective factors, is the way in which ideologies support, or attempt to bolster, objective social structures, organizational arrangements, and systems of stratification and authority.

As noted at the start of the chapter, the labor input to production is unlike other inputs because of its ability consciously to reflect on its role and situation. Certain beliefs and ideas are therefore required if the energies of people are to be exerted toward the process of production. These ideas cannot be understood or imposed independently of the structural organizational arrangements of society. The Weberian model, for example, links belief systems with the objective interests of economic actors and the existing conditions of economic organization. Similarly, Marx identified the dominant ideology as that which corresponds to the interest of dominant classes. Without a sense of the broader organizational and economic structures, and the social relations of these structures, it is difficult to establish the single best subjective disposition for the purpose of development.

This idea is well illustrated in various writings on Western culture that link individualism, consumerism, and economism to socio-economic crisis, stagnation, and decline. These very values, which earlier had been elevated to the level of cultural prerequisites for growth, are today deemed problematic. The argument that the liberal tradition is now "dysfunctional" for capitalist development can be found in the influential works of Bowles and Gintis (1982) and James O'Connor (1984). The neo-Marxist argument, exemplified in these theoretical accounts, contends that the most recent phase of economic crisis and decline in the United States is the result of the liberal doctrine of "possessive individualism" that encourages economistic behavior and excessive demands for property and material goods.

For example, Bowles and Gintis (1982) maintain that working-class political demands in liberal democratic capitalist societies tend to revolve around economistic demands aimed at redistribution, the expansion of social welfare programs, higher wages, and greater job security. The success of these efforts, while stimulating economic growth in the immediate post-World War II period, has had the long-term effect of creating impediments to sustained capital investment, accumulation, and economic growth. (See Piven and Cloward 1982 for a similar argument.)

O'Connor (1984), in perhaps the most comprehensive statement of this general thesis, argues that the liberal ideology of individualism has served, over the long haul, to undermine the social fabric of capitalism. The contemporary crisis involves the intensification of the persistent contradiction between capitalism's requirements for production and consumption. Capitalist profitability requires, on the one hand, costs low enough to encourage investment in production and, on the other, wage levels sufficient to allow consumption of the goods produced. These dual requirements of capitalism could not be simultaneously satisfied in the broader context of possessive individualism.

> The fact that "individualism" was a national ideology meant that individuals regarded themselves as "American citizens" or "Americans." . . . needs were construed as individual demands for entitlement to individualized services and income . . . the working class and salariat developed individualistic economic and social needs, pluralistic forms of economic and social struggles and political organization and activity which increased the size and value content of the consumption basket. . . . The only practical unity in the highly individualistic context of U.S. capitalism was the development of political means to individual ends. To the degree, therefore, that working class struggle broadly defined created unfavorable conditions for capital accumulation, the result was unplanned and unintended. (1984:94, 105, 215–18)

Consumption-oriented values, associated with liberalism and modern Western development, have resulted in a system of economic reward and redistribution for workers that leads to an excessive drain on profits, disinvestment, and slowed growth.

The tension between the culture of individualism and the institutions of modern capitalism is further noted in the work of Abercrombie et al. (1986). Given that modern corporate organizations place the greatest emphasis on

> conformity to rules, deference and obedience to superiors, custodianship of other people's property, and collective organization instead

of individual autonomy . . . individualistic traits bear no obvious functional relationship to the organizational forms typical of more recent capitalism. (1986:138)

The broader point is that the functional relationship between individualism and capitalism has been overstated and that the former is not a necessary prerequisite for the latter. As the issue applies to the modern corporation, it has been argued that a non-individualistic corporate structure and collective orientation among employees is now more appropriate for effective corporate success in a highly competitive, complex, and uncertain world economy (Dore 1973).

It is not that individualistic cultural traits played no role in the expansion of capitalism, but that in the present phase of capitalist development they may be impediments to economic growth. One of the basic arguments of this chapter is that the "functionality" of individual attitudes, beliefs, behaviors, and cultural traits can be assessed only in relation to other structural features of society (or levels of analysis). Because these structural features have been transformed and altered, what had previously been regarded as a cultural necessity is now being called into question. In fact, the individualistic and instrumental orientation of Western workers is currently being countered by the development of specific types of organizational structures designed to engender a more diffuse attachment to the corporate firm. The relationship between work organizations and development is the subject of Chapter 3.

NOTES

1. The fundamental and unique features of the human labor input in production can also serve as obstacles to effective collective action. See Offe and Wiesenthal (1980) on this point.

2. The relationship between the Protestant ethic and the rise of capitalism is a long-debated issue in sociology, and in social theory more generally. For further discussion of this issue see Eisenstadt (1968b).

3. On the question of the relationship between individualism and capitalism, see Abercrombie et al. (1986).

4. For discussion of the work ethic concept, see Barbash et al. (1983).

5. In the contemporary study of development this segment of the population is often referred to as "comprador" or "pariah" capitalists; they find a niche in underdeveloped nations through their subservient relationship with foreign-owned multinational corporations (see Chirot 1986:113–14).

3

ORGANIZATIONS AND DEVELOPMENT

Although organizations are only one type of institution . . . they are critical
to economic development. Most goods and services are produced by organizations and most development projects are implemented by them. In fact,
the production function actually takes place in organizations, because capital,
labor, technology, human capital, and materials are utilized by organizations
and transformed into goods and services. Therefore, if organizations can be
made more productive, the economy will grow and people will be better off
generally. (Hage and Finsterbusch 1987:2)

This chapter examines how organizations influence the process of socio-
economic development. Economic production requires human activities
that are carried out within organizations that specify, implicitly and
explicitly, obligations, duties, roles, functions, tasks, specialties, means
and ends, and rules and regulations. More specifically, the primary focus
is on formal work organizations that have been deliberately formed for the
production of goods and services for direct consumption and/or sale in a
market.

Organizations influence development in two important ways. First, the
efficiency and productivity of formal work organizations contribute to the
gross national product (GNP) and the rate of economic growth. Second,
individual interests and motives are shaped by organizational forces and
the resulting patterns of behavior may have significant consequences for
social and political change.

In Chapter 2 individual-level explanations were criticized for focusing
on values and attitudes as determinants of socio-economic development
without an adequate consideration of broader structural forces. One of the
purposes of this chapter is to fill in some of the gaps by considering
organizational structures, organizational arrangements, the interests that
are served in work organizations, and the relationship between organiza-

tional forms and economic development. We begin with a discussion of agricultural organizations and their impact on socio-economic and political behavior. The second section takes up the question of the transition from rural to urban organizational forms and some of the consequences of this transformation. This is followed by a review of organizational theories and techniques that have been linked to economic development in advanced Western nations. The chapter concludes with a consideration of the multinational corporate organization.

AGRICULTURAL ORGANIZATIONS

Agriculture, as a sector, accounts for well over half the labor force in less-developed countries. Among the low-income economies (those with a per capita GNP of less than $400) an average of 77 percent of the labor force is employed in the agricultural sector. For these nations, the organization of agriculture is a central determinant of individual-level motives, interests, and behavior, as well as a critical factor influencing the growth rate of the economy. Where agricultural organizations produce for export, they are linked to international market forces and serve as a leading source of foreign exchange. Changes in the organization and productivity of agriculture also will affect the migration of populations from rural to urban areas. In short, many of the forces of social change in less-developed nations are tied to the organization of agricultural enterprises.

Land Tenure Systems and Socio-economic Development

Individual-level modernization models have been used to explain the agricultural performance of less-developed economies. The logic should now be familiar: the traditional and backward beliefs of farmers discourage productive agricultural development. Agricultural development requires modern entrepreneurial values that promote the utilization of modern productive technology and encourage a shift from subsistence to surplus agricultural production. In the absence of such a value structure, agricultural producers will be unable to respond to dynamic market opportunities, and agricultural development will stagnate.

In this chapter organizational forces and structures are introduced as causal factors shaping human values and behavior. This represents a first step in transcending narrow individual-level models of development and social change. From this perspective, if we look beyond the presumably deficient cultural values held by farmers, we may discover some structural factors related to the organization of work that account for their behavior.

For example, one observer provides alternative explanations for the cautious economic behavior of subsistence farmers when he remarks, "The economic advantages turned out to be illusory—the landlord secured all the gain; the moneylender skimmed off the cream; the government guaranteed price was not in fact paid; the cost structure made the new innovation unprofitable" (Wharton 1983:235). These observations point to the rural experiences and property systems that create certain disincentives and uncertainties, and reduce the likelihood that economic risks will be undertaken. Rather than blaming agricultural producers and subsistence farmers for holding the wrong values, their behavior should be interpreted in light of organizational structures and economic experience. This requires an analysis of the effects of organizational arrangements. In the case of agriculture this means, first and foremost, a consideration of land tenure systems.

Land tenure systems refers to the ownership, reward, and utilization pattern of agricultural enterprises and the relationship between the owners and the producers of agricultural output. Patterns of land tenure have changed dramatically over the course of history and vary widely from country to country. What is clear is that land tenure systems exercise an enormous influence on the behavior of producers and the social, economic, and political development of nations.

Grasping the behavioral impact of organizational arrangements requires returning, for a moment, to the point made in Chapter 2 about the unique nature of labor. Workers are conscious and reflective, and are able to respond to their environment, unlike other factors of production. What might appear as irrational or unresponsive behavior in the face of economic opportunities is, in fact, rational and reasonable when patterns of land tenure and their associated incentive systems are taken into account. The incentive to invest time, money, and/or human energy is likely to depend upon the system of land ownership and the way in which the fruits of labor are distributed and utilized. Under conditions of coercion, poor treatment, exploitation, or inequitable distribution, peasants are apt to behave, using conventional language, in irrational, unmotivated and unproductive ways. Yet that behavior may be quite rational in the context of particular organizational systems.

The "tenure and incentive problem" is a fundamental fact of agricultural development. In a widely used economic development text, Gillis et al. (1987) point to the disincentives that emerge when farmers are unable to receive benefits from increased effort because they do not own the land. Under a wage labor system, where owners hire workers for a set wage, special techniques have to be utilized to motivate the work force. A "piece rate" method might be employed that pays workers by the number of units harvested. This system tends to be less successful in agriculture than in industry, however, given the lag time between cultivation and harvest, the difficulties in supervision, and the inability to measure output accurately.

Other tenure systems, such as communal and collectivized agriculture, also have built-in incentive structures. Under communal systems there is common land ownership but a disincentive to improve the land because benefits are widely distributed rather than returned directly to the individual. Collectivized agriculture joins common ownership with an accounting system of labor input that provides the basis for a distribution of output based on the amount of time and effort expended. In the end, many advocate the family farm as the system best able to motivate farmers, but the economies of scale make this system less feasible and inherently inefficient for large-scale agricultural needs.

The structure of land tenure also serves as the central explanatory variable in a study of land reform and political development by Prosterman and Riedinger (1987). The authors regard land tenure as the most useful predictor of revolutions and political upheavals in less-developed nations. Land tenure is said to influence the probability of civil violence through its effect on the individual-level sentiment of "relative deprivation," defined as "deprivation relative to one's own expectations for oneself" (1987:7). Thus, in their model, inadequate tenure arrangements affect the individual judgment of deprivation, which is then a potential source of political action.

Prosterman and Riedinger also link land tenure arrangements to productivity and the rate of economic growth. They divide land tenure systems into three major types: tenant farm/agricultural labor systems, small owner-operator farming systems, and collective farming systems. With few exceptions, the authors conclude, based on their cross-national data, that the owner-operator systems are the most productive, followed by collective farming and, as the least productive, tenant/labor systems. These differences in productivity are attributed to the differential incentive structures of the tenure systems. The incentive to invest time, energy, and resources in enhancing the productivity of the land is strongly related to the perception that these investments will be rewarded by a share of the output. Under the owner-operator system, expected and actual returns are greatest and most certain. Under sharecropping and tenant systems the returns are both smaller and less certain.

A more elaborate typology of land tenure systems is found in Stinchcombe's (1961) model of agricultural enterprises. Stinchcombe confines his analysis to commercial agriculture and describes five types of enterprise. Four of these are considered here: the manorial system, family-size tenancy, the family small holding, and the plantation. Stinchcombe's purpose is to demonstrate that each of these enterprise types gives rise to a distinct rural class system. The rural class systems can then be distinguished by the class differences in legal privileges, style of life, knowledge of the technical culture, and political activity between owners and producers.

The *manorial* or *hacienda system* is characterized by feudal social and political arrangements. The manor lord has legal rights over the land, the peasant population, and the agricultural product cultivated by the peasants. Peasants are given access to small plots of land that provide for subsistence consumption needs. The landed elite pursue an aristocratic style of life influenced by international fashion and the conspicuous consumption of material goods. They also tend to be heavily involved in political affairs and depend on the political apparatus to enforce their rights over land and peasants. The peasants, in contrast, are isolated and excluded from national affairs, and are politically weak and unorganized. The one asset possessed by the peasantry is knowledge of cultivation practices and techniques, but the independent exercise of these skills is not widely entertained.

In the *family-size tenancy* enterprise, labor is carried out by an extended family unit but the land is owned by rentier capitalists. Thus the agricultural laborers pay a rent in the form of money or a portion of the agricultural product. Prosterman and Riedinger (1987) have suggested that levels of relative deprivation may be most pronounced under this type of system. Stinchcombe (1961) emphasizes that this enterprise is the most politically unstable. A number of structural features contribute to the political volatility of this arrangement.

First, the division of the agricultural product is clear and apparent, in that the rent paid to the landowner is a direct deduction from the farmer's potential income. Second, rental arrangements usually include provisions ensuring that the risks of failure are borne by the farmer rather than the rentier. Though many conditions affecting the agricultural yield are beyond the control of farmers, they are under constant pressure to meet their rent obligations. Third, there are sharp distinctions between the farmer and rentier styles of life and residential location. Rentiers are absentee in the sense that they tend to live in urban centers and have little direct contact with tenants. Finally, under this system the farmer is perfectly capable of performing all required agricultural tasks independent of the rentier, who is regarded more as a parasitic than as a productive force. For all these reasons, the political interests of the two classes tend to diverge sharply, and the farmer has a visible object toward which to direct discontent. As Stinchcombe remarks, "It is of such stuff that many radical populist and nationalistic movements are made" (1961:168).

The *family small holding* can be distinguished from the family tenancy enterprise in that the farmer is able to secure all or most of the agricultural product. As indicated above, this system is most likely to create the greatest incentives among the direct producers for enhancing productivity and output. Since there are no lords or rentiers to skim off the surplus, the primary concern of farmers under this system is the market price of their agricultural commodities. There are, however, creditors who may have loaned the small farmers significant sums. Thus, stable prices are often necessary in order to meet regular debt payments. Politically, then, these farmers can be quite active in pushing for stable commodity prices and opposing banking interests. Differences between family farmers and the rural upper classes in legal rights and style of life tend to be small.

Plantation agricultural enterprises are typically found where labor-intensive crops, such as coffee and sugar, are cultivated. The plantation system comes closest to approximating the industrial factory. Workers are hired and paid a wage (though in some instances slave labor may be used), and they are directed by managers and administrators. In this sense the laborers do not possess the technical know-how required to cultivate and harvest the crop. The large-scale nature of plantation agriculture also involves substantial capital investment. Under this system landowners have a direct interest in, and make a direct contribution to, the productive and efficient use of resources. There are sharp divisions between the landowner class and agricultural laborers. The latter often come from racial/ethnic minority groups who are highly exploited and systematically excluded from urban industrial job opportunities. Where the labor force is recruited from other regions or nations, and employed on a seasonal basis, they may also lack basic citizenship and residence rights. Landowners, in contrast, usually possess considerable political clout and, as capitalists, may own enterprises in a variety of other industries.

Stinchcombe's typology of rural enterprises provides a useful framework linking organizational structures with socio-political behavior. Some of its basic elements are found in the rich and sophisticated study of export agriculture and political movements by Jeffery Paige (1975). Paige examines the social relationships between, and the sources of income for, rural cultivators (farmers) and noncultivators (landowners) in the export sector of less-developed economies. Based on the income source of the two classes, Paige offers some expectations about the likely form of political conflict and development. Paige's theoretical and empirical account represents the best of multi-level social science research.

Individual level motives, forms of land tenure, socio-economic systems, and world-economic forces are brought together in his theory of rural class conflict. Rural relations and conflict are empirically examined using both cross-national and case study data. In its most simplified form, Paige's theory of rural class conflict hinges on the different income sources of cultivators (agricultural workers and/or peasants) and noncultivators (landed aristocrats or capitalist property owners), and the political interests and motives that stem from these organizational and social class positions.

Table 2, adopted from Paige, summarizes the four forms of land tenure that emerge from the land-wages/land-capital income basis of cultivators and noncultivators, and the likely course of socio-political movements. For the commercial hacienda, land is the income source for both cultivators and noncultivators and this determines their political behaviors. The noncultivators derive their income from land and tend to be economically weak. They therefore must rely upon extra-economic or political forms of intervention and coercion in order to control cultivators and maintain their privileged position. They are also likely to view conflict in zero-sum terms. This means that any gain by or concession to cultivators in the form of land or income is regarded as a direct loss to the noncultivating class. The cultivators or peasants, who depend on access to land for their survival, are hesitant to take political risks, are more prone to competition rather than cooperation with other peasant cultivators, and are more closely integrated with and dependent on non-cultivators than their fellow cultivators.

Table 2
Paige's Model of Agricultural Organizations and Agrarian Social Movements

Type of Land Tenure System	Source of Income for: Labor/ Cultivators	Owners/ Noncultivators	Political Outcome
Commercial Haciendas	land	land	Agrarian Revolt
Sharecropping/Migratory	wages	land	Socialist/ Nationalist Revolution
Small Holding	land	capital	Commodity Reform
Capitalist Plantation	wages	capital	Labor Reform

SOURCE: Adapted from Jeffery M. Paige, Agrarian Revolution. New York: Free Press, 1975, p. 11.

All this adds up to a peasant population that is unlikely to engage in collective political organization and struggle. However, the combined effect of a peasantry heavily dependent on access to land and an intractable landed elite creates a certain form of conflict: "The form of social movement most common in the commercial hacienda system might be best described as an agrarian revolt—a short intense movement aimed at seizing land but lacking long-run political objectives" (Paige 1975:43).

In contrast with the hacienda, the plantation is an agricultural system in which cultivator income is derived from wages, and noncultivator income from capital investments. These income sources also have consequences for political behavior. Noncultivators who rely on returns from capital investment in machinery and factories do not define conflict in a zero-sum manner. The application of capital investments implies increasing productivity such that concessions can be granted out of an expanded agricultural surplus. Because the noncultivators rely on wage labor, they tolerate the free movement of cultivators and assume that labor market forces will ensure an adequate supply of workers. In this way they are less dependent on the direct coercion of the state to maintain an adequate labor supply. The wage-labor cultivators under this system also can be distinguished from their hacienda counterparts by their inclination to take greater political-economic risks because they do not depend on access to land and are not involved in direct competition with their fellow cultivators. The net result is a greater incentive and likelihood for political organization and solidarity.

Paige notes that the agricultural organization of the plantation satisfies many of the conditions that Marx associated with the development of proletarian political action:

Payment of wages in cash or in kind . . . creates economic incentives for collective political action, intense class solidarity. . . . The agricultural export economy . . . creates a homogeneous, unskilled labor force with little or no internal stratification and no prospect for upward mobility. Economic gains can seldom be realized at the expense of other workers but rather in most cases, only through economic pressure on the employer. . . . The agricultural wage laborer seems to illustrate the characteristics that Marx believed were essential for the mobilization of the industrial proletariat. . . . While it has become commonplace to observe that Marx's revolutionary prediction remains unfulfilled in industrial societies, this fact does not invalidate his original hypothesis concerning economic conditions and class consciousness. . . . In the agricultural export economy, however, these economic conditions have persisted long after they have disappeared in industrial societies. The homogeneous poorly paid, concentrated mass of workers that Marx saw as the vanguard of the revolution are found not in industrial societies, but in commercial export agriculture in the underdeveloped world. It is in such societies that the greatest incentives for class-based organization and class conflict exist. (1975:33–34)

In order to understand why a more radical outcome does not actually occur, we must consider the interests and behavior of the noncultivating class. The expected form of political social movement emerging from the plantation is what Paige (1975:49) calls the "reform labor movement because the powerful non-cultivating class in this agricultural system is in a position to make economic concessions to a well-organized agricultural proletariat."

For the "mixed types" of agricultural organization, the small holding and sharecropping systems, there are also distinct political movements. In small holding agriculture, where labor continues to receive income from control and access to land, and noncultivators receive returns from capital, a reform movement also emerges. However, the conflict is not distributional but over agricultural commodity markets and prices.

In the sharecropping system, the most explosive results are nurtured because it pits a rigid noncultivating class against a politically mobilized agricultural proletariat. The result is "agrarian revolution" in which the demands of cultivators can be met only through the forceful appropriation of land and political power from the noncultivating elite.

The study by Paige is an especially outstanding example of the relationship between land tenure systems and socio-economic development. The results of his case study and cross-national analyses indicate the significant influence of organizational arrangements on individual motives and interests, political movements, and social change.

Transition to Capitalist Agriculture

Much of the writing on the changing organization of agricultural production in less-developed societies employs the standard traditional-modern dichotomy, or what is often called the *dual-society thesis*. This perspective views less-developed nations as transitional, containing distinct modern industrial and traditional agricultural economic sectors. The traditional agricultural sector is assumed to be backward, feudal, subsistence-oriented, stagnant, and archaic. The feudal landowning elite are, in this model, inefficient in their use of the surplus appropriated from the peasants. Excessive consumption and minimal capital investment are the twin character flaws of the feudal elite. Their behavior, and that of the peasants, is tied to the precapitalist organizational structure that dictates near subsistence production by peasants and surplus squandering by feudal landowners.

The solution to the problem of inefficiency in agriculture, according to the dual-society thesis, involves the diffusion of capitalist market forces. These will stimulate the efficient use of productive resources. Landowners will reduce costs, introduce modern productive techniques, expel redundant peasant labor, and, overall, expand the size of the agricultural surplus and the rate of profit. This scenario and prescription parallel the logic of the cultural diffusion or modernization model, only here it is applied to sectors within a single nation. Agricultural development and expansion require the influence of capitalism on feudal sectors. The spread of capitalism will transform agriculture from a traditional and stagnant to a modern, prosperous, and productive economic sector.

While there are many critiques of the dual-society thesis (some of which lay the basis for dependency theories examined in Chapter 5) the feudal/capitalist division, as we have seen, informs many of the existing typologies of agricultural organization. Studies of Latin American agriculture typically draw the distinction between the hacienda and the plantation (Wolf and Mintz 1957; Stinchcombe 1961). The hacienda is the large estate that maintains vestiges of feudalism in the social relations between the large landowners and the dependent peasant labor force. This means that the labor force is not free and mobile but "tied to the land" and in a servile relationship with the landowning elite. The hacienda, in this typology, retains feudal peasant social relations, maintains highly inefficient forms of production, and directs a large portion of the surplus to conspicuous forms of consumption in order to enhance the symbolic image of the aristocracy.

At the other end of the typology are the plantations, which more closely resemble capitalist forms of organization in that the labor force is hired for a wage, owners are oriented toward the maximization of profit through modern cultivation techniques, and the surplus is reinvested in production. For these reasons the plantations are said to be more efficient and dynamic.

In addition to differentiating the capitalist from the feudal land tenure system, there is the issue of how agricultural organization evolves from feudal to capitalist forms, and the consequence of this process for political and economic development. Lenin presented a model of two roads to capitalist agricultural development based on experiences in Prussia and the United States. In the former case, known as the "Junker road," feudal landowners become capitalists as they convert production to large-scale commercial purposes, evict peasants from the land, hire wage laborers, and modernize production techniques. This account is based on the history of the Prussian Junker class.

A different path to capitalist agriculture is represented by the "farmer road." In this model capitalist agriculture emerges from the activity of small farmers who gain access to land through social revolution, land reform, or redistribution programs. In the United States small farmers gained a foothold through the colonization of western territories and the homestead acts that encouraged the movement of individual farmers to previously remote and uncultivated locations. This is usually considered the most progressive and productive road.

The various roads to commercial agriculture have also been linked to national political development. Perhaps the most elaborate theoretical and comparative historical account of the various "roads" is provided by Barrington Moore (1967). Moore explains the political outcomes in a number of different nations (Britain, United States, France, Japan, India, Germany, and China) with reference to the class structure and the class alliances that existed and emerged in the transition to commercial agriculture. He identifies three major routes.

The first path is the "bourgeois revolution," which was followed in the United States and Britain. The bourgeois road involves a fairly thorough transformation of the landed elite into capitalists such that they dissolve feudal peasant relations and apply rational production methods to agriculture. These conditions are said to promote the flowering of liberal democratic institutions.

The second path, the "revolution from above," is associated with the historical experience of Germany and Japan. This path entails a strong landed elite who resist liberal reforms and maintain their hold over commercial agricultural production under conditions of serfdom or slavery. The strong and repressive political methods required to enforce this system, typically in alliance with a weak bourgeoisie, are said to lay the groundwork for the associated political system of fascism.

The third path, represented by the experience of China and Russia, is labeled "peasant revolutions." The absence of a commercial revolution in agriculture initiated by a landowning elite results in the persistence of feudal peasant institutions. These institutions, unchallenged by a significant bourgeois sector, are unable to manage the stress and strains of prolonged repression. The end result is said to be a peasant revolution and the institutionalization of Communism.

The Formal Subordination of Labor and Functional Dualism

One of the preconditions for capitalist agricultural production is the *formal subordination of labor*, the process by which individuals are separated from control over and access to productive property. Without any independent means of survival, individuals are forced to work for someone else or "sell their labor power for a wage." In short, capitalist production and profit require workers who can be hired and exploited. In the rural context this means the hacienda must be dismantled, peasants must be evicted from their plots of land, and small independent farmers must be bought out or driven out of business. A labor force of workers is then created who can be hired by capitalist landowners interested in agricultural production.

There are three possible outcomes from the formal subordination of labor. First, there might be a *labor equilibrium*, in which all the workers released from the hacienda and other agricultural arrangements find work and are absorbed by the plantation system as wage labor. A second possibility is a *labor shortage*, in which the plantations are unable to find significant sources of labor and therefore must recruit workers from other areas either voluntarily or coercively. The third and most common experience is a *labor surplus*, in which the number of formally subordinated individuals exceeds the number of jobs in plantation agriculture. This results in an extended transition to capitalist agriculture and a system of "functional dualism."

The system of *functional dualism* is described by deJanvry (1981) in his analysis of the changing patterns and resulting crisis of Third World agriculture. Based primarily on the experience of Latin America, de Janvry notes that a significant portion of the evicted peasant population, unable to find employment in rural areas, is forced to settle on unclaimed plots of land in proximity to capitalist plantations. On these plots, peasant families cultivate crops for home consumption and, if a surplus is produced, for sale in a local market. It is not uncommon for some of the members of the family to be employed on the plantation while other members work the plots. The "dualism" refers to the fact that in this agricultural system capitalist plantation agriculture and family subsistence agriculture exist side by side.

In contrast with the dualism described by dual-society theorists, under functional dualism the capitalist and peasant forms of production depend upon each other and are closely linked. This dualism is regarded as "functional" in the sense that profit levels in capitalist agriculture are enhanced by the existence of the subsistence sector.

DeJanvry describes the labor force in capitalist agriculture as only *semiproletarianized* because many of the workers and/or their families have access to, and derive income from production on, subsistence plots. They are not fully proletarianized because they have access to and control productive property. This allows wages in the plantation sector to be kept very low because the workers and/or their families grow much of their own food and therefore do not require money income to purchase foodstuffs. The "subsistence" plots may also produce a marginal surplus that can be sold in local markets. This further contributes to low wages in the capitalist plantation sector because relatively cheap food is available to those workers who purchase food from local producers. Finally, the settlement of peasant families in proximity to the capitalist plantation sector creates a "reserve army of labor" that undercuts the bargaining power of plantation workers and further reduces wage levels in the capitalist sector. The local peasant subsistence economy, therefore, serves to subsidize wage costs and increase profit, and is a vital ingredient in the logic of the transitional rural economy. The long-term effect of this arrangement, however, is the eventual and total subordination of the rural masses and abject rural poverty.

This outcome is based on the behavior of rural producers, which is a consequence of the survival strategies dictated by the system of functional dualism. In addition to interpeasant competition for wage labor positions, as well as for the sale of foodstuffs in local markets, there are pressures to increase the volume of production on the subsistence plots. Over time the intensive use of the soil produces progressively smaller yields as the land becomes less and less fertile.

Human fertility, on the other hand, is quite high because children are required as part of the family labor force that produces for home consumption and, where possible, the local market. Again, it is imperative to note that the fertility behavior of peasants is in large part a consequence of the economic organizational arrangements under which they live. DeJanvry describes it thus:

Individual economic rationality does not exist in the abstract—it is conditioned by the social position of the household relative to productive resources and to the social division of labor. It is also conditioned by the absolute income level relative to the consumption and security needs of the couple. In peasant agriculture, poverty implies pressure to seek control over additional productive resources. Since producing children is often the only means whereby peasants can secure access to additional resources, more children are raised in order to increase the labor applied to a fixed piece of land so that it will not fall below subsistence level. (1981:89)

As deJanvry clearly documents, the net result of this process is rural overpopulation, impoverishment, and misery.

The lesson to be learned from the various studies of land tenure systems and the transition to capitalist agriculture is that the organization of production is an important explanatory variable for understanding human political-economic behavior and socio-economic and political change. Cultural values and motivational systems cannot be taken as given but must be linked to the conditions of material existence and modes of economic survival. It is difficult to isolate these factors from the broader structures of national social systems or the forces of the world economy. A complete and systematic analysis requires that connections be made both downward—to the individual-level—and upward—to the level of the social system and of the international economy.

INDUSTRIALIZATION: FROM RURAL TO URBAN ORGANIZATIONS

The process of industrialization involves the geographic migration of the population from rural to urban areas and the organizational shift from agricultural to industrial employment. There are many neat and abstract theories that describe these processes as smooth and self-regulating, in which workers migrate from rural labor surplus to urban labor-shortage sectors of the economy, in which labor supply and labor demand reach equilibrium. There are also expectations about the relationship between industrial development and urbanization.

What should first be emphasized is that the allocation of labor from rural to urban economies in less-developed nations has not conformed to the conventional models. A great deal has been written about the population explosion in the less-developed world, the crowded cities, the massive squatter settlements, and the urban shantytowns. The term "overurbanization" refers to excessive urban population growth relative to the carrying capacity of the industrial urban economy. At one time it was common to equate urbanization with progress, modernization, and development. This association was based on experiences in Western Europe and North America during the major phases of industrial expansion. However, for the contemporary Third World, industrial development and employment have not kept pace with urban population growth. In many less-developed nations, particularly middle-income countries, urbanization rates approach or equal those found in the advanced capitalist states, but it is "urbanization without industrialization." In Peru, for example, 68 percent of the population resides in urban areas but only 18 percent is employed in industry. Most observers agree that this type of "hyperurbanization" is the result of massive rates of rural-to-urban migration alongside the sluggish growth of the urban industrial economy.

Standard models of population migration explain the geographic shift of human population as a combination of "push" and "pull" factors. *Push factors* are those forces at the point of departure that encourage the population to leave a geographic location. In rural-to-urban migration these are characteristics of the agricultural economy and rural enterprises, such as the mechanization of agriculture, the erosion of the soil, rural poverty, the eviction of peasants, the shift to export cash crops, and rural overcrowding. These factors affect the ability of the rural population to work and survive in the countryside.

Pull factors are those features of the urban environment, such as "city lights," income opportunities, higher wages, industrial jobs, and kinship ties, that encourage population settlement in urban areas. While the explanation for migration involves some combination of these push and pull factors, the failure of the rural economy is the necessary condition facilitating excessive rates of rural-to-urban migration. Where prospects for rural survival are deteriorating or have evaporated, labor is forced to migrate to areas where income opportunities exist. These are usually the urban centers.

Once migrants arrive at their urban destination, they must deal with the problems of finding employment and housing. Expectations for employment are often dashed because the urban labor market is unable to generate a supply of jobs to meet the swelling demand. Survival in the urban economy often requires, therefore, innovation and resourcefulness. This is reflected in the informal economic activities that are engaged in by a substantial portion of the urban population. Studies of these activities in less-developed nations indicate a massive, vibrant, and highly functional informal sector.

The rural "functional dualism" identified by deJanvry, which promotes the eventual migration of labor from rural to urban centers, is reproduced at the urban level. The "urban dualism thesis," described by Portes and Walton (1981), delineates a dual urban structure made up of "formal" and "informal" economies. In the formal sector workers are hired by employers and paid a wage or salary. The large-scale rural-to-urban migration creates a labor surplus in the city, and the formal sector is incapable of absorbing all those seeking employment in urban areas. This means that a substantial portion of the urban population, falling outside formal-sector economic activity, must devise alternative means of survival.

The proliferation of these urban survival strategies contributes to the burgeoning informal sector. The urban informal sector is made up of myriad street vendors, peddlers, and hucksters who offer goods and services to the urban cash market. These goods are produced cheaply with individual and family labor and are sold under conditions of intense competition. Consequently, the price of informal-sector goods is quite cheap. The existence of the informal sector, then, is functional to the profitability of the formal sector. It supplies cheap wage goods (the basic goods that urban workers consume, such as food and clothing) to formal-sector workers at very low prices. This reduces the cost of living, allowing employers to pay lower wages than would otherwise be the case. In this way informal-sector activities serve to subsidize the wage costs of formal-sector employers. Further, the informal sector serves as a huge reserve army of unemployed and underemployed labor that weakens the bargaining position of formal-sector workers and drives down wages. Thus, many rural-to-urban migrants experience a shift from formal and/or informal rural production to informal urban production. Whether this represents a loss or a gain in living standards is difficult to assess.

Both classical and contemporary social theory have a great deal to say about the social psychological and political effects of the rural-to-urban transformation. Durkheim believed that this transition would threaten the foundations of social order unless new modes of social solidarity developed in the industrial setting. In Durkheim's relatively optimistic view, the mechanical solidarity regulating members in traditional societies on the basis of social similarity is superseded by an industrial version, organic solidarity, based on the division of labor and functional interdependence among members. Anomie and alienation are, therefore, minimized and social order is maintained.

For the less-developed economies, where urbanization outstrips industrialization, one might plausibly expect a less harmonious scenario. Effective organic solidarity can hardly be established where the mass of migrants exists outside the formal economy. *Mass society theory*, applied to less-developed nations, has offered a modern version of the Durkheimian concern, but with a more explosive outcome. In this contemporary account, the transition from traditional to modern economies creates social psychological strain due to the breakdown and absence of social control mechanisms. The severed communal and kinship bonds of traditional society are not replaced in the modern urban setting. Thus the masses are said to be isolated, atomized, unattached, and poorly integrated. The net effect of this process of social change is the creation of a politically volatile population. Crowded into urban areas, lacking employment, discontented, the urban masses presumably will engage in unconventional and disruptive political activity as a means to redress their grievances. Less-developed nations, therefore, will inevitably and perpetually be plagued by mass political uprisings, riots, revolutions, crises, and political paralysis.

The apocalyptic visions of mass society theory have not come to pass. In most cases the Third World urban masses have been relatively quiescent and politically conservative. Their moderate political behavior can be attributed to their organizational location in the informal urban economy and the nature of their economic existence (Petras 1970). The urban residents engaged in informal-sector activities are organizationally isolated and individually competitive in their day-to-day struggle to eke out a living from the cash economy. There is little basis for collective political action. Many aspire to and identify with the position of the petit bourgeois shop owner who has achieved a relatively secure station in the urban economy. When political demands are made, they tend to be rather modest, involving access to basic services. Studies of the political movements of urban squatters (Cornelius 1975) indicate that the major issues revolve around legal titles to squatter lands, permits to construct housing, and access to water and sanitation services. In short, the scenario of the urban powder keg, ready to explode at the slightest provocation, though a plausible expectation, must be qualified in light of the actual behavior of the masses in question. In most cases, urban survival strategies preclude revolutionary and collective forms of social disruption.

A different perspective on the transition to industrial society is offered by *convergence theory*, which assumes that the process of industrialization requires the application of modern technology, trained labor, and rational planning to industrial organizational tasks. As industrial capital penetrates less-developed societies, or governments make conscious efforts to launch national industrial ventures, these features of industrialization are regarded as necessary and inevitable. In this view, the process of industrialization has a single logic that results, over time, in a convergence across societies in patterns of production, decision-making, conflict resolution, and technological application. An important consequence of this process, which weds the organizational and individual levels of analysis, is the impact of industrial employment on individual workers. Not only is there a convergence in organizational practices under the industrialization process, but there is also an assumed convergence in the subjective beliefs of industrial workers. A study by Form and Bae (1988) attempted to assess the validity of this component of convergence theory, which they label the "industrial worker hypothesis." This hypothesis states:

> that the exposure of workers to industrial technology and organiza-tion socializes them everywhere to adopt similar patterns of behavior and beliefs. Whatever their cultural socialization, they will respond to machine technology and industrial organization in much the same way. . . . The more workers participate in organizations in work and outside organizations, the more they internalize the urban-industrial milieu and their place in it. Thus, industrial working classes everywhere emerge with some common political dispositions and world views. (1988:621)

A key question guiding Form and Bae's research is whether exposure to modern industrial technology will have an independent influence on adaptation to and acceptance of modern urban life and political ideology, above and beyond the effects of traditional origin and socialization. Based on a sample of South Korean workers employed in a Hyundai auto plant, their results support many of the expectations of the industrial worker hypothesis. Those workers exposed to the most complex technology, and for the greatest duration, were the best adapted to industry and the most likely to participate in organizations outside the factory. It was also found that despite the traditional Confucian ethic that legitimates hierarchical authority patterns, the workers in this plant tended to support strong unions and expressed an oppositional working-class consciousness.

These findings point to the role of organizational forces, in this case a modern industrial complex, in shaping the attitudes and beliefs of workers within the formal sector. Locations and experiences within organizations can "create" people who fit the image, at least partially, of the "modern human." The reaction of workers to these industrial conditions, however, does not necessarily conform to the overly optimistic expectations of convergence theory. Rather than ideological consensus on the organization of production and the distribution of rewards, a "modern" working-class consciousness develops in opposition to the industrial system. This less functional feature of industrialization has required, in the case of South Korea, a repressive state apparatus. One might wonder, given the interna-tional prevalence of such authoritarianism, whether this, too, is part of the package deal of industrialism.

Frederic Deyo's (1982) research on export-oriented industrialization (EOI) is instructive on this question. Examining the cases of Korea, Taiwan, Hong Kong, and Singapore, Deyo notes that all four nations are under pressure to impose controls over the cost and political organization of labor. This is because much of the production is labor-intensive and foreign investors are attracted to these nations because they can gain access to a cheap and reliable labor force. The export-oriented strategy (which will be further elaborated in Chapter 5) hinges on the availability of cheap, highly competitive labor and smooth, depoliticized labor relations. This strategy typically requires the political repression of workers.

However, the relative levels of state repression vary significantly across the four countries. Deyo attributes these differences to the nature and strength of the labor movements prior to the institutionalization of the export-oriented strategy. In Hong Kong and Taiwan the labor force is quite docile, conservative, and intensely anti-Communist. Immigrants from mainland China make up a significant portion of the work force in each nation. The pattern of industrial organization also militates against collective labor organization. Deyo describes the system of industrial production in Hong Kong and Taiwan as "dispersed EOI," meaning that production is dispersed across a large number of smaller enterprises. This fragmentation of industrial workers makes labor organization more difficult and allows for greater employer control over the work force. The net result is a less militant, politically weak, and poorly organized labor movement that does not require heavy-handed state repression.

Singapore and South Korea represent the contrasting cases where there is a historical legacy of left-leaning labor organization and political involvement and where, in response, the state has been quite authoritarian. The pattern of industrial production, "consolidated EOI," further encourages a more cohesive labor movement. Under this form of export industrialization, production is carried out in large, modern enterprises, bringing thousands of workers together in a single factory. Levels of worker communication and consciousness are enhanced under these conditions, and political action is more likely. For this reason the governments of Korea and Singapore have been forced to play a major role in the regulation of labor relations.

A consideration of these different cases suggests that, first, the process of industrialization in less-developed nations is driven by a logic different from that in the developed states due to the heavy dependence on foreign investment and foreign markets; and, second, the pattern of industrial organization, whether it is dispersed or consolidated, has a significant effect on the development of industrial worker consciousness.

In sum, the historical process of the decline of agriculture and the rise of industry, and, accordingly, the movement of labor from rural to urban organizations, has been a critical part of the development process. As a number of studies indicate, this transition has been anything but smooth. The integration of the labor force into industrial organizations involves periods of conflict and economic dislocation. In order to illustrate further the role of organizations in the development process, we turn to the patterns of industrial organization and labor control in the advanced capitalist states.

INDUSTRIAL ORGANIZATIONS AND WESTERN DEVELOPMENT

The Rise of Bureaucracy

The best-known theory linking organizational structure with economic development is Weber's theory of bureaucracy (Weber 1947). Although the bureaucratic system existed under the Roman and Chinese empires, it was with the rise of industrial capitalism, Weber emphasizes, that its superiority as the most efficient organizational arrangement, compared with traditional forms of social organization, became clear: "Experience tends universally to show that the purely bureaucratic type of administrative organization . . . is, from a purely technical point of view, capable of attaining the highest degree of efficiency" (Weber 1947:337).

Weber developed the conceptual notion of the "ideal type" to emphasize the most salient characteristics of bureaucracy. The fundamental features of the bureaucratic organization are (1) a division of labor with specialized positions and tasks occupied and carried out by experts; (2) a hierarchical structure with authority flowing from the top down and each position responsible to a higher-level supervisor; (3) formal rules and regulations outlining official procedures, responsibilities, and relations between positions; (4) recruitment, promotion, and treatment of personnel based on universal rather than particular criteria.

These characteristics need not be an operative part of all bureaucratic organizations. Weber's point was to show that together they advance efficiency and that under capitalism, where production and economic decisions are based on the rational calculation of profit, the tendency to employ bureaucratic methods is enhanced.

Capitalism in its modern stages of development strongly tends to foster the development of bureaucracy, though both capitalism and bureaucracy have arisen from many different historical sources.

Conversely, capitalism is the most rational economic basis for bureaucratic administration and enables it to develop in its most rational form. (Weber 1947:338)

In addition to the objective structural characteristics of bureaucracy, Weber placed a great deal of emphasis on the system of legitimate authority or "voluntary submission." Systems of authority cannot simply be imposed on a reflective and conscious labor force; they must also be accepted to some extent as fair, just, and legitimate. Weber notes that bureaucratic *rational-legal* systems differ qualitatively from earlier traditional and charismatic forms. In a bureaucracy, differences in power and authority, and the fact of subordination, are accepted because the hierarchical authority structure is regarded as formally *rational*. That is, members of an organization, who presumably share the same goals and objectives, view the hierarchical arrangement as a necessary means to achieve the desired ends. If the ends (goals) are agreed upon, and the best way to realize these is to institute some type of hierarchical structure, then this will be regarded as acceptable by the members of the organization.

The *legal* side of this authority system involves the explicit rules and regulations that define the relations between positions and offices. Authority relations are formalized in a legalistic way and thus they do not reflect the personal tastes or whims of supervisory personnel. This lends further credence to the fundamental rationality and fairness of the organizational system. The importance of subjective legitimacy for the operation of objective organizational structures will be emphasized throughout our discussion of various industrial organizational systems.

The explanation for the rise of bureaucracy as an organizational system cannot be reduced exclusively to its relative efficiency. It must be understood as an effective system of control and exploitation, which the emerging system of capitalism also required (see Clawson 1980). As Weber also noted, ability to exercise hierarchy, control, and discipline over workers, which profitable production requires and bureaucracy assists, was facilitated by the rise of the free labor market and the dependence of labor on capital. We now turn to the development of this industrial system and the organizational strategies designed to maximize profit, which in turn contributed to the rate of economic growth.

The Labor Process and Capitalist Development

It is usually taken for granted that in order to survive and make money, people must work for someone, and that once they agree to work in that organization, they follow the rules laid down by owners and managers. However, prior to industrial capitalism, this was an entirely foreign concept, one that produced a great deal of resistance and stress among industrializing populations. As already noted, the process of the formal subordination of labor involves the progressive loss of control over land and productive property by rural laborers, peasants, and independent artisans. As these populations are forced off the land, denied access to fertile soil, outcompeted by larger producers, and cut off from markets, they can no longer exist independently. They must now sell their labor to an employer for a wage. That is, they must depend on the owners of the means of production for income and survival. The resulting wage-labor relationship ushers in the capitalist mode of production and the development of the primary social classes—the capitalist class that hires labor and the working class that is hired by capital. The formal subordination of labor is a precondition for capitalist production and accumulation.

Once workers are within the confines of the capitalist work organization or factory the *real subordination of labor* begins. This involves the organizational methods and techniques that are applied to the task of extracting the greatest work effort from employees. Much of the remainder of this chapter will be devoted to a consideration of these strategies. It should be emphasized that these techniques were (are) aimed at increasing the organization's level of productivity and profit margin. In the aggregate, this translates into economic growth and development.

Scientific management, popularized by Frederick Winslow Taylor, was the first and most systematic attempt to carry out the real subordination of labor. Simply bringing workers into the factory did not solve the problems of control for owners and capitalists because craftspersons, and the workers they hired, still retained the knowledge and the know-how regarding the methods of production. Although workers could be watched by the owners, there was still no way to determine whether they were producing as fast and efficiently as possible. A great deal of control, and with it power, remained in the hands of workers.

Taylor developed a system whereby each production process could be studied and dissected scientifically, using basic principles derived from engineering. The aim of these studies was to show that there existed a "one best way" to organize production, and that managers could impose these techniques on the factory workers and thus gain control over the labor process. Using what came to be known as "time and motion" studies, Taylor demonstrated that the logic used to design a machine, involving repetitive motions, could be applied to the production of a product.

Once supervisors and managers dissect the production process into a series of simple components, they begin to impose an alternative organization of production on the workers and thus establish themselves, the representatives of owners, as efficiency experts. Knowledge and know-how are shifted from the workers to the managers, who now determine the "one best way" to produce a product. This organizational innovation weakens the power of workers and increases the rate of output. The basic stages of this process involve the division of production into a sequence of simple tasks. Workers are then assigned to these tasks and given basic instructions by the managerial stratum. With this latter process, conception and execution, or mental and manual labor, are distinct and separate activities. This organizational division of labor can be seen as an integral part of the development of capitalism.

A number of studies of the labor process place great importance on the role of scientific management as a major stage in the process of capitalist development. For example, Harry Braverman (1974:86–87) argues that:

It is impossible to overestimate the importance of the scientific management movement in the shaping of the modern corporation and indeed all institutions of capitalist society which carry on labor processes . . . its fundamental teachings have become the bedrock of all work design.

The struggle over these organizational systems, and the new conditions that emerge from these conflicts, are fundamental parts of capitalist development. There are many examples of this dynamic. The factory system, where workers are brought together under one roof so that they can be monitored by the owners, lays the basis for working-class communication, solidarity, and union organization. The struggle by labor to limit the length of the workday forces owners to develop more sophisticated technological methods to increase the rate of productivity. The struggle over control of work, and the imposition of scientific-management-type systems, creates a permanent stratum of managerial employees and excessive hierarchy in the organization. In short, each organizational "solution" or outcome contains problems and tensions that ultimately emerge as obstacles to continued production and development. The history of the development of industrial capitalism is replete with many instances of this "dialectical" process.

An extended example of the general point is provided by Burawoy (1983) in his consideration of "factory regimes." These are the particular political and ideological arrangements that support and legitimate the social relations between workers and managers and regulate the struggle between social classes within organizations. Burawoy refers to the early stage of capitalist industrial organization as "market despotism."

> In fact, market despotism is a relatively rare form of factory regime whose existence is dependent on three historically specific conditions: (1) Workers have no other means of livelihood than through the sale of their labor power for a wage. (2) The labor process is subject to fragmentation and mechanization so that skill and specialized knowledge can no longer be a basis of power. . . . (3) Impelled by competition, capitalists continually transform production through the extension of the working day, intensification of work and the introduction of new machinery. Anarchy in the market leads to despotism in the factory. (1983:588)

The conditions supporting the despotic factory regime have been modified significantly by modern developments involving state intervention. The first condition cited by Burawoy, in which workers are in a totally dependent position vis-à-vis employers, have no alternative to wage labor, and are especially vulnerable to excessive exploitation and domination, has been altered in the modern era by the expansion of the welfare state and the provision of social welfare benefits. One must also consider, as it applies to the second and third conditions, the role of formal credentials, professionalization, and trade union/collective bargaining rights. These are enforced and regulated by the state, and they protect workers from arbitrary despotism. These changing conditions result in a shift in the forms of organizational labor control from the despotic regime to what Burawoy calls the "hegemonic regime." Under the hegemonic regime, workers are less vulnerable and must be persuaded to cooperate with management. Efforts are aimed at eliciting worker consent. In short, organizational arrangements, like scientific management or market despotism, are more difficult to sustain given modern political-economic conditions. Organizational strategies of development are constantly changing to accommodate a shifting environment.

The unique nature of labor (as outlined in Chapter 2) is another reason why organizational arrangements like scientific management and market despotism are a source of conflict and are subject to transformation. Machines and raw materials can be molded to the structure of industrial organization; they do not need to be convinced or persuaded that the system is legitimate. Workers, on the other hand, are not so easily controlled and require a rationale for existing organizational arrangements.

Coercion is not enough, for it is costly and inefficient; what is needed is acceptance and legitimacy. Work organizations are like mini social systems; their viability requires ideological support, a belief that the methods of production are fair and just, a feeling of cohesion and solidarity.

James Coleman (1988b) has chosen the term "social capital" to describe the important role played by human interaction and social relations in contributing to collective welfare and productivity. He distinguishes social capital from the more familiar financial, physical, and human capital. In contrast with money, machines, and individual skills, all of which are typically required in the production process, "social capital exists in the relations among persons" (1988b:100–101). It is not a tangible good like physical capital, nor one that resides at the individual level, like human capital; rather, it emerges out of the interaction and perceptions of social actors.

Among the forms of social capital, Coleman cites obligations and expectations based on trustworthiness, information flows, and norms accompanied by sanctions. All of these are elements that emerge only through the conscious and reflective interaction among humans. As Coleman notes:

> Just as physical capital and human capital facilitate productive activity, social capital does as well. For example, a group within which there is extensive trustworthiness and extensive trust is able to accomplish much more than a comparable group without that trustworthiness and trust. (1988b:101)

The progressive recognition of the importance of social capital informs the historical evolution and application of organizational strategies and managerial ideologies promoting socio-economic development. Recognition of the value of social capital requires systems of industrial organization that appear fair and equitable in an effort to quell resistance and opposition. It is for labor that such ideological infrastructures are erected, and by the subsequent reaction of labor that they are transformed. Managerial methods and ideologies are part and parcel of the continuous system of organizational labor control required for the production and accumulation of wealth in all societies.

Richard Edwards (1979) has documented the historical evolution of organizational "forms of labor control" designed to maximize levels of work effort, productivity, and profit. The three systems are simple, technical, and bureaucratic control. *Simple control* is typified by the direct supervision and oversight of workers within an organization. In this personalized system the managerial role is one of immediate sanction and reward. This system is associated with the early stages of industrial production in which the owner carried out the managerial duties of oversight, encouragement, and discipline. *Technical control* replaces direct managerial supervision with a machine-based accounting system for the labor process. Technological innovations, most notably the assembly line, are introduced as non-personal methods of pace setting. Labor is forced to adjust to the mechanical and technological tempo of production. Under *bureaucratic control*, work effort is extracted through the use of systematic rules and procedures for promotion, wage increases, and job security. These bureaucratic incentives are said to promote consent, satisfaction, and commitment, which in turn should increase individual and collective work effort.

The evolution of organizational strategies is driven by a fundamental contradiction inherent in all productive systems—the pressure to rationalize as much of the production process as possible, on the one hand, and the need to elicit human cooperation, on the other. The basic dilemma is outlined in a work by Evan (1976) on the effects of organizational hierarchy. Most large, complex organizations that produce goods and services are hierarchically structured with a stratified system of positions. This hierarchical arrangement is regarded as either indispensable for a rational bureaucratic system of administration (the Weberian position) or inevitable in all large organizations (Michels' iron law of oligarchy). In either case there tends to be general agreement that hierarchical administrative positions enhance organizational productivity.

However, the inequality in the distribution of resources associated with the hierarchical structure—inequality in skills and knowledge, rewards, and authority (Evan 1976)—which tends to be cumulative, results in alienation, disaffection, and a lack of commitment among those who lack some or all of these resources. These subjective reactions to hierarchical arrangements may actually serve to undermine the positive effect of hierarchy on organizational effectiveness. Again, it is the unique nature of labor that yields this organizational dilemma for systems of production.

Rational methods involving differentiation, specialization, chains of command, and evaluation/accounting systems limit the freedom and autonomy of employees. Where the subjective response counteracts the potential advances in efficiency and productivity, efforts must be made to develop systems that placate workers and facilitate their attachment to the enterprise. This can be accomplished through symbolic rewards, ideological appeals, human relations gimmicks, or genuine systems of worker control. In some cases, at the national system level, where this dilemma also applies, political repression and the labor market serve to discipline workers and submerge the contradiction. Ultimately, however, the contradiction is never entirely resolved.

In advanced capitalist states today we see organizational developments that often seem inconsistent. Elaborate technological systems of work place accounting and surveillance exist alongside efforts to involve workers in decisions on quality and the organization of production. These tendencies are responses to different but coupled forces. The imperative to plan and control production encourages the drive to rationalize; the subjective response to rationalization systems often defeats the purpose and must be confronted with a human strategy. The ebb and flow of the socio-economic development process finds much of its source within this basic organizational-level contradiction.

MODERN ORGANIZATIONAL FORMS AND ECONOMIC SUCCESS

Contemporary organizational studies are concerned with emerging organizational strategies that facilitate profitable production in a modern, complex, and uncertain world economic environment. "Open-system" theories emphasize the relationship between environmental demands on organizations—such as shifting markets, the location of required resources, the rate of technological change, intensified competition, and internal organizational arrangements. It is assumed that internal organizational structures can be developed to cope with changing environmental conditions. Two notable examples of this trend in organization theory are the obsession with Japanese management techniques and approaches prescribing hierarchical solutions to organizational uncertainties.

The Transition from Fordism to Toyotaism

The current U.S. fixation on Japanese-style management techniques is a striking acknowledgment of the link between organizational structure and socio-economic development (see Boswell 1987). There appears to be no end to business press publications based on the premise that U.S. organizational practices have become obsolete and must be modified if the United States is to remain a globally competitive economic force. The Japanese system serves as the logical model for industrial success, given Japan's remarkable economic record since the 1970s and its exceptional ability to compete in world markets. We now have a case where continued

Western modernization may require the diffusion and adaptation of Eastern patterns of social organization (Ouchi 1981).

The U.S. model of industrial organization that fueled the rapid economic expansion of the 1950s and 1960s has apparently outlived its usefulness. Often referred to as *Fordism* (Aglietta 1979), this industrial model emerged alongside the transition to a mass-production economy and is associated with the innovative production techniques introduced by Henry Ford and the Ford Motor Company. The organizational system of Fordism has two central ingredients. First, it extended the principles of Taylorism to the mass production of commodities. The driving technological innovation was the semi-automatic assembly line, which created a rigid division of labor with job position and work pace determined by locations on and the speed of the assembly line. As with the principles of scientific management, Fordism involved a distinct separation between manual and mental labor as well as between specialized and repetitive work tasks. These features of Fordism have long created problems with employee motivation, commitment and satisfaction.

A second ingredient of Fordism served to compensate for some of the more unpleasant aspects of this industrial system. This was the relatively high wages paid industrial workers and the ability of industrial unions to engage in collective bargaining. The mass-production system required the enlargement of working-class buying power and a consumer market. Unions fought for and gained regular wage increases in accordance with gains in productivity, as well as work rule and job classification systems that reduced the arbitrary discretion of managers. Overall, labor-management relations were regulated through institutional channels, but they remained fundamentally adversarial.

Today, Fordism is contrasted with a presumably more appropriate form of industrial organization named *Toyotaism* (Dohse et al. 1985). The key facets of Toyotaism are the organization of the labor process and the nature of labor-management relations. As most studies indicate, Japanese workers have a greater affective emotional attachment to their work organization. Levels of commitment, loyalty, and identification with the firm are greater than for Western workers. While much of this attachment has been explained as a cultural phenomenon, Japanese managerial practices are clearly related to the positive orientation of employees. Key among these is the human relations orientation toward the labor force that engenders the creative involvement of workers in the tasks of production and quality control. Greater efforts are made to integrate production workers into areas of managerial concern and to spread the responsibility for productivity and quality among a broader cross-section of the work force. Bonuses, lifetime employment guarantees, and long-term career ladders further serve to attach employees to their place of work. Under this general system there is a stronger likelihood that workers will view their interests as consonant with those of managers, and thus comply with managerial efforts to promote greater productivity and efficiency.

A variant of the Fordism-Toyotaism model is the comparative analysis of Ronald Dore (1973). Dore focuses on the organizational and employment system characteristic of British/U.S. industrialization versus the contemporary Japanese system. Dore uses the term *market individualist* to describe the Anglo system. The market individualist system consists of weak communal ties in the relationship between worker and organization. Workers are not emotionally attached to the enterprise and, therefore, *inter*organizational mobility is routine. Wages tend to be determined by the labor market rather than by intraorganizational factors; this results in individualistic career planning, in which workers gravitate toward the highest-bidding enterprise. The market individualist system also gives rise to occupational and/or class forms of solidarity rather than enterprise-level forms of attachment.

Welfare corporatism describes the Japanese system, which, in contrast with the Anglo model, is said to facilitate the necessary conditions for production and growth in the modern world economy. Welfare corporatism promotes *intra*organizational mobility and careers, internal labor-market-based wage structures, and a high degree of company loyalty and consciousness. While welfare corporatism has historically been associated with the Japanese system, Dore contends that its superiority as an organizational form encourages its adaptation in Western societies. This claim is no doubt true, since Western firms have incorporated many welfare corporatist mechanisms into their organizations.

The key components of welfare corporatist organizational structures are summarized by Lincoln and Kalleberg (1985). First are structures facilitating participation, which involve expanded opportunities for input in the decision-making process in an effort to gain consensus on the goals and methods of production. Second, workers are integrated into the organization through numerous divisions and hierarchies that tend to cut across class and status lines, and thus defuse potential worker solidarity and class polarization. Third, an elaborate constellation of mobility and career ladders is used as a bureaucratic control technique engendering long-term organizational attachment, motivation, and loyalty. Finally, there is a broad sense of all organizational members as "corporate citizens" with legal rights and obligations within the organization, as well as social and recreational ties outside the factory. Together, these structures are said to foster diffuse and specific employee attachment to and support for the organization, and to make for a highly efficient and productive work force.

The glorification of the Japanese system implied in many of these accounts must be balanced with a few critical comments. The indisputable world market success of the Japanese economy has had the effect of distorting the nature of labor relations and the actual contribution of the managerial system. There is a tendency in much of the organizational literature to elevate the Japanese organizational system to a utopian status where labor has the best of all worlds, managers are benevolent and trusting, and the industrial order approximates Shangri-la. In reality, the production system is intensive and fast-paced, and workers are not well protected from managerial abuse. Work loads are subject to few restrictions, and managers are able to distribute, transfer, and allocate workers across a variety of positions, responsibilities, and tasks. While the organizational flexibility that results from these arrangements may be a critical structural feature of the modern competitive corporate organization, it is also one based on significant managerial latitude.

Other descriptions of Toyotaism (Dohse et al. 1985) emphasize the pressure and stress created by heavy work loads, daily production quotas, individualized wage systems, frequent evaluations, and intraorganizational labor market competition. Further, unions—the organizations most able to alleviate these negative work place features—are company specific and exist as part of the larger administrative structure of the firm. They are based on the principle of integration and consensus rather than on the adversarial role typical in the United States. Thus, they do not serve as viable political organizations able to represent the grievances of workers.

What we have, then, is a remarkably effective (at least temporarily) system of labor control that is based on a set of organizational structures that are keenly tuned toward facilitating consensus and organizational attachment. Many of these mechanisms are regarded as progressive, and in comparison with historical U.S. patterns this is an apt description. Nonetheless, one should not be blind to the basic fact that Japan is a capitalist economy engaged in production for private profit; there are many features of the employment arrangement that would be undesirable from the standpoint of U.S. workers.

There are also a number of structural features of the Japanese corporate organization, apart from the management system, that account for the positive economic performance. One of the most important is the size and scope of the major industrial corporate units. Major production in all sectors of the economy is carried out by industrial groups, or coalitions of enterprises, that are tightly integrated and include a symbiotic relationship with a major bank and trading company (Zimbalist and Sherman 1984:ch. 2). The close relationship with a major bank promotes a unique lending pattern that is oriented toward long-term projects and gestation periods. This "patient capital" is said to facilitate entrepreneurial risk in projects that require large start-up costs (Thurow 1985). Given the world market orientation of Japanese industry, the trading companies have played an integral role in the provision of imports and the facilitation of the export of goods to foreign markets. While it is the management/employment system that receives the greatest hype, these kinds of nonmarket coordination mechanisms are an essential key to the industrial success of Japan.

This vertically integrated system is also characterized by a significant level of internal dualism that delineates a core and peripheral structure within the industrial group. For example, while Toyota maintains lifetime employment policies and the other organizational benefits/structures outlined above, the subcontractors in these industrial groups are the organizations that bear the cost of slack demand and, therefore, establish a much less secure relationship with their employees. In short, the costs of market fluctuations and uncertainties are passed on to the peripheral members of the industrial group while the core is relatively protected and thus is able to project the image of the stable, trouble-free organization.

The Hierarchical Solution

The success of the vertically integrated Japanese system and the way in which these organizations deflect market uncertainty has not gone unnoticed by Western organizational theory. The work of Oliver Williamson (1975) is one of the most prominent examples of the current trend in organizational theory and research analyzing managerial strategies designed to buffer organizations against the uncertainty of markets. According to the transaction cost model, markets are cost-efficient allocators of goods and services when transactions are short-term, one-time, and transient. They are less effective where long-term commitment and exchange are required.

In a turbulent and complex environment, economic conditions can change quickly and it is difficult, if not impossible, to incorporate all these contingencies into a market contract. Thus, contracts can be broken, altered, or continued even after they have outlived their purpose. All of these potential uncertainties make market transactions costly and enhance the incentive for the construction of organizational hierarchies that incorporate the former market transaction within the planning apparatus of the firm. Vertical integration is the process whereby upstream and downstream transactions and the associated uncertainties are coordinated and controlled within a single hierarchy. This involves the merging of buyers and suppliers into a single enterprise or hierarchy. Quality, price, and supply presumably are more predictable, and long-term planning can be carried out with greater confidence within the organizational hierarchy.

This logic of the hierarchical solution to market transactions is extended to the labor market in the relationship with employees. In order to reduce the uncertainty associated with the labor component of production, where workers may not be totally qualified or committed to the firm, *internal labor markets* are erected. These bureaucratic structures of control, noted by Edwards (1979) and included in the welfare corporatist model, allow the organization to promote and select the known quantities that have also developed an allegiance to the firm. This presumably is the most effective way to reduce the transaction costs inherent in external market contracts that are based on incomplete information about the quality of the labor input.

Several considerations cast doubt on the inherent cost efficiency of the hierarchical strategy. These involve the variation in market forces across geographic areas and the ability to exploit advantageous market transaction conditions. For example, in the employment relation it may make much more sense for a firm involved in routine unskilled production to shift to a location or country where the labor market is characterized by less militant, unorganized workers than to internalize the labor market within the hierarchy of the firm (Clark 1981). The spatial separation of the various functions of the firm takes advantage of existing labor market conditions in particular areas. It also eliminates the "demonstration effect," in which bundles of bureaucratic incentives aimed at attracting and retaining highly skilled technical personnel are often demanded by less skilled production workers. While functions of the firm may be under a single corporate hierarchy, it may be most advantageous to decentralize the various functions spatially (see Massey 1985).

Further, from the perspective of the cost-conscious firm, it may be more cost-efficient to acquire supply inputs from independent producers located in low-wage, unregulated environments. General Motors provides a striking example of this situation. In an effort to become totally integrated along hierarchical lines, General Motors expanded into parts production for its line of automobiles. These parts producers came under the bargaining umbrella of the United Auto Workers, thus raising costs for parts. Foreign competitors obtained parts through low-wage peripheral producers. The ensuing crisis in the auto industry and the recent efforts at restructuring have prompted moves toward eliminating the General Motors' parts production and the sourcing of these functions to low-cost foreign and/or domestic producers. The whole movement toward off-shore production in cheap-labor countries is part of the spatial logic of organizational restructuring. This strategy has obvious implications for the socio-economic development of investing and host nations.

ORGANIZATIONAL STRATEGIES FOR LESS-DEVELOPED NATIONS

It may have occurred to the reader that our discussion of organizational strategies has been confined almost exclusively to developed industrial societies. This is because, with few exceptions, the vast literature on managerial intervention and organizational strategies promoting productivity and development has been directed primarily toward the modern industrial corporation, with the problems of the industrialized economies as their major focus. Organizational-level theorizing aimed at the development problems of less-developed economies is far less common.

There are, however, a number of exceptions to this general neglect of the organizational problems of less-developed nations. One of these is the work of Hage and Finsterbusch (1987), who advocate organizational change as a Third World development strategy. They subscribe to what is known as the *contingency theory* of organizations (Lawrence and Lorsch 1967; Burns and Stalker 1961). This approach advances a rather common-sense principle to the question of organizational structures and success—the success of organizational structures depends on the kinds of tasks that organizations have to carry out and the markets to which goods and services are directed. In short, there is no single best way to organize the production process. The appropriateness of an organizational strategy is contingent on the specific goals and needs of a particular organization and the particular setting.

This open-ended approach to organizational strategy is qualified significantly by the elaboration of a few principles guiding the contingency model. First, a number of possible contingencies are specified, and then the appropriate organizational structure for that contingency is prescribed. For example, where an organization is providing a good or a service to a stable and constant market, it is appropriate to use a rigidly bureaucratic organizational structure. Where production is for a rapidly changing, dynamic market, the organization must be more flexible and institute a decentralized system of production (Burns and Stalker 1961). Other contingency theorists have focused not so much on the market as on the form of technology applied to the production task (Woodward 1965). This leads to a second principle of contingency theory: that organizations using simple technological processes can institute a bureaucratic system, and those using complex technology require a more flexible organizational structure.

These fundamental principles of contingency theory are extended by Hage and Finsterbusch to yield a fourfold table of contingency pairs and what might be the appropriate organizational structure for each case:

Simple technology/small market equals craft organization; simple technology/large demand equals mechanical organization; complex technology/small demand equals organic organization; and complex technology/large demand equals mechanical-organic organization. (1987:4)

The term "mechanical" implies a rigid, formal bureaucratic structure, while "organic" refers to a decentralized and informal organizational structure. This basic typological model guides the analysis of, and suggestions for, organizational strategies of development in less-developed nations.

Hage and Finsterbusch (1987) take the rather abstract precepts of contingency theory and propose a set of change tactics designed to facilitate social and economic development. The basic strategy involves the following steps. First, it is important to demonstrate that a performance or output gap exists. That is, the owners and controllers of organizations must be made aware that their organization is operating far below capacity and/or is not adequately reaching the market of clients it is designed to serve. Second, some solution to the output gap must be devised. The solution, for Hage and Finsterbusch, involves the application of contingency principles and the proposal of a strategy that brings the organizational structure in line with the environmental and technological demands. Third, the proposed solution should be tested prior to wholesale implementation. This stage includes data collection, evaluation, and the revision of the original proposal, where needed, as well as extensive training of personnel in new roles, skills, and procedures. Last, a successful model is shaped and implemented, using proven methods and trained personnel.

The Hage and Finsterbusch approach represents one of the clearest examples of an organizational-level approach to the study of Third World development. It is also unique in the extent to which theoretical ideas are used to guide a very applied, nuts-and-bolts strategy for development. One of the major problems with their model, which they try to address in an epilogue to their work, is the neglect of the other levels of analysis, particularly the societal level constraints related to the power and position of particular social classes and political elites. Hage and Finsterbusch hold the somewhat overoptimistic—one might say naive—belief that those who control organizations are willing to recognize the performance gaps and to restructure the organization to alleviate these problems. While they make a fairly plausible argument that "influentials favor performance improvement," it is also important to consider the fact that "output gaps" are not necessarily unintentional or the product of irrational organizational processes. They may be deliberately intended because they serve the interests of particular groups. Underlying many, if not most, of Hage and Finsterbusch's proposals is a set of assumptions about the universality of the technocratic ideal and the neutrality of science.

Much of what Hage and Finsterbusch propose might yield significant organizational and societal gains, especially in the public sector projects on which they focus. However, as the contingency model suggests, the applicability and success of formal prescriptions depend upon another set of factors. Many of these other factors lie at a level of analysis that is to a large extent entirely ignored in their work. When societal-level forces are included in the model, the notions of "performance gap," "efficiency," and "scientific evidence" become politicized, and are often used as tools to advance particular interests.

THE MULTINATIONAL CORPORATION

The multinational corporation (MNC) might be considered the ultimate organizational structure because of its international reach and global power. Its impact on development can be viewed from a variety of perspectives. Nations that headquarter these large firms are placed in a relatively powerful international position, given the ability of MNCs to dominate international markets, contribute to a favorable trade balance, and influence social and political events worldwide. However, it is also the case that these firms, being multinational or transnational, have no loyalty to any single nation-state, and thus act to advance their own narrow self-interest, often at the expense of the economic health of the nation of origin.

Their impact on the nations in which they invest and operate is also a source of heated debate. Most conservative political economists view the spread of multinational capital as a positive development, one that can improve the economic performance and quality of life of less-developed nations. Third World nations should, therefore, encourage and accommodate foreign investment. Neo-Marxist theorists, with few exceptions (see Warren 1980), regard MNCs as exploitative, profit-maximizing firms that dominate and distort less-developed economies, hamper independent forms of development, and ultimately retard prospects for long-term economic growth. (Some of these issues will be reviewed in Chapter 6.) For the moment, it is worth considering the organizational characteristics of the MNC that allow it to function as a leading source of capital accumulation.

Stephen Hymer's (1972) influential and insightful analysis of the MNC views this organizational form as the logical and contemporary product of the tendency toward ever larger units of production. This evolutionary process dates to the Industrial Revolution and involves a movement of the organization of productive forces from "the workshop to the factory to the national corporation to the multidivisional corporation and now to the multinational corporation" (1972:113).

Hymer notes a critical distinction between these various capitalist forms of organization and precapitalist organizational arrangements. Under precapitalist production, the "macro" or societal level was structured in a hierarchical fashion by caste, class, and guild. At the "micro" or organizational level there was little coordination and a significant degree of autonomy. In contrast, under capitalism the central spheres of production are the *market* and the *factory*. This is the mirror image of the precapitalist society. Now the macro level is governed by the decentralized "invisible hand" of the market, while the micro level involves a progressive and systematic tendency toward coordination, control and hierarchy within the firm. It is at the organizational (or "micro," in Hymer's scheme) level that cooperation and the division of labor yield an ever-growing economic surplus. As with Williamson's transaction cost theory, managers are intent upon bringing much of the uncoordinated market activity within the hierarchical framework of the firm.

Efforts to deal with the problem of market uncertainty and flux promoted, according to Hymer, the precursor of the MNC—the multidivisional corporation. The strength of this organizational structure is its ability to produce for various markets simultaneously, expanding and contracting divisions as the market dictates while leaving the larger corporate structure intact. The essence of the MNC phase involves the *spatial expansion* of the multidivisional corporation to foreign locations that serve both as sources of supply and as outlets for demand. Through the mechanism of direct investment the MNC secures control over those environmental resources that were formerly acquired through world market exchange. What we have is the hierarchical strategy advocated by transaction-cost theory, but on an international level. As Hymer suggests:

"Multinational corporations are a substitute for the markets as a method of organizing international exchange" (1970:441). The combination of size and international scope allows MNCs to coordinate production and exchange worldwide, to produce in cost-efficient locations, and to extend markets beyond national confines. In this way and akin to the strategy of hierarchy, MNCs "enlarge the domain of centrally planned world production and decrease the domain of decentralized market directed specialization and exchange" (1970:443).

The various functions of the MNC also undergo a systematic spatial distribution. Hymer uses the basic insight of location theory, along with a model of administrative levels, to depict a spatial division of corporate tasks. Level I activities, the highest level of management and strategic planning, is located in the world-class cities and capitals that also house the centers of finance capital and governmental support structures. Level II—the intermediate administration level, composed of middle management, white-collar, professional, and information-processing tasks—deals with the coordination activities that also tend to be located in the larger international cities. At the lowest level, Level III, the actual operational management of production is carried out; this is located where appropriate raw material and labor market conditions exist. This means that the MNC system represented at Level III is decentralized and spread widely across the globe. In short, the internal hierarchy of the firm is reproduced spatially and internationally, which, according to Hymer,

represents an important step forward over previous methods of organizing international exchange. It demonstrates the social nature of production on a global scale. As it eliminates the anarchy of international markets and brings about a more extensive and productive international division of labor, it releases great sources of latent energy. (1972:133)

A broader question is how these organizations, international in scope, affect the development of their nations of origin and those that they penetrate. As we shall see, dependency theory has a great deal to say about this latter question. Hymer's assessment of the developmental role of the MNC is based on the application of a marketing cycle model to the international economy. In this model, innovation and new product development originate at the center of the international administrative hierarchy—the advanced capitalist states and the central international cities. Production and consumption patterns are then transferred to less-developed economies by MNCs interested in expanding the market for their products. These products then trickle down to other groups and locations, giving the sense of material advancement when, in fact, their relative position remains unchanged.

In this scheme the less-developed economies serve as a source for the extension of the cycle. Hymer's analysis of this process is related to that advanced by Vernon (1966), who uses a "product life cycle" model to analyze the changing nature of international production. According to this thesis, product development begins in the advanced industrial economies and, therefore, the economically dynamic effects and positive spin-offs are also felt in this location. Once these areas have reaped the benefits of product innovation, satiated center markets, and routinized production methods, the products and techniques are exported to the hinterlands. In both cases it is implied that the spatial extension has sustained the cycle while diffusing few of the dynamic by-products.

Given this view of the process, Hymer argues that MNC activity in the less-developed nations is not particularly beneficial and may actually reduce developmental options. He notes that MNC-generated forms of industrial development create little demand for highly trained and educated labor in the host country. In addition, MNCs tend to contribute little government revenue, since they either avoid significant taxation through transfer pricing or are granted major tax concessions as a condition for locating in the less-developed country. Hymer concludes that

A regime of multinational corporations would offer underdeveloped countries neither national independence nor equality. It would tend, instead, to inhibit the attainment of these goals. It would turn the underdeveloped countries into branch-plant countries, not only with reference to their economic functions but throughout the whole gamut of social, political and cultural roles. (1972:129)

MNCs can also have a negative effect on the development objectives of the advanced capitalist nations in which they originate. Hymer (1970) cites as the major contradiction the fact that the international scope of MNC operations precludes effective nation-state control or regulation of the most significant source of capital investment. Economic policy instruments are unable to capture much of the economic activity that takes place outside the borders of the nation-state. There are no international governmental institutions able or willing to control these giant corporations.

It has become clear that the internationalization of capital contributes to the mobility of foreign investment, jobs, tax revenue, and industries from the advanced to less-developed nations (see Portes and Walton 1981: ch. 5). While this was, for a long time, part of the product life cycle and trickle-down process, it is now clear that much of the industrial base is not being replenished and that other, significantly less dynamic, sectors have taken the place of manufacturing industry. The current consequences of MNC mobility and disinvestment have stimulated debate over the net impact of deindustrialization and the question of a national industrial policy.

4

SOCIETAL-LEVEL EXPLANATIONS I: STRUCTURAL MODERNIZATION AND ECONOMIC GROWTH MODELS

The societal level of analysis contains the greatest assortment of explanatory models of development. This is because it is commonly assumed that national development is a function of national (or societal-level) characteristics. In societal-level theories the causal factor (some national characteristics) and the effect (socio-economic development) are observed at the same level of analysis. Development, according to this framework, is the result of the organization of political, economic, and social institutions, or national socio-economic policies. The review of these theories covers two chapters. This chapter considers the influential structural modernization approach to development as presented by sociologists and political scientists. This is followed by an examination of economic growth and social welfare models of development.

STRUCTURAL MODERNIZATION AND SOCIO-ECONOMIC DEVELOPMENT

Chapter 2 considered the individual-level modernization approach that explains socio-economic change in terms of the diffusion and adaptation of Western values and beliefs. Closely related, but aimed at a different level of analysis, is the *structural modernization* approach, which identifies a set of social and political structural characteristics that define and are required for the realization of economic development. As in the individual-level approach, many of the requisite structural features represent ideal-typical patterns of social organization found at the ends of the traditional-modern continuum. To the extent that less-developed societies can incorporate these elements of modernity, the potential for sustained development is presumably enhanced.

Structural-Functionalism and Social Change

The structural modernization model, like the individual-level version, is heavily influenced by structural-functionalist theory. While the role of functionalism's value-normative factor loomed large in the individual-level model, the functionalist logic is even more pronounced in the structural renditions, given the converging levels of analysis—the social system. Many elements of Talcott Parsons' (1951) structural-functionalist systems theory have been incorporated into structural modernization models. We will not consider all the aspects of Parsons' work, but restrict our attention to those concepts of structural-functionalism used in theories of social, economic, and political development.

One of the central concepts in Parsons' evolutionary model of social systems and social change is *differentiation*. This refers to the proliferation of new structures and roles that emerge out of previously multifunctional structures. For example, in traditional societies the family structure combines a multitude of functions and roles—biological reproduction, economic production, education, medical care, and so on. In the course of modernization, and indicative of the process of development, there is both structural and role *specialization*. Specialized institutions and structures develop for the purpose of producing goods and services, training the population and providing health care. These institutions are composed of specialized and trained personnel.

Structural differentiation is one of the leading indicators of socio-economic development in Smelser's (1963) widely cited model of structural modernization. He defines structural differentiation as the process whereby

> One social role or organization . . . differentiates into two or more roles or organizations which function more effectively in the new historical circumstances. The new social units are structurally distinct from each other, but taken together are functionally equivalent to the original unit. (1963:106)

Contributing to the process of structural differentiation, according to Smelser, are a number of fundamental transitions: technologically, the shift from simple traditional techniques toward the application of scientific knowledge; economically, the evolution from subsistence to commercial farming and the transition from human/animal to industrial power; ecologically, the migration from farm to urban areas.

Each of these changes further serves to differentiate various structures and systems. Smelser cites numerous examples. Scientific knowledge provides the basis for new forms of secular rational understanding that promote the differentiation and specialization of religious systems. Commercial farming contributes to the differentiation of the kinship-family-community unit as specialized economic units emerge and are directed toward market production. The rise of the urban industrial system contributes to the decline of the multi-functional extended family unit, leaving it as a more specialized structure formed by choice and providing for expressive needs.

Establishing the causal ordering of these various processes, or the precise determinants of socio-economic development, is no easy task in Smelser's functionalist model. Causes and consequences are routinely confounded. While scientific knowledge, commercial farming, industrial power, and urbanization are seen as harbingers of economic progress and expansion, they merely describe the most common stereotypical elements of modern society. The socio-economic origin of these modern characteristics is not clearly delineated. Referring to these as "interrelated processes" that "frequently accompany development" sheds further darkness on the causal priority of the various forms of differentiation and modernity.

A second popular application of structural-functionalist theory is the employment of Parsons' pattern variables. These define the fundamental forms of social interaction and organization in social systems, and borrow heavily from Weber's ideal-type bureaucracy. The three variables most often selected and used to compare and differentiate modern and traditional societies are *specificity-diffuseness, achievement-ascription,* and *universalism-particularism.* These three polar concepts have been used to describe value systems, interaction patterns, modes of organization, and social systems. Consequently there is a great deal of ambiguity in their meaning. For the present purposes, however, we can consider the three variables as defining the different ways in which roles are organized, allocated, and evaluated in traditional and modern societies. The pattern variables are correlated with the level of differentiation and specialization.

Specificity-diffuseness refers to the extent to which roles are either narrowly or broadly defined. It is assumed that in modern differentiated societies people occupy specialized roles that carry formal and explicit expectations and responsibilities. In a modern society, with a complex and interdependent division of labor, role specificity contributes to the effectiveness of the larger system. This is contrasted with diffuseness, presumably common in traditional societies, in which people perform many roles simultaneously. Diffuseness is said to create difficulty in defining and accounting for areas of authority and responsibility.

Achievement-ascription, the second pattern variable, embodies two of the most widely used sociological concepts defining the basis for role allocation and reward. In modern societies achievement is regarded as the primary means by which positions are rationed and rewarded. People achieve positions in society through education, the development of skills, competent performance, and experience. In this way the specialized roles are carried out by the most able and the society, as a result, is more productive. This is contrasted with role reward and allocation on the basis of ascription, which involves recruitment to positions and the distribution of rewards on the basis of family background, race, sex, and other unachieved or ascribed characteristics. Traditional societies, in this model, are ascriptive, and this pattern of reward and allocation is seen as economically irrational and inefficient because positions are not filled on the basis of competence and merit.

The third pattern variable, *universalism-particularism*, has also assumed the status of a classic sociological dichotomy and is used to differentiate traditional and modern organizations. In modern universalistic organizations all members are subject to the same rules and regulations. As a feature of modern bureaucracy universalism guarantees that universal and impersonal standards will guide the allocation of rewards and sanctions. Universalism is said to contribute to organizational effectiveness and legitimacy. Particularism, in contrast, is a system in which rewards and sanctions favor some groups and individuals over others. The application of rules and regulations is not universal but selective and discriminatory. It is assumed that particularism characterizes less-developed societies and impedes the effectiveness of their social institutions.

The general argument of the structural modernization school is that less-developed nations must adopt the structural patterns of modern society—universalism, achievement, and specificity—if they hope to develop socially and economically (Hoselitz 1960). One illustration of the application of these concepts is found in the work of Theodorson (1966), who believes societies must move toward the modern end of the pattern variable continuum if they are to industrialize effectively. He uses the pattern variables to define and describe the different orientation and interaction patterns of individuals. Theodorson contends that in a society driven by industrial machines—a "machine society"—people must conform to modern patterns of interaction. What most distinguishes the modern industrialized world from traditional societies is the location where people work: the factory. Thus, according to Theodorson, people must adjust to the fact that work is no longer carried out with family and community members but with unfamiliar people who must be dealt with on a *specific* and *universalistic* basis. Relations and interactions with coworkers are explicitly and formally designed for instrumental purposes: to achieve organizational goals. Therefore, the diffuse, nonwork roles of workers are irrelevant in the machine society.

Theodorson further combines the pattern variables in arguing that, because machines are expensive and complicated, there is no room for anything but *achievement*-based recruitment to industrial positions. The ability to operate machines is a *specific* demand; diffuse or ascriptive standards of selection and evaluation have no basis in the machine society.

This society is also characterized by a complex division of labor, specialization, and considerable interdependence among producers of goods and services. Impersonal market exchanges are required in order for workers to secure access to food and clothing, and to satisfy various other needs. Accordingly, individuals must approach these market interactions and exchanges with a *specific* orientation with regard to the buyers and sellers of goods. The only relevant considerations are the adequacy of a person as a supplier of some product and the ability of the buyer to pay for the product. Again, diffuse roles and ascribed characteristics are irrelevant. In Theodorson's model, then, the brave new world of the machine society is characterized and driven largely by instrumental rather than expressive interactions, secondary rather than primary groups, specificity rather than diffuseness. All of this fits squarely into classical sociological accounts of modern urban industrial life.

Theodorson includes a fourth pattern variable, not defined above, in his analysis of the machine society: *affective neutrality-affectivity*. This further complements the instrumental-expressive distinction and refers to the extent to which one gives open expression to immediate desires or, in contrast, suppresses these desires for a long-range goal. The suppression of desires, according to Theodorson, is required in the industrial milieu because

One of the most serious problems facing the new factory in the underdeveloped area is that of absenteeism and labor turnover due to the reluctance of the workers to accept the new factory discipline. The worker must do his work regardless of his private desires of the moment. Gratification must be postponed. (Theodorson 1966:303)

In sum, structural differentiation and role specialization, which stem from the process of industrialization, require congruent patterns of interpersonal behavior and interaction. The expressive freedoms of multifunctional roles give way to the instrumental, goal-directed constraints of role specialization. These social structural patterns both define and promote socio-economic development.

Criticism of the Structural Modernization Model

Because the social-structural modernization models are based heavily upon the tenets of structural-functionalist theory, an attack on the foundations of functionalism would go a long way toward a critique of structural modernization approaches. However, functionalism-bashing, while still a favorite pastime among many sociologists, has become somewhat passe.[1] Rather than restate the accumulated litany of charges against structural functionalism, it is more fruitful to select those major shortcomings of the structural modernization approach that relate specifically to the question of socio-economic development, social change, and the level of analysis.

One of the most forceful critiques of the modernization model is provided by Andre Gunder Frank (1969). In his strident assault Frank takes the theoretical model to task on the basis of its empirical validity, theoretical adequacy, and policy effectiveness. His "gloves-off" style makes for a stimulating and entertaining critique.

Frank directs a large part of his attack at the "pattern variables"—universalism-particularism, achievement-ascription, and specificity-diffuseness—outlined above. As already noted, the use of the pattern variable logic is consistent with the general tendency among modernization theorists to compare the ideal-typical traits of equally ideal-typical societies. Using this theoretical strategy, the modernization model leaves itself wide open to charges of empirical irrelevance and invalidity. Certainly all theories are, to one degree or another, susceptible to the accusation that reality has been compromised and oversimplified. Such is the nature of theory construction. Yet modernization theory goes further. There is the clear implication that the ideal-typical characteristics of the modern society are superior to the patterns prevalent in traditional systems and social structures. The ethnocentrism of the modernization model incites critics and invites attacks on the empirical validity of such invidious comparisons. If claims for the superiority and inferiority of societies are based on fictitious accounts, then the theory "deserves what it gets."

Frank, in his critique, wastes no time attacking the empirical weakness of the pattern variable system. He points to the indisputable fact that universalism and achievement are more accurately normative ideals than behavioral realities in modern industrial societies. The persistence in almost every empirical study in advanced capitalist societies of "statistically significant" effects of family background, race, and sex on occupational prestige and income should put to rest the traditional-ascriptive versus modern-achievement societal comparison. The effects of ascription are especially strong, as Frank points out, in the recruitment to roles at the upper and lower reaches of the stratification system. The fact that particularism and ascription are pervasive facts of life in modern industrial societies, which remain modern and industrial, suggests that these factors are much less critical for development than structural modernization theorists assume. In fact, there may be many rational reasons to select people on the basis of particular and ascribed criteria. Institutions and organizations may benefit greatly from the appointment of personnel who have outside connections that can advance the goals of the institution (see Perrow 1986). In this instance their technical administrative competence is much less important than "who they know" and "where they have been." To put it succinctly "to deplore particularism is only to advance an ideal and to neglect the reality of organizational affairs" (Perrow 1986:11).

As for the presumed necessity of "functional role specificity," Frank points to the common pattern of role diffuseness that exists in modern industrial societies at the highest and most critical institutional levels. He uses the example of the "power elite" who, as documented by C. Wright Mills (1956) and William Domhoff (1971), carry their power and influence across and into political, economic, and educational organizations. Indeed, it is their role in numerous spheres, most notably the corporate, that often qualifies them for positions in other institutions. Role diffuseness, in this case, is an asset that legitimates role recruitment; it is viewed as a strength rather than a weakness. Likewise, in traditional societies, normative universalism holds considerable sway. Universalistic norms have had the effect of spawning, according to Frank, the radical anti-colonial and nationalist movements and protests that frighten the very modernization theorists who claim devotion to the universalistic ideal. Similarly, both normative and behavioral achievement patterns are apparent in traditional societies in the mobility and recruitment of comprador capitalists and military elites who have *achieved* their positions through extortion, speculation, exploitation, murder, and torture.

Frank also takes issue with structural modernization theorists for failing to identify which of the many social roles are the most decisive for socio-economic development. It is often implied that structural differentiation and functional specificity must characterize all institutions and social roles. Frank believes that certain political-economic roles are more important and therefore should be assigned greater weight in a model of development. Specifically, if one examines the top economic and political roles in modern societies, which have the greatest influence on socio-economic development, the claims of achievement, universalism, and specificity simply cannot be sustained.

An important level-of-analysis question is also raised by Frank. He accuses structural modernization theorists of moving from one set of variables or units of analysis to another. The version of modernization theory reviewed here is considered by its advocates to be a social structural and systemic model, yet it tends to identify smaller units (tribes and families), particular roles, and patterns of interaction as explanatory variables, suggesting that to "produce development it is only necessary to change particular variables, roles or parts of the social system—that it is not necessary to change the structure of the system itself" (Frank 1969:37). This, claims Frank, is a betrayal of the very structuralist model they seek to employ. Further, Frank (1969:35) contends that the selection of roles and interaction patterns is "empirically unacceptable" because it draws attention from "the system whose characteristics are the determinant ones for development and underdevelopment."

There are a number of points that can be added to those raised by Frank. The traditional-modern antithesis presented by structural modernization theorists, and the mutually exclusive polar traits associated with these ideal types, obscures the fact that a combination of traditional and modern traits coexists in all societies. This is true not only in the transitional sense but also in a functional sense, as the example of "functional dualism" in Chapter 3 indicated. In deJanvry's account, family subsistence agriculture, with its likely constellation of traditional pattern variable traits, coexisted alongside modern rationalized plantation agriculture. The traditional kinship economic unit contributed to the viability and profitability of the modern sector. This mutually reinforcing system of traditional and modern elements is reported in many other contexts.

The critical point to emphasize is that there is no necessary reason why modernization and industrialization should automatically shatter traditional patterns based on particularism and ascription. This kind of teleological argument is difficult to sustain in the face of the various modes of industrial development existing in the contemporary world. The case of South Africa illustrates the point. South Africa is, by any measure, an industrialized society. Yet it is hardly driven by universalism—normatively or behaviorally. The racial caste-like system that exists there may be "dysfunctional," but that has not led to its demise. One of the major dysfunctions of the racial system of apartheid is its effect on the labor market. Excluding the black majority from higher-status positions has resulted in a severe labor shortage as well as an inflated wage structure for white workers, who, having a monopoly over the best jobs, do not compete with black workers.

The economic irrationality, from the standpoint of capitalist logic, of such a system has failed to create anything close to a universalistic achievement-based society. Instead, alternative non-universalistic arrangements have been devised. As Randall Stokes's (1975:131) analysis of the South African system indicates: "Racial particularism is the parameter within which rational solutions are sought." Any solution that involves the upgrading of the position of blacks to deal with the labor shortage is typically accompanied, according to Stokes (1975:132), by two general but unspoken principles:

First, the "principle of contamination" holds that whites must not be put in intimate contact with Africans unless there is a clear superiority of rank to insulate whites. . . . Second, the "principle of preserving relative position" holds that whites must retain their traditional income and status advantages over Africans.

In sum, the traditional-modern dichotomy, and the various social processes presumed to accompany the movement from one extreme to the other, offer little in the way of an analysis of the socio-economic forces responsible for development. The societies described by structural modernization theorists are fictional. The praiseworthy traits of modern society are not found in real-world industrial societies, and the inferior traits of traditional society are equally difficult to find in most nations of the world. The assumed logic of industrialism and modernity has not inevitably resulted in universalism-achievement, nor are these types of pattern variables required for economic development. The structural modernization perspective provides little more than a bundle of interrelated concepts that describe imaginary societies. The explanatory power of this model is severely limited.

Structural-Functionalism and Political Development

The impact of structural-functionalism is not confined to sociology. Political scientists have borrowed elements of structural-functionalism to describe political structures, delineate the function of political institutions, and explain the way political structures contribute to socio-economic development. In the structural-functionalist model political institutions assume a critical role in the structural evolution of social systems. As societies become increasingly differentiated structurally, they require institutions that *integrate* and *coordinate* the differentiated structure. A number of subsystems emerge for this purpose and permit the system to adapt and maintain continuity and stability (Smelser and Parsons 1956). One of these subsystems is the *polity*, which is designed to facilitate the attainment of collective goals. Because these goals may be economic, there are direct links between the structure of the political subsystem and the process of economic development (Spengler 1966).

The language and logic of structural functionalism have become an integral part of comparative politics and the study of political development. Perhaps the most striking example of this interdisciplinary germination is found in the work of Gabriel Almond and his colleagues (Almond 1960, 1965; Almond and Powell 1978). The process of political development, according to Almond, involves *differentiation* and *secularization*. These terms mean for the political structure what has already been described for the social system: roles change and become more specialized and autonomous, social patterns of behavior are more oriented to cause-and-effect relationships, belief systems come under the sway of science and technology (Almond and Powell 1978). Almond and Powell's basic argument is that, "A structurally differentiated political system with a secularized political culture will have an increased capability to shape its domestic and international environment" (Almond and Powell 1978:20). Needless to say, modern political systems are characterized by high levels of structural differentiation and cultural secularization.

Lucian Pye (1968) offers a similar set of structural-functionalist concepts. After reviewing all of the various definitions of political development, he reduces the concept to three key elements. The first indicator of political development is *equality* in the form of mass participation and citizenship. The principle of equality is said to ensure that the legal system is guided by *universalistic* laws and procedures and that recruitment into positions is based on *achievement* rather than ascription. The second element of political development, according to Pye, is an increased *capacity* of the political system. This involves the implementation of policy outputs, effective and efficient governmental performance, and a rational and secular orientation toward administrative matters. The final feature of political development, according to Pye, is the familiar *differentiation* and *specialization* of political structures. Political development entails both the functional specificity of political roles and institutions and the integration of the various structures and specialties.

As with Smelser's model of structural modernization, the causal relationship between political development and socio-economic modernization is not clearly formulated. Political development is seen as both a cause and a consequence of modernization. While political differentiation and secularizaton may promote socio-economic development, it is also the case that the forces of social change prompt further political development. For example, Almond and Powell (1978:21) assert: "Development results when the existing structure and culture of the political system are unable to cope with the problem or challenge without further structural differentiation and cultural secularization."

In identifying the source of "problems and challenges" for political systems, Almond incorporates additional elements of structural-functionalism. He frequently conjures up the familiar "black box" image of the polity as a system receiving various inputs, converting and aggregating them and, ultimately, manufacturing outputs in the form of government policies and actions. Inputs are both governmental supports (symbolic forms of support and loyalty, financial resources) and political demands. Problems and challenges are said to result when there is a decline in input supports, an imbalance between supports and demands, or the oft-cited "demand overload." These forms of disequilibrium presumably are less likely where the political system has developed the appropriate (read "modern") structures that carry out the necessary functions of political socialization and recruitment, interest articulation, interest aggregation, and political communication. Because modern political systems are structurally differentiated and culturally secularized, they have developed a diverse set of institutional structures that serve these various and imperative functions.

Among the many challenges that might confront a political system, Almond and Powell cite three specific types: nation-state building, participation, and distribution. They note how each of these challenges contributed to the structural differentiation of Western political systems. Thus, the ages of "absolutism," "democratization," and "welfare" in the West are interpreted as structural responses to the challenge of nation-state building, participation, and distribution, respectively. However, as Almond and Powell indicate, there is no guarantee that these challenges will be handled as effectively by less-developed political systems. Where political systems are unable to develop sufficient levels of structural differentiation to absorb these demands, system maintenance is threatened.

This brings us to yet another concern of structural-functionalist theory: "social disturbances." These are the potentially negative consequences of modernization such as hysteria, violence, religious outbursts, and political movements (Smelser 1963). These types of challenges to political systems are seen as a largely inevitable result of "social mobilization" (Deutsch 1966:205):

> Social mobilization is a name given to an overall process of change which happens to substantial parts of the population in countries which are moving from traditional to modern ways of life. It denotes a concept which brackets together a number of more specific processes of change, such as change of residence, of occupation, of social setting, of face-to-face associates, of institutions, roles, and ways of acting. . . . Social mobilization can be defined . . . as the process in which major clusters of old social, economic and psychological commitments are eroded or broken and people become available for new patterns of socialization and behavior.

While social mobilization might be regarded as a positive indicator of socio-economic development, both structural-functionalist and political modernization theorists tend to place a greater priority and value on social order and stability. Therefore, social mobilization is not always a good sign because it may result in social and political disorder. Consequently, political development theorists informed by structural functionalism have spent a great deal of energy attempting to identify the requisite political structures able to contain social mobilization and thus prevent instability. If such a political capacity is established, it is believed that socio-economic development will proceed more smoothly.

The fear of instability has a long legacy in post-war U.S. sociology and political science. The rise of fascism in Germany and Italy and the institutionalization of socialism in the Soviet Union shaped the pro-order bias of structural-functionalist theory. This bias is reflected in the obsession with stability, order, integration, consensus, and harmony. In the underdeveloped world modernization and social mobilization are feared because they may result in just the opposite—instability, disorder, disintegration, dissensus, and dissonance. These negative consequences are potential obstacles to socio-economic development. Thus a definition of a "modern," correct, and adequate political structure must include the "capacity" to deal with social disturbances, prevent political chaos, and promote gradual, peaceful, and harmonious change.

It was in this context that Samuel Huntington produced his classic and controversial work *Political Order in Changing Societies* (1968). Huntington's model of political development incorporates not only some of the basic elements of structural modernization logic but also some healthy pessimism and apprehension concerning the ability of nations to modernize in a smooth, painless, and orderly manner. In this latter sense his account departs in a constructive way from the naive optimism of evolutionary modernization models (on this point see Leys 1982).

Huntington's basic premise is that development and modernization are not necessarily progressive forces, because they can breed instability and disorder. The essence of political development, therefore, is the creation of *effective states* that are able to govern authoritatively and legitimately in the face of social change. Huntington cites the United States, Great Britain, and the Soviet Union as effective political structures that differ from the "debile" political systems of Latin America, Asia, and Africa. His primary thesis is that instability and violence are due to "rapid social change and rapid mobilization of new groups into politics coupled with the slow development of political institutions" (1968:4). The relationship between these two variables—social mobilization and political in-stitutionalization—determines the pace of development and modern-ization. While social mobilization is viewed as a relatively inevitable feature of social change, political institutionalization is susceptible to active intervention by elites and nation builders. As structural requisites for development, then, Huntington cites those which promote the in-stitutionalization of political systems and organizations.

Institutionalization is defined as "the process by which organizations and procedures acquire value and stability" (1968:12). The level of institutionalization can be measured by a set of ideal-type criteria of the pattern-variable variety. These criteria are *adaptability-rigidity, com-plexity-simplicity, autonomy-subordination,* and *coherence-disunity.* As one might expect, adaptability, complexity, autonomy, and coherence are the desiderata of political modernization. *Adaptive* political organizational structures are able to handle changing demands from the environment and shift functions as new situations arise. In this sense it is not functional specificity but functional adaptability that characterizes effective political organizations. *Complex* organizations are more highly institutionalized. Complexity refers to the hierarchical and functional subunits of an or-ganization that allow for multiple bases of support and attachment, and a greater capacity for adjustment. *Autonomous* political organizations pos-sess higher levels of institutionalization because they exist independent of other social groupings and methods of behavior, are able to maintain their integrity, and are not simply the expression of the interests of particular social groups. Finally, according to Huntington, institutionalized or-ganizations exhibit a high level of *coherence.* This refers to the degree of consensus and agreement among members of political organizations and political participants. This facilitates unity and discipline, and thus reduces the likelihood of conflict.

It is Huntington's contention that highly institutionalized political structures, characterized by adaptability, complexity, autonomy, and coherence, are best able to handle social mobilization and, therefore, to provide for the smooth and stable modernization of their societies. However, in most less-developed nations such effective political structures are absent, and this results in political instability and "political decay." Political institutions, under this condition, are unable to absorb the expansion of political demands and political participation. Huntington describes these societies as "praetorian"—combining low levels of institutionalization with high levels of participation. In praetorian societies a variety of socio-political movements, often resorting to unconventional methods, act directly on the political system. The political intervention of military, religious, and student groups is cited by Huntington.

> What makes such groups seem more "politicized" in a praetorian society is the absence of effective political institutions capable of mediating, refining and moderating groups' political action. . . . Each group employs means which reflect its peculiar nature and capabilities. The wealthy bribe, students riot, workers strike, mobs demonstrate, and the military coup. (1968:196)

These activities are a common part of the "praetorian polity." This is contrasted with a "civic polity," in which political institutionalization is high relative to political participation, stable patterns of institutional authority exist, political organizations such as political parties mediate the involvement of different social groups, and structures of political socialization are present. Under the civic polity the conditions for socio-economic development are enhanced insofar as political participation is institutionalized and managed, and political disruption is avoided. The praetorian-civic comparison is akin to the various other traditional-modern dichotomies that have been discussed. In Huntington's model the explanation for development or decay resides at the political system level of analysis, the implication being that a civic polity is the most appropriate political structure for development.

Problems with the Political Development Model

Huntington's formulation has been the target of numerous critiques. One rather glaring logical weakness is its extreme circularity. As in individual modernization models and many renditions of structural functionalism, the empirical presence or absence of certain attributes determines the cause. In this case, the level of institutionalization is determined by the presence or absence of political stability. Systems that are politically stable are highly institutionalized; instability reflects low levels of institutionalization.

Several additional comments are in order. First, it is difficult to find, in a single work, a more representative statement of the spirit of mainstream post-war U.S. social science. There are many samplings throughout the book that reflect the dominant themes of the day. In deference to structural functionalism there are the polar-type variables that define the appropriate and inappropriate structural system requirements. Huntington devotes considerable space to the familiar "functional differentiation," "integration," and "rationalization" processes. The model also borrows systems theory language. For example: "A well-developed political system has strong and distinct institutions to perform both the 'input' and 'output' functions of politics" (1968:84).

As already noted, there is an unmistakable reverence for social and political order in Huntington's work. Indeed, there are few pieces of social science that rival his obsessive concern with stability. It seems that, for Huntington, maintaining order is the raison d'être of political systems. The quality of a political system is based, in Huntington's account, on its ability to handle participation, absorb demands, assimilate opposition, and, more generally, buffer the system from any external challenges. Political effectiveness is not measured by the capacity of the political system to "deliver the goods," provide a high quality of life, allow for the exercise of democracy, or promote the greatest good for the greatest number. It is defined, instead, by the extent to which structural mechanisms exist to protect political institutions and authority from external domestic threats. It is for this reason that Huntington, though a cold war anti-Communist, regards the political systems of the United States, Great Britain, and the Soviet Union as equally effective and deserving of admiration. A respect for order and authority makes for strange political bedfellows.

Finally, the assumptions of mass society theory (Kornhauser 1959; Lipset 1960), a guiding doctrine of post-war political sociology (see Chapter 3), are firmly embodied in Huntington's model. The fear that social change will unleash an insatiable and undemocratic mass leads Huntington to view mass political participation suspiciously and to favor, instead, political institutions that demobilize and co-opt the population and political movements. In the end, if the choice is between political democracy and political order, it is quite clear that Huntington comes down in support of the latter. There is a political-economic rationale for this choice. Democracy, political demands, and mass participation are often viewed as antithetical to economic growth and development because these inconvenient consequences of social mobilization may reduce the freedom of economic and political elites. Huntington is careful to avoid stating it quite in these terms and, like many of his fellow political scientists, prefers to couch the issue in the neutral-appearing language of systems theory.

The obsession with social and political order in Huntington's model and, more generally, in contemporary versions of structural functionalism deserves one final remark. Order, as a developmental objective, may appear to be a perfectly reasonable goal. However, it is not, as many theorists would have us believe, an entirely value-free or unbiased objective. The political implications of the call for order have been most clearly elaborated in Alvin Gouldner's (1970:251–54) sweeping critique of structural functionalism. He argues that the political conservatism of a social theory can be gauged by the value placed on the maintenance of social order. This is indicative of conservatism not only in a literal sense—that is, conserving the existing society and order—but also in a more explicitly political sense. To express a preference for the maintenance of the status quo over some possible alternative is to endorse those features of the existing order and the corresponding privileges accorded to some and denied to others.

In this context, as Gouldner's argument clearly implies, the defense of social order is a political position. Not all parties have an equal interest in the maintenance of social order. Those who benefit from the existing arrangements—the elite or ruling class—have an interest in preserving the system. Those at the bottom do not share equally in this interest. They may, in fact, prefer a major structural overhaul in which the rules are changed and their chances of obtaining valued resources are enhanced. In short, the advocates of social and political order are defending the privileged position of the existing elite. This is obviously not a politically neutral or value-free undertaking.

It is also worth considering Gouldner's argument about the source of disorder. In many models of political development "social disturbances" are said to arise out of the mass "mobilization of excessive demands." Thus, those who make demands and seek change are regarded as the agents of disorder, chaos, and disruption; the change seekers are "the problem." As Gouldner notes, "it takes two to make disorder." One must consider not only the demanders but also the resisters of change. Elite rigidity and inflexibility in the face of political demands often force insurgent groups to utilize "unconventional" political tactics. These disruptive and sometimes violent strategies are not the result of inadequate political institutionalization or the failure of effective political socialization, but the direct product of deliberate attempts by elite segments to deny political access to particular groups or to outlaw more "conventional" forms of political expression.

The "Bureaucratic Authoritarian" Solution to Political Disorder

One "solution" offered to deal with the problem of mass mobilization is the establishment of a "bureaucratic-authoritarian" state. The model of "bureaucratic-authoritarianism," developed by O'Donnell (1973), differs from Huntington's in that it is based on specific historical cases (Brazil and Argentina) and is more explicit about the class interests that are served by this particular political development strategy. However, the model of bureaucratic authoritarianism is mentioned here because it is informed by elements of structural-functionalist logic and is seen as an antidote to Huntington's nemesis, political disorder.

O'Donnell, tying the case histories of Argentina and Brazil to major currents in political development, relies heavily on the concepts of differentiation and integration. He argues that industrialization creates a pattern of social differentiation that has *political pluralization* as its political expression. Out of the proliferation of political actors and social units come "competing interests, conflicting normative claims, and divergent behavioral expectations. Insofar as some 'fit' is not achieved among these aspects and across social units, social integration lags behind social differentiation" (1973:76). All of this contributes to a "demands-performance gap"; there are "low levels of social cohesion"; the "capacity" of the political system is diminished—the net result is "mass praetorianism."

> The political tendency, thus, was toward a highly authoritarian political system, but the specific characteristics of such authoritarianism, as well as the major goals of the winning coalition, were deeply influenced by the degree of [high] modernization and the type of [mass] praetorianism. (O'Donnell 1973:78)

The authoritarianism to which O'Donnell makes reference is defined as an exclusionary coercive system that seeks to deactivate the masses and allow for governmental autonomy unconstrained by mass demands. At the same time, the system lacks any coherent ideology or solid basis of legitimation. Because the model is based upon the experience of the more modernized Third World states, O'Donnell adds the "bureaucratic" dimension to his political system type. The implication is that the authoritarian state system is, like other parts of the modernized social system, highly differentiated and composed of greater role specificity. He emphasizes the emergence of *technocratic* roles in all institutions, including the state. The value orientation of these role incumbents is said to be toward rational and efficient solutions to economic and social problems. This rational orientation, which O'Donnell links to the diffusion of technical expertise from the advanced to less-developed nations, leads to a technocratic alliance in opposition to mass political participation:

> Technocratic role-incumbents in situations of high modernization are likely to act in contrast to their usually politically liberal role-models, and to constitute the core of the coalition that will attempt the establishment of an authoritarian, excluding political system. . . . This coalition will aim at reshaping the social context in ways envisioned as more favorable for the application of technocratic expertise and for the expansion of the influence of the social sectors that the role-incumbents have most deeply penetrated—i.e., an "excluding" authoritarian system. (1973:87–88)

It is here that O'Donnell employs the kind of language, akin to Huntington's, that obscures more than it illuminates. With all the talk about "technocratic role-incumbents," it is implied that the disdain for democracy is nothing more than a desire for efficiency. It is also suggested that exclusion and coercion are pursued because they facilitate the efficient formulation and implementation of government policy, allowing technocrats to "get things done." The banning of unions and strikes, the curtailing of consumption, and the abolition of government social programs, however, must be linked to the interests of particular class segments and the enhancement of the rate of private profit. O'Donnell makes this connection quite explicit in his case studies, but the theoretical model, with its propositions and hypotheses, lapses into the obscurantist jargon of structural-functionalist systems theory. As Petras (1981:126) put it:

> In some ways, the bureaucratic structure is a facade, an alibi that disguises the multiple forms of repression and the arbitrary nature of the state. In this sense, the notion of bureaucratic authoritarianism itself is an ideology that serves to mystify the violent and arbitrary nature of the state.

In fairness to O'Donnell, it should be mentioned that his more recent work (1978, 1979) points directly to the foreign and political class interests served by the authoritarian regime. This "political economic" perspective will be discussed in greater detail later in this chapter and in Chapter 5. For the moment we turn to a different system-level explanation that focuses upon economic structures and institutions.

ECONOMIC MODELS OF DEVELOPMENT

There are many economic models of development that operate at the societal level. These typically focus on, as explanatory variables, national economic structures, economic processes, and financial conditions. The major dependent variable, or indicator of development, is the level of and change in the gross national product (GNP). Many of these economic models are quite technical and complex. The presentation is confined to theories and arguments accessible to readers unfamiliar with formal microeconomic and macroeconomic theory.

The GNP Growth Model

At the most basic economistic level, development can be defined simply as an increase in GNP—the change in the value of the output of goods and services between two points in time. If the development objective is to expand GNP, then one must identify those factors which have the greatest influence on this measure. The problems of the less-developed nations are often framed in this way. Their economies do not produce enough commodities and services, enough value, or enough income. The key to expanding the value of output involves the manipulation of a set of other factors.

Most GNP models place the greatest weight on the role of *capital formation*. This is defined as the net investment in capital assets, such as factories, machinery, and productive equipment. Holding many variables constant, the basic GNP model assumes that economic growth is a direct function of the amount and rate of capital formation (Domar 1957). In this theory of "capital fundamentalism" (Gillis et al. 1987:253–54), the solution to underdevelopment involves an increase in the volume and rate of capital investment.

Like so much of economics, however, the causal chain extends further backward, such that the level of capital formation is itself a function of the *rate of savings*. The rate of savings is the level of available financial capital that can be used for investment. It is based on the degree of surplus at the governmental, corporate, and household levels. Government savings require that revenue exceed expenditures; corporate savings are based on the retention of earnings and profits; household savings are based on the income remaining after consumption expenditures. Where a surplus exists and savings occur, resources for capital formation are available. The ability to produce surplus income, however, requires advances in the *level of productivity* such that the level of output increases with constant inputs of labor. In turn—and it is here that the model comes full circle—the level of productivity depends upon the rate of capital investment and formation.

We have sketched some of the basic elements of Ragner Nurkse's (1962) famous "vicious circle" model. The deficient state of each factor in the model is the product of the insufficient level of some other factor. There appears to be no way out of this developmental trap. Poverty breeds poverty. We have outlined the "supply side" of the dilemma, but there is also a "demand side" (Smelser 1963). On the demand side the incentive to invest in capital formation is weak because the internal market (domestic buying power) is too narrow. The lack of buying power is due to the low level of productivity, which, as we have seen, is due to insufficient capital investment. And so the cycle is complete.

The trick is somehow to break the cycle by intervening at some point in the circle. The level or quantity of one of the variables must be increased, and this will then generate expansion of the other factors and, ultimately, the GNP. This requires the intervention of some exogenous force. Nurkse suggests a variety of solutions. For example, production can be geared for export, which gets around the problem of insufficient internal demand. Or nations can borrow investment resources from international lending agencies to build the stock of capital formation. Each of these proposals—export-oriented growth and a reliance on external capital—has been instituted, in some form or other, in most less-developed nations. However, they have not entirely solved the problems of economic development, and some theorists (see Chapter 6) argue that these policies have, in fact, reinforced the state of underdevelopment. Nonetheless, the logic of Nurkse's formulation necessitates the entry of some external force to break the circuit.

Smelser's (1963) treatment of Nurkse's model attempts to demonstrate the central role of sociological variables in the "vicious circle" problem. He notes that the problems of savings and consumption are intimately tied to the modes of social organization and social class structure. Thus, in feudal societies the controllers of the surplus—the feudal oligarchy—consume rather than invest savings and therefore do not contribute to advances in productivity. The unproductive use of labor is also due, according to

Smelser, to the kinship ties in rural areas that discourage workers from moving to the geographic locations where they can be used most productively. And the entrepreneurial spirit, which would encourage capital investment and risk taking, is hindered by traditional religious beliefs and institutions. Here we see some of the modernization arguments linked directly to the GNP model and, more generally, to the idea that the circle can be broken only through the diffusion of Western capital, social organization, and culture.

Paul Baran (1957) presents a theory of growth that revolves around some of the variables in the GNP model. In his thesis the key factor in generating the expansion of per capita output is new net investment or capital formation in the means of production. This depends on the availability of capital and savings, which are drawn from a nation's economic surplus. The concept of economic surplus plays a major role in Baran's theory of economic growth. He distinguished between the actual and the potential economic surplus. The *actual* economic surplus is "the difference between society's actual current output and its actual current consumption" (1957:22); the *potential* economic surplus is "the difference between the output that *could* be produced in a given natural and technological environment with the help of employable productive resources, and what might be regarded as essential consumption" (1957:23).

Baran assumed that the difference between the actual and the potential surplus could be realized under alternative forms of economic and social organization. This basic idea provides a useful way to conceptualize the fundamental problem of socio-economic development: organizing society in such a way that all available resources are productively directed toward economic production, while wasteful consumption is minimized. It is unlikely that many students of development would object to this definition. The battle would begin over which factors are responsible for the inability to realize the potential surplus.

In Baran's view, the potential surplus is unrealized because of excess consumption, loss of output from unproductive workers, wasteful and inefficient organizations, and chronic unemployment and underemployment. These various explanations for the inability to realize the potential surplus, and their elaboration in Baran's work, extend across all levels of analysis. At the individual level there are the values and behavior patterns of the landowning elite and their tendency to squander surplus through the inordinate consumption of luxuries. At the organizational level Baran pointed to the lack of investment in modern technology, which retards the productive use of labor. At the level of national socio-economic systems, Baran distinguished between Western European capitalism and the hybrid feudalism/capitalism of underdeveloped societies. Baran also pointed to a number of world/economic forces that will be considered in Chapter 6. The multilevel scope of Baran's work distinguishes it sharply from conventional economic GNP-growth models.

The emphasis on the expansion of gross output or GNP as the ultimate developmental goal has a number of political and social implications that must be considered. First, it is often assumed that growth in per capita GNP will automatically trigger progress in the political and social spheres. In this scenario, an economy that expands its output of goods and services will industrialize, provide jobs, promote democracy, and improve the quality of life. While many of these economic deterministic claims have been called into question, the belief in economic growth as a panacea remains widespread. The universal faith in the inevitable benefits of growth has allowed national policymakers to impose programs in the name of growth that are contrary to the interests of the vast majority of citizens.

For example, advocates of the GNP-growth model often oppose policies of progressive taxation or those aimed at equalizing the distribution of income. This *growth first, redistribution later* approach is an integral part of the conventional GNP model (Lewis 1958). Redistributional policies should not be pursued, it is argued, because they will stifle growth. Taxes and restrictions on the income of the wealthy should be minimized or abolished so that the entrepreneurial spirit can be unleashed and the elite will retain the necessary funds for the purpose of investment in productive property and technologies. In this formulation, income inequality is a necessary functional condition for economic growth. These costs of growth, paid disproportionately by the working classes, will eventually yield dividends once the society takes off and income begins to "trickle down." There was a time when this prescription for growth was confined to the economies of less-developed nations. What we now know, all too well, is that this ageless policy for capitalist growth periodically comes home to roost, most recently under the guise of "supply-side" economics. The same growth-oriented logic that has championed laissez-faire for the Third World has been used in advanced capitalist states to justify recession, unemployment, tax breaks for the rich, and a frontal assault on the living standards of workers. Again, all in the name of growth.

While there is considerable evidence from the Third World experience that such policies promote economic growth, enhance profit rates, and enrich landowners and capitalists, there is less support for the presumed "trickle-down effect" on the incomes of the lower and working classes. A number of Third World nations have experienced remarkable growth rates while making little progress in alleviating poverty. In fact, in some cases we find a "trickle-up effect," in which wealth is concentrated in fewer hands and the proportion of income accruing to the bottom wage earners actually declines.[2] Such experiences are often accompanied by political regimes of the "bureaucratic-authoritarian" type. Social and political order through government repression often ensures the priority of growth over redistribution. One is hard pressed to find a clearer illustration of the "political economy of growth."

The fraudulent claims of the growth first, redistribution later policy, refuted by sustained expansion in GNP coupled with increasing income inequality, has necessitated a consideration of alternative growth strategies (Stewart and Streeten 1976). Growth may be necessary but it is hardly a sufficient condition for improving the overall standard of living. Rather, as Samater (1984:4) argues: "the problem of mass poverty is more one of the *pattern* of growth rather than the *rate* of growth per se. As a result, arguments for 'functional' inequality are now rarely heard, and we find a widespread acceptance of the necessity for new development strategies."

What has recently emerged is a series of GNP-growth-oriented models that do not require income inequality as a prerequisite for economic development. One alternative is to reverse the causal ordering of the variables; thus, the *redistribution first, growth later* strategy. In this approach growth requires significant reforms or revolutionary changes in the distribution of wealth and property. Again, these involve not simply technical economic but fundamental political issues.

This growth strategy is often associated with socialism, as in the People's Republic of China, where the property of capitalists and landlords was confiscated and either redistributed among small producers or converted to collective enterprises. As with the growth-first approach, there are clear winners and losers under this economic policy. This development strategy, however, does not necessarily require the wholesale appropriation of property. Many nations have experimented with *land reform* versions of the model, which can take a variety of forms but have as their basic objective the institutionalization of laws that enforce the right of workers' access to land. Such policies range from legal limits on the ability of landowners to evict and extract rent from tenant farmers, and the amount of land that can be controlled by a single landowner, to the confiscation of property and its redistribution to small producers. These policies have many objectives. The reforms may ensure a more intensive utilization of land, reduce the rate of rural poverty and underemployment, prevent massive rural-to-urban migration, head off rural unrest, or encourage the production of foodstuffs for domestic consumption.

Another growth strategy that challenges the assumption of a rigid trade-off between growth and distribution is the *redistribute-with-growth* approach. This strategy involves a combination of policies ensuring that the gains of growth are distributed to the working and lower classes (see Weaver et al. 1978). Active government intervention is required in order to direct the use of human resources, encourage geographically balanced capital investments, expand the supply of human capital, enforce progressive forms of taxation, and subsidize the cost of basic necessities. Such policies not only may provide for more equitable growth but also may further fuel economic expansion by improving the productivity of human resources and widening the internal market, encouraging further investment in production for domestic consumers.

Finally, there is what has come to be known as the *basic needs* approach. Advocates of this strategy question the ability of the growth-with-redistribution model to meet the basic needs of the population adequately. One of the most forceful advocates, Paul Streeten (1977), argues that the growth-with-redistribution approach relies too heavily on income policies intended to increase the buying power of the poor. This approach, according to Streeten, leaves a great deal to chance. Significant portions of the population may fall outside the income stream, and many basic needs may be unmet through market mechanisms. Therefore, what is advocated in the basic needs approach is direct governmental provision of basic services, which usually refers to "satisfying minimum levels of material needs such as consumption of food, shelter, and clothing, and access to such essential public services as pure water, sanitation, public transport, health and education" (Samater 1984:4). The governmental provision of these basic services obviously requires both economic growth *and* available sources of revenue.

This points to a basic bind for capitalist economies. On the one hand, growth requires promoting the confidence of and encouraging investment by private capitalists, which usually necessitates a restricted government role in the economy; on the other hand, the state must gain access to a share of the surplus in order to finance basic social needs. This "dilemma of the state" is hardly confined to less-developed nations; it plagues all capitalist economies (questions of capitalism versus socialism will be taken up shortly). In this sense it is not surprising to find that socialist states have a far better record of combining economic growth with the provision of basic needs. Evidence for this relationship is provided in a study by Jay Mandle (1980:186), who points to a basic distinction between the two kinds of systems as it affects the growth-equity question:

A shift of resources from the population generally to the public sector in order to finance welfare does not represent a reallocation away from would-be investors. The converse is true in the context of capitalist under-development. . . . The financing of public sector-provided basic needs must therefore come from the relatively affluent. But these are the potential savers and investors in the community. It is recognition of this conflict which is the source of the belief that growth and equity are in conflict under capitalism.

Rostow and the "Stages of Growth" Model

Rostow's (1960) model of economic growth provides a greater elaboration of the precise factors and stages that must be present and completed as a nation becomes a modern industrial society. The "stages of growth" outlined by Rostow are based on the experience of the industrialized West. Because today's advanced capitalist states passed through a series of economic stages, these stages must be initiated and completed if less-developed nations are to reach the promised land of a mass-consumption, industrial society. In this respect Rostow's thesis shares the ethnocentric and Eurocentric bias of countless other recipes for economic success.

The first stage of the model conforms to the standard descriptive category found in theories of modernization—the "traditional society stage." In this stage methods of production are backward and inefficient. There are no advances in the level of productivity, and economies are relatively stagnant. Since things can hardly get any worse, the next stage, almost by definition, must entail sowing the seeds of growth. Rostow terms the second stage the "preconditions for take-off." The most outstanding feature of this stage is the emergence of a "leading sector" in the economy that has a positive influence on other economic sectors. It is usually assumed that an industrial sector or set of enterprises will emerge, encouraging expansion and productivity in the agricultural sector as well as improvements in transportation and other forms of infrastructure. In short, the leading sector stimulates the forces of supply and demand, and this sets the nation on the road to economic development.

The third and most important stage is the "take-off." During this stage all the past obstacles to growth presumably are removed and overcome. Growth becomes a "normal condition" for all sectors of the economy, the ratio of savings and investment to national income increases, and political and social institutions support the growth mode. Rostow emphasizes the role of the entrepreneur during the "take-off" phase. He believes, like many of the individual modernization theorists reviewed in Chapter 2, that an elite segment of risk takers driven by the profit motive is a requirement for "take-off." As income shifts into the hands of the entrepreneurial elite, spending is said to be more productive because it is plowed back into new capacity and modern innovations.

Once the "take-off" stage is complete, the economy moves into the home stretch—the "drive to maturity stage." In this phase there are long periods of sustained growth, with minor fluctuations, and 10–20 percent of national income is steadily reinvested. In addition to continuous growth and investment, new sectors emerge to replace the aging leading sectors.

The drive to maturity is followed by the terminal "age of high mass consumption stage." In this final phase, structural changes are less rapid, and the leading sectors are those specializing in the production of consumer goods and services. In the end, once nations "take off," they are essentially destined to complete the stages and follow the Western pattern toward a mass production/consumption economy. In Rostow's optimistic account all nations will eventually join the ranks of the advanced consumer societies. It is implied that this is the end of the line and, once it has achieved mass consumption status, a nation's problems are solved and the society can shift into cruise control. The recent imposition of austerity-type policies in advanced Western nations indicates that the joy ride may be over. There are future stages to confront.

Rostow's model had a major impact when first presented in the early 1960s—it attracted both praise and criticism. I shall focus on the shortcomings of Rostow's work, since it is unlikely that even the most avid fans would today exhibit much enthusiasm for the model. The most obvious difficulty with his theory of growth is his assumption that all nations will travel along a single unilinear developmental path. On this count Rostow has a great deal of company, for many of his contemporaries, equally optimistic and ethnocentric, believed that any nation was capable of following the industrialization model if it adopted the cultural and economic patterns of the West. Today, given the vast number of historical case studies and the critical contribution of dependency theory, it is relatively easy to identify this fault. Yet it is quite pronounced in Rostow's stages-of-growth scenario. These stages effectively deny the non-Western, non-industrial world its history. In 1960, when Rostow decided to proclaim them "traditional societies," still in the starting blocks, these nations had already run a few hundred laps under conditions that now distinguish their social structures from anything that ever existed in the presently advanced nations. This legacy, in essence, assures that they will pass through a number of qualitatively different stages on a very different trajectory (see Frank 1969). This point will be extended further in Chapter

6 when we consider the international level of analysis that links stages of growth in the West to the stages of underdevelopment in the Third World.

Perhaps the most thorough and devastating critique of the stages-of-growth thesis can be found in the polemical review by Paul Baran and Eric Hobsbawm (1961). Because a great deal of fanfare surrounded the release of Rostow's work, and it was hailed as an alternative to Marxist theory, Baran and Hobsbawm hold it up to a rather high standard and, on this basis, essentially conclude that Rostow's "manifesto" is worthless as an explanatory model of economic development. While Baran and Hobsbawm clearly have a larger axe to grind, they raise some very valid points on deficiencies in the stages-of-growth logic and theoretical strategy.

One of the fundamental weaknesses they identify is the wholesale inability of the stages-of-growth model to explain anything because it is more *a descriptive account* of an ideal sequence of economic changes than a coherent theoretical framework that allows one to understand how nations actually move from one stage to another. They note:

> There is no particular reason why the "traditional" society should turn into a society breeding the "preconditions" of the "take-off." . . . Nor is there any reason within the Rostovian stages why "preconditions" should lead to the "take-off" to maturity. (1961:236)

They also point to what is by now a familiar flaw in many explanatory models of development: circular logic. Once we assume that all forms of national development proceed along the path outlined in the stages of growth, a nation's "take-off" automatically presumes that the prior "preconditions" have been established and instituted. Effects determine cause. The claim for the existence of any stage implies a prior as well as a subsequent stage.

Baran and Hobsbawm further denounce the model for its lack of utility as a tool to illuminate the empirical world of underdevelopment. That is, placing a nation within any one of the stages proposed by Rostow hardly advances our understanding of the social, economic and political forces responsible for the realization of that particular stage or the prospects for further development. This can be done, according to Baran and Hobsbawm, only by using the historical materialist (Marxist) framework that Rostow seeks to transcend. Much of the review is an attempt to demonstrate that Rostow's rejection of the Marxist concepts of forces and social relations of production renders the model entirely useless. The social and political forces, and social class behavior and motives, shaped by existing social structures, cannot simply be shoved aside and replaced by

a deterministic sequence of stages that contain very indeterminate propositions, or none at all, about why capitalists invest and exploit, why workers
struggle and rebel, why elites resist change, and why few nations ever
actually travel on the "stages of growth" line. Finally, as Baran and
Hobsbawm make clear, it is important to place the Rostovian edifice in its
social historical context: "It demonstrates in a particularly striking way
the low estate to which Western social thought has declined in the current
era of the cold war" (1961:242).

Today, neither the structural modernization thesis nor the GNP/stages-
of-growth model claims many adherents. The traditional/modern
dichotomy guiding the modernization approach has lost its attraction as
an explanatory framework. The increasingly important qualitative features
of development have rendered the fixation on GNP obsolete. In place of
these theoretical models one finds a preference for particular socio-
economic arrangements and policies as the central societal-level dimensions responsible for development. These are examined in Chapter 5,
where we continue our review of societal-level theories.

NOTES

1. For the best and most comprehensive critique of structural functionalism in
general, and Parsonian functionalism in particular, see Gouldner (1970).

2. On the complicated relationship between economic growth and income equality,
see Adelman and Morris (1973).

5

SOCIETAL-LEVEL EXPLANATIONS II: COMPARATIVE SOCIO-ECONOMIC SYSTEMS AND STRATEGIES

> Here and elsewhere, we must never forget that perfect systems exist only in books, that the real world in East and West abounds in irrationalities, misallocation, misemployment of resources, various forms of waste. In the real world, whether socialist or not, some intractable problems and contradictions will exist. Indeed, it is well that this is so, for a world without contradictions would be an intolerably dull place, and social scientists would be threatened with unemployment. . . . We must learn from the things that go wrong, in the hope that by doing so we will diminish the ill-effects of predictable troubles. (Nove 1983:141)

This chapter continues examining societal-level explanations for development within a comparative analytic framework. Most of the chapter is devoted to a review of theories of capitalism and socialism as systems facilitating socio-economic development. The real-life problems and experiences confronted by these systems also are addressed. The chapter concludes with a discussion of societal-level strategies for development that are currently being proposed for some advanced capitalist and less-developed nations.

SOCIO-ECONOMIC SYSTEMS AND DEVELOPMENT: CAPITALISM

The most common comparison of socio-economic systems is between capitalism and socialism, with claims made for the relative superiority and appropriateness of each system as a strategy for growth.[1] Up to this point much of the discussion has assumed that nations are organized along capitalist lines or are pursuing a capitalist development strategy. However, it is important to note that there are not only significant variations within the capitalist mode but there are also compelling reasons why nations opt for or experiment with socialist principles.

Describing the fundamental characteristics of socio-economic systems, such as capitalism and socialism, is a difficult task for at least two reasons. First, there are no "pure" socialist or capitalist societies existing anywhere in the world. By "pure" we mean societies that conform to the abstract theoretical models of what capitalism and socialism are supposed to be. For this reason, as one lists the characteristics of these societies, many reservations and qualifications are in order. A second, related problem that often emerges is the tendency, when comparing different societies, to select the ideal features of one society and compare these with the actual and often undesirable features of the other (see Burawoy and Lukács 1985). This "selection bias" frequently is politically motivated because it is often the case that comparative analysts have a (unspoken) preference for one or the other of the different systems. Students of comparative social science should be aware of this tendency and make efforts to present both the ideal-typical features of socio-economic systems and the day-to-day problems, inefficiencies, and inequities that emerge in all systems to one degree or another.

In an attempt to follow this lofty advice, we shall consider some of the theoretical arguments for the advantages of both capitalism and socialism, and then confront some of the real-life deviations from these abstract models.

Capitalism in Theory and Practice

Capitalism is a socio-economic system that allows the private owner-ship of productive property (property that produces goods and services). Individuals who own the means of production make up the capitalist class; those who work for capitalists make up the working class. Arguments favoring capitalism as the best socio-economic arrangement for develop-ment hinge on the role of markets and the concept of incentives.

Markets determine the production and allocation of goods and services in a capitalist society. Buyers and sellers come together to exchange goods, services, labor, and money. Prices serve as the leading piece of information in markets and determine how much of a good will be bought and sold. When the supply of goods exceeds demand, prices tend to fall; when demand exceeds supply, prices tend to rise. Thus, through the market mechanism goods are assigned a value or price, and this results in the most efficient allocation of resources. Where a commodity is in plentiful supply, the low price will stimulate demand for that good and it will be used; where a good is scarce, the high price will discourage demand and buyers will seek alternative goods. The use and allocation of resources are both efficient and noncoercive, requiring no direct government intervention. The "invisible hand" of the market directs the economy and, in the process, preserves liberty and freedom.

A second argument for capitalism rests on the inherent incentive structure that prevails in competitive market systems. Because individual capitalists and workers are able to control the profit or income derived from their economic activity, there is an incentive to invest money and energy, take risks, work hard, and, ultimately, create wealth. The competitive nature of capitalism gives it its dynamic efficiency. Capitalists are competing with other capitalists for profits and markets, so they are driven to be as productive as possible and as accommodating to buyers as possible. Innovative production techniques are constantly developed, pressure is exerted to use resources as efficiently as possible, and high-quality products are required if capitalists are to secure markets for their goods. In short, the incentives of market competition guarantee expanding investment, productivity, wealth, jobs, and quality products for consumers.

Let us now consider some of the common arguments *against* capitalism (Zimbalist and Sherman 1984:10–11). First is the issue of inequality between workers and owners. Only a small proportion of the total population in a capitalist society owns means of production and therefore is able to reap the profits from production. The vast majority are workers who are hired by capitalists. The same market competitive forces that result in dynamic efficiency may also provide an incentive for the severe exploitation of workers as a means to cut costs and produce efficiently.

Second, because decisions about production are based on supply and demand, the investment behavior of capitalists tends to fluctuate, and so the "invisible hand" creates periods of recession and depression that result in long periods of production well below the actual capacity of the economy. Production of goods based on market criteria—that is, the presence of demand backed up with cash—means that those with the most income have the greatest influence over which goods will be produced. The supply of goods is not determined by actual human needs.

Third, the process of competition inevitably results in some winners and some losers. Over time wealth and power become concentrated in the hands of the largest and strongest firms and thus competition, the motor of innovation, is replaced by oligopoly and monopoly. The liberty and freedom presumably advanced by competitive capitalism are threatened as the economy and polity are dominated by individuals and firms who use their economic muscle to advance their own ends, set prices, control supply, and dominate the economy.

It should be clear from these critical comments that the assessment of the desirability of different socio-economic systems rests not only on economic growth criteria but also on a set of other, equally compelling values and priorities. These include efficiency, fairness, equality, democracy, freedom, choice, control, and quality of life (see Bowles and Edwards 1985:20–24; Zimbalist and Sherman 1984:23–29).

There is one final critical comment that deserves mention. Capitalist economies do not always utilize resources in the most efficient manner. As was argued above, market-based prices are said to provide for the most efficient use and allocation of resources. A major problem arises, however, when resources have no price tag and can be used at no cost. In this sense they appear to be infinite and can be used in unlimited quantities. Air is such a commodity. Since it can be used by producers at no cost, it is rational and profitable to use, and in the process pollute, this environmental resource. There is no price disincentive to do otherwise even though the pollution of air exacts enormous social costs.

This is the classic case of a *negative externality*. An externality is an action taken by a firm in one location that affects other firms in other locations. In this case it is negative because the effects on other areas, firms, or people are *costs*; someone else has to pay the price. This is also referred to as an *external diseconomy*.

There are also *positive externalities*. These occur when the effect of an activity in one place or firm transfers not costs but *benefits* to other places and firms. For example, converting a burned-out factory into attractive condos may enhance the property values of surrounding buildings and homes. This is also known as an *external economy*. Externality is an important economic concept that can be applied to the economic actions of many different organizations in various societies. The increasing incidence of negative externalities is a major reason for government intervention in the economy and the development of socio-economic systems that do not conform to the pure capitalist model. In the case of a negative externality such as pollution, the state must "internalize" the external cost by penalizing firms for air pollution through fines, or by requiring pollution control devices that increase the production costs of firms using natural resources. The increasing role of the state in capitalist economies is probably the single most important reason for challenging the ideal-theoretical depiction of capitalism. We should therefore examine the question of state intervention in greater detail.

Theories of the State and Development in Capitalist Economies

The state plays a major role in the development of all capitalist economies. In this section we consider some of the theories offered to explain the expansion of the state apparatus in advanced and less-developed capitalist societies and the socio-economic effects of this intervention.

State Expansion in Advanced Capitalist Economies

"Theories of the state" have proliferated over the past two decades (see Alford and Friedland 1985; Evans et al. 1985) with the major contributions coming from neo-Marxist theorists. While most of these theories claim loyalty to the intention, if not the writings, of Marx, there is considerable variation in the extent to which they employ a rigid *base-superstructure dichotomy*. The orthodox Marxist contention that the economic base (the forces and social relations of production) determines the form and nature of other social institutions (superstructure), such as the state, has thwarted the development of a Marxist theory of politics (see Miliband 1977 on this problem). In this base-superstructure formulation one need only examine property and production relations in the economic sphere in order to understand the role of the political system. As we shall see, this one-way determinism has been largely supplanted by a more realistic, some might say dialectical, approach.

As a point of departure, however, it is worth considering the Marxist proposition concerning the fundamental contradiction in all societies—the contradiction between the *forces of production* and the *social relations of production*. The forces of production are the buildings, machines, technologies, and organizational/corporate arrangements devoted to the production of goods and services. The social relations of production are the relations that exist between the two major social classes—the owners of the forces of production (in capitalist societies, the capitalist class) and the actual producers of goods and services (the working class). These include the property and legal rights of the two social classes and the authority relations between them. During certain periods the forces and social relations of production are compatible and consistent. However, according to the Marxist logic, as societies develop, they come into conflict or become incompatible, prompting major societal-level transformations.

To take one example, during the early stages of capitalism the emerging forces of production—the urban industrial factory system—begin to conflict with the social relations of production associated with feudal society. The factory system required a free and mobile labor force that could migrate to factory locations and be hired for a wage (a social relation). Yet a large part of the population remained under the sway of feudal social relations as peasants having access to, and residing upon, manorial lands with servile obligations to feudal landowners. In order for the social relations of production to be compatible with the developing capitalist forces of production, peasants had to be evicted from and denied access to the land, and forced to take employment for a wage in the urban industrial centers.

In the modern era we find a different kind of contradiction that prompts the expansion of government intervention. As capitalism has developed economically, the corporate units (forces) of production have grown enormously. Corporations control greater and greater proportions of the nation's wealth, and the size and scope of their actions affect larger and larger numbers of people. The increasing interdependence of the economy also means that the actions of larger corporate units will have ripple effects, or external effects, on the entire society, population, and economy. In this sense production takes on more and more of a "social character." In spite of the increasingly social character of production, and the wide-ranging social impact of corporate actions, decisions about production and investment remain in the hands of private capitalists—individuals motivated by self-interest and profit. As part of the social relations of production of capitalism, private capitalists exercise legal sovereign rights over the use of their property. Tension develops between the forces of production, as embodied in the immense corporate units that dominate the economy, and the social relations of production allowing private control over these socially influential units.

The expansion of the state can be seen as a means to resolve this contradiction. Given the wide-ranging impact of private decisions on significant sectors of the population and various communities, the government is compelled to act to ensure both that corporate decisions are not socially destructive and that certain segments of the population are cushioned from the negative effects of corporate actions. This represents one perspective on the growth of the state. The production-based concepts driving this thesis are important to understand, as are the tensions that result from the coexistence of a highly interdependent, complex economy and a legal apparatus that places the economy beyond the direct control of public or democratic forces.

O'Connor's "fiscal crisis of the state" thesis (1973) posits a somewhat mechanistic and functionalist account of the expansion of state activity in capitalist societies. His analysis, like the forces-social relations thesis, links the expansion of the state to the changing organizational forces of production, most notably the rise of the monopoly sector. It is the monopoly sector of capitalism, made up of the large, highly profitable corporate firms, that has the greatest influence on the actions of the state. The powerful role of the monopoly sector in the overall economic health of the system prompts state intervention to stimulate investment, enhance the rate of profit, and ensure the viability of this pivotal sector. O'Connor calls this the *accumulation function* of the state. Through subsidies, tax breaks, industrial development incentives, educational training, and the provision and maintenance of a physical infrastructure, to name only a few activities, the state assists in financing the accumulation of capital.

The consequences of capital accumulation, on the other hand, are not necessarily socially beneficial or distributed equitably. This prompts additional state activity in the form of the *legitimation function*. This refers to government spending and programs designed to create and maintain harmony, mass loyalty, and an image of fairness. Welfare services, progressive taxation policies, and redistributive programs are some of the major components that serve to legitimate both the state and the capitalist economic arrangements.

One of the major contributions of O'Connor's analysis is the connection drawn between the accumulation and legitimation functions and the inevitable fiscal crisis of government. His basic point is that the combined expenses of accumulation and legitimation exceed the revenue capacity of the state. Budget shortfalls are the direct product of a state apparatus that publicly finances capital accumulation but, at the same time, does not directly control any of the subsequent profit. In this sense his thesis is founded on the forces-social relations contradiction. The social property relations allowing private corporate units to control their surplus guarantees that state expenses and social costs supporting these units will not yield proportionate financial returns to state institutions.

Supply-side economic theorists in the United States have offered one way out of the fiscal crisis of the state, based on the now infamous "Laffer curve." This curve, graphing the relationship between tax rates and government tax revenue, embodies a fundamental tenet of supply-side economics: less government intervention means more economic growth. It posits a curvilinear relationship between tax rates and tax revenues. The relationship at first is *positive*—the greater the tax rate, the greater the tax revenue. However, at some point (no one really knows where) tax rates become excessive. This results in a decline in capital investment by private capitalists because returns on investment, after taxes, are insufficient to serve as an incentive. Workers presumably will cease working as the government extracts too large a share of their income in the form of taxes. The net result of the excessive rate of taxation is a decline in economic activity, less income being produced and distributed, and, therefore, less tax revenue for government coffers. The relationship between the tax rate and tax revenue, therefore, becomes *negative* as tax rates reach too high a level.

The policy implications of the Laffer curve are clear: Lower tax rates not only will stimulate economic growth but also will increase state revenue. The best of both worlds is assured. This supply-side logic guided Reagan's economic policy during the early 1980s and, in retrospect, it is now clear that the supply-side claims were (and are) fraudulent (see Thurow 1983). The record budget deficits registered during the 1980s provides ample disconforming evidence for this component of supply-side economic doctrine (once labeled "voodoo economics").

The ability to sell supply-side solutions to capitalist governments is based on the fundamentally dependent relationship that exists between the state and the private economy. This relationship is often described in *structuralist theories of the capitalist state* (see Gold et al. 1975). In attempting to answer the question of why the state in a capitalist society tends to act in the interests of the capitalist class, structuralist theories point to the dependence of the state on economic growth and vitality. State managers have an objective interest in presiding over an expanding economy because economic growth and the accumulation of income and wealth result not only in greater amounts of tax revenue to fund state projects and programs but also in greater levels of public support necessary for winning reelection (see Block 1977). In order to ensure adequate revenue and public support, the state is "structurally constrained," regardless of its ideological predilections, to institute policies that advance economic growth. In a capitalist economy growth is based, in large part, on the investment behavior of private capitalists, and so the state must act in a manner that is consistent with this economically critical constituency. To do otherwise is to risk disinvestment and capital flight, which, in the end, will create unemployment and recession. In this sense, most government policies designed to facilitate private capital investment are "supply side" in nature.

Keynesianism and the Political Economy of Crisis

While the more recent economic crises of advanced capitalism, particularly in the United States, have prompted efforts to curtail state action, it is important to understand the historical forces responsible for state expansion in the first place. This brings us to a consideration of *Keynesianism*, named for the economic theories and policy prescriptions of John Maynard Keynes, a British economist. Keynesianism advocates state intervention as a means to prevent economic crises and promote sustained economic expansion. For Keynes one of the central problems of a capitalist economy was the tendency to periodic bouts of unemployment and recession. He believed that these economic problems resulted from the investment behavior of capitalist firms under conditions of insufficient aggregate demand for goods and services (Sidelsky 1979; Martin 1979). Fluctuations in mass buying power created disinvestment, layoffs, unemployment, recession, and depression. In order to prevent these economic cycles Keynes advocated state intervention as a means to manipulate aggregate demand, thus encouraging investment and employment. The major tools for ensuring growth in the Keynesian model are taxation, state spending and the redistribution of income. These serve to stimulate demand and encourage capital investment. If levels of demand are adequate, firms will be motivated to invest in the production and supply of goods and services.

The economic depression of the 1930s is often viewed as a crisis of overproduction or underconsumption; that is, a crisis in which the supply of goods and services is not matched by a corresponding level of demand. During the expansion that preceded the depression, major advances were made in the methods and organization of production. The most notable development was the rise of the assembly line and the beginning of the mass production of consumer goods. The enormous gains in productivity associated with this organizational innovation, along with the relatively low wages paid to production workers made for an attractive investment climate. Goods could be produced rapidly and at low cost, but the enormous profit embodied in each commodity went *unrealized* because there was insufficient demand for the products. What followed was disinvestment, layoffs, and economic crisis—a demand-side crisis.

The logic of Keynesianism dictates a solution that involves progressive taxation, the redistribution of income, the expansion of social welfare programs, support for labor organization, collective bargaining, and higher wages. These components, and the legislation supporting them, make up what Bowles and Gintis (1982) describe as the "post-war capital-labor accord." One of the remarkable accomplishments of Keynesian economics was to convince the capitalist class that economic struggle was not necessarily a zero-sum game. Higher wages to workers, while increasing the costs of production, were beneficial to the extent that they served to stimulate aggregate demand and mass buying power. Thus a compromise between labor and capital came out of the post-Depression–World War II period that linked gains in productivity to income gains for workers. As the pie expanded, each could secure a larger and larger slice. The "institutionalization of class struggle" (Lipset 1960), celebrated during the so-called "end of ideology" phase of U.S. capitalism, involved in effect the conversion of labor into an additional and viable interest group, making claims on the economic surplus through collective bargaining contracts and demands for social welfare legislation.

According to various neo-Marxist political economists, the economic crises of the 1970s and early 1980s in the United States were due to the success and logical extension of the very forces that provided the economic prosperity of the post-war period. The argument that contemporary economic crises are the unintended consequence of the Keynesian/ labor-capital accord of an earlier period is to apply a basic Marxian premise concerning the way in which solutions to economic crises at one point in time emerge as obstacles and impediments to continued capital accumulation at a later point in time (see Harvey 1982:ch. 6).

Bowles and Gintis (1982) present one version of this general thesis. In opposition to the standard Marxist view that the capitalist state functions exclusively to counteract crisis tendencies and support the interests of capitalists, they argue that actions of the state also can precipitate and reinforce economic crisis tendencies. This is due, in particular, to the success of working-class demands for redistributional social programs and the institutionalization of collective bargaining agreements. These efforts have resulted in the expansion of the social wage or "citizen's wage"— "that part of a person's consumption supplied by the state by virtue of his citizenship rather than directly by the sale of labor" (Bowles and Gintis 1982:53)—and the ability of labor to protect and expand wages and job security in the post-World War II period. While these two developments provided the basic foundation for the Keynesian-based economic expansion of the 1950s and 1960s, they have more recently served as impediments to sustained capital accumulation and economic growth.

Long-term labor agreements make it more difficult for capital to reduce wages and lay off workers. Even when they are laid off, unemployment benefits and other social welfare provisions allow workers to collect income without working or entering the labor market. This means that fewer workers enter the labor market than would be the case if there were no alternative sources of income available. The supply of labor is reduced, and this serves to keep wages higher than would be the case if public support were unavailable. Therefore, the normal wage-reducing impact of unemployment is significantly moderated. High unemployment rates do not have as strong a negative effect on wages as was true prior to the expansion of the welfare state. All of these factors, according to Bowles and Gintis, strengthen the bargaining power of labor vis-à-vis capital and reduce the rate of profit and exploitation. This discourages capital investment.

In this interpretation of the recent economic crisis, the institutionalization of Keynesian economic policy and the related economistic demands of labor, originally seen as part of the solution to the economic crisis of the 1930s, are held responsible for the economic stagnation of the 1970s and 1980s. Using a slightly different approach, Weisskopf et al. (1985:259) state: "Capitalist economic crisis may occur either because the capitalist class is 'too strong' or because it is 'too weak.' " Where the capitalist class is too strong, the supply side prospers and the demand side suffers; where the capitalist class is too weak (in a relative sense), the demand side is vibrant and the supply side is inadequate. It is the latter condition that is said to characterize the most recent phase of economic crisis. The reemergence to prominence of supply-side economics and the initial policies associated with Reaganomics, are developments consistent with this interpretation.

A similar position is advanced by Piven and Cloward (1982). In their original formulation of the determinants of social welfare fluctuations (1971), they argued that social wage welfare payments served a regulatory function for capital—payments were expanded to "cool out" the poor and defuse potential class conflict during hard times, and were cut back to force workers into the labor market during growth periods. The manipulation of welfare expenditures appears, in this model, to be "functional" to the interests of capital.

In a more recent extension of this thesis (1982), Piven and Cloward readjusted the basic logic to explain the recent attack on welfare during a period of economic crisis. In the revised formulation, the welfare state is viewed as "dysfunctional" for capital, as the social wage welfare payments are institutionalized to the point that the state practically provides a floor on minimum incomes. Thus, economic hard times associated with the late 1970s and early 1980s do not bring an expansion of welfare, as might be expected from the old model, since it is the existence of the now institutionalized welfare apparatus that is partially responsible for the economic crisis. According to Piven and Cloward, the social wage now competes with the private low-wage competitive sector labor market. Income can be derived not only from the sale of labor power but also from social welfare entitlement programs. This "artificially" raises the average wage level required to attract labor and contributes to declining rates of profit. The "new class war" is aimed at eliminating this working-class subsidy and forcing workers back into the low-wage labor market.

This neo-Marxist interpretation (see Clegg et al. 1986 for a dissenting view) of the source of economic crisis—the product of expanding welfare expenditures and economistic demands of labor—converges with some conservative accounts. However, the political and policy implications of these respective analyses are quite distinct. Among neo-Marxists the lesson is that there are structural limits on the expansion of social welfare programs under capitalism. Therefore, the economy must be reorganized or transformed along socialist lines. Among conservative economists the recent economic crises vindicate their general opposition to government intervention, point to the bankruptcy of liberal Keynesian formulations, and justify the institutionalization of pro-growth supply-side policies. A basic axiom of this position is that scaling back the state and "getting government off people's backs" is the key to growth and prosperity.

In spite of the widespread acceptance of this latter claim, particularly in the United States, there is little empirical evidence to support it (Katz et al. 1983). In fact, a cross-national analysis of the United States, West Germany, Japan, and Sweden since 1960 (Gorham 1987) indicates that the United States, with the consistently lowest level of public-sector spending among the four nations, ranks last in per capita economic growth, industrial productivity, average unemployment, and the "misery index," which combines unemployment and inflation rates. These and similar results from other studies clearly call into question the simple claim that less government intervention means more prosperity. What all the studies suggest (Katz et al. 1983; Apple 1983) is that under certain structural arrangements, state intervention can enhance not only the rate of growth but also the quality of life.

Statism in the Less-Developed World

The active interventionist state is not a phenomenon confined to advanced capitalist economies. In the less-developed world, state actions also are a major determinant of socio-economic development. The universal extension of governmental intervention and regulation has prompted one observer to describe the second half of the twentieth century as the "era of the state" and to argue:

The active penetration of society and economy by agents of the state is as extensive as at any previous period in the several-centuries history of the modern state, including the so-called "age of absolutism." This situation is widely recognized and is true virtually of all countries. "Statism" is pervasive. (Duvall and Freeman 1981:99)

Explanations for the expansion of the state in less-developed economies differ from those offered for advanced capitalist nations. While in both cases the state is concerned, first and foremost, with facilitating the process of capital accumulation, in less-developed economies there is a greater tendency for the state to play the role of entrepreneur, hence the term "state entrepreneurship." This is defined as

the expansion of the state into *productive* sectors of the economy (as distinct from infrastructural provision), the *degree* to which (public) management conforms to standard capitalist performance criteria, and the general *commitment* of the state to capitalist development. These features—state ownership of noninfrastructure enterprises, the relative importance of capitalist performance criteria, and the extensive commitment to capitalism—define the entrepreneurial state. (Duvall and Freeman 1981:105)

The hyperactivity of the state in less-developed economies and its encroachment into productive sectors are developments best understood in the context of the global economic structure and the historical position of less-developed nations within this system.

The term "entrepreneur," as was seen in Chapter 2, is usually reserved for private individuals who are innovators and risk takers, and, by virtue of these actions, stimulate economic growth and production. Public organizations are, if anything, seen as a hindrance to this entrepreneurial process. However, where no independent class of entrepreneurs actually exists or is willing to act according to the capitalist ideal, other institutions may be required to fill the void in order for economic expansion to occur.

According to dependency theorists (who are considered in detail in Chapter 6), an indigenous entrepreneurial capitalist class is largely absent in less-developed nations. The shortage of a national bourgeoisie possessing the economic and political autonomy to shape the development of less-developed economies is, in this view, the historical product of domination by, and subservience to, the international market and multinational corporations (Cardoso and Faletto 1979; Evans 1982). A national capitalist class is unable to emerge or exert itself in the face of domination by these external forces. The weakness of this class is reflected in its inability to initiate a truly bourgeois revolution and its lack of control over sufficient economic resources to transform the forces of production. In order for the economy to modernize, therefore, substitutes for the national capitalist class must be found. There are three basic options: (1) allow the economy to be developed and controlled by the external forces of multinational corporate capital; (2) use the state as an institutional substitute for the absent national capitalist class; (3) align the state with foreign capital in an effort to encourage and direct capital investment.

This developmental dilemma is not unique to contemporary less-developed nations. As Gerschenkron's (1962) theory of "delayed industrialization" outlines, both Germany and Russia faced a similar choice in their effort to "catch up" with England. In fact, Gerschenkron believes there are advantages to late industrialization because many of the painful evolutionary stages have been faced, and technological innovations developed, by the leading international economies. The state can then, as entrepreneurial substitute, select the proven and most productive technologies and organizational methods as strategies for economic growth.

Gerschenkron's thesis provides a rationale for the state as an institutional substitute for the capitalist class. Evans (1979; 1982) indicates that the actual situation for less-developed nations is somewhat more complex and usually involves a tripartite arrangement composed of the state, multinational corporations (MNCs), and the national bourgeoisie. His analysis of the Brazilian experience (1979; 1982) represents a major contribution to the development literature.

Evans notes that the precise configuration of the tripartite alliance varies at different historical moments, and there are periods when the state favors MNCs to the detriment of the national bourgeoisie. Such an alliance—between the state and MNCs—existed in its strongest form in Brazil during the post-import-substitution industrialization phase as part of the development of the bureaucratic-authoritarian regime (described above). At the height of the dual alliance version of the bureaucratic authoritarian state (in Brazil, from 1968 to 1973), government policy was aimed at establishing an attractive business climate for international capital by financing infrastructural projects that complemented the needs of foreign capital and repressing popular political movements and working-class demands. During this period the national bourgeoisie exerted little impact on government policies, many of which were carried out at the expense of local capital.

However, both Evans (1982) and O'Donnell (1978; 1979) believe that while the "dual alliance" phase advanced the rate of economic growth and capital accumulation, the national bourgeoisie had to be reinserted into the alliance because the state must appear as the representative of national, versus foreign, interests. In this respect the state in less-developed nations is faced with a contradiction, not unlike that identified by O'Connor (1973) for advanced capitalist states, between the conditions for growth and accumulation, on the one hand, and public support and legitimacy, on the other. If the state appears overly subservient to foreign capital, it risks not only the opposition of domestic elites but also political disruption by anti-imperialist nationalist movements.

The course of events in Brazil, as described by Evans (1982), supports this theoretical expectation. The dual alliance was followed by a period of government activity designed to "reinvent the bourgeoisie." Policies included the expansion of loan capital at generous terms for domestically owned firms and projects, preferential interest rates for activity in particular industrial areas, and fiscal incentives. These efforts, however, met with limited success. Evans attributes the failure of these programs to a fundamental contradiction faced by less-developed states: the simultaneous attempt to maintain good relations with international capital and to strengthen the domestic capitalist class. Opening an economy to world market forces, as we shall see in Chapter 6, often means compromising national autonomy and domestic control.

The statist strategy has also contributed to the international debt crisis—less-developed nations owing billions of dollars to Western banks with virtually no prospect for repayment. Historically, many less-developed nations relied on foreign investment to stimulate industrialization. As greater and greater portions of these economies come under the control of foreign interests, prompting a nationalistic political reaction, the state was compelled to intervene and direct the process of industrialization. This included supporting the economic interests of domestic capitalists, as described by Evans, and using state resources to expand the productive infrastructure and provide financial support for large-scale economic projects. All of these activities required substantial funds. In response, less-developed states turned to Western banks to finance their industrialization policies. During the 1970s Western banks went on a lending, and less-developed states on a borrowing, binge. The banks were quite eager to lend dollars, at high interest rates, to cash-starved governments. The net result is what Frieden (1981) terms "bank debt-financed government-led industrialization"—less developed states relying on borrowed capital to finance their industrialization:

In the pursuit of local control over local investment, the state has taken over; yet, paradoxically, this state involvement in the economy has been based on borrowing from foreign banks. In short, the state sectors in these LDCs have in effect been mortgaged to the Eurobanks, and both the banks and their client states have staked their fortunes on rapid national economic development. (Frieden 1981:413)

As Frieden suggests, the borrowing required to finance industrialization has produced a new form of external debt dependence.

The expansion of the state in less-developed nations is frequently accompanied by an authoritarian political arrangement. "Neo-fascist" may be a more apt description of the regimes analyzed by Evans and O'Donnell, authoritarian right-wing states that have become an almost permanent fixture in the political landscape of the less-developed world (Petras 1981). Examples include Brazil, Argentina, Singapore, Uruguay, Chile, and South Korea. Authoritarian neo-fascist regimes maintain their political power through the exercise of force, violence, and terror rather than through political responsiveness or ideology. Popular forces are demobilized, political parties are outlawed, and political participation is discouraged. The total suspension of democratic procedures is part of a comprehensive socio-economic development policy aimed at long-term economic growth in service to the international market and MNC capital. Outlawing the active participation of political organizations, particularly working-class and labor unions and parties, is one step toward establishing an attractive international business climate. Making the world safe for capital is often hazardous to the economic welfare of workers. Among the specific types of policies typically instituted by the neo-fascist state, Petras (1981:133) cites the following:

1. *Control over labor*: imposition of labor bureaucrats; restrictions or abolition of strikes, meetings, elections; wages fixed at low levels to maximize profit; job security weakened, giving employers absolute freedom to change the composition of the labor force and intensify exploitation.

2. *Freedom from fiscal obligation*: low tax rates; tax holidays; exemptions on exports; import of machinery.

3. *Public subsidies*: land grants free; industrial parks constructed and leased at little or no cost; infrastructure constructed (ports, railroads, communications); loans provided at low interest; access to local savings.

4. *Guarantees against expropriation*: nationalization partial or for expedience is accompanied by market-value compensation.

5. *State development complements development of private enterprise*: no risk of competition or absorption by state.

It is important to note that these regimes receive not only tacit blessing but also direct military and economic support from advanced capitalist nations, most notably the United States. Anti-Communist rhetoric and free-market economic policies are the standard litmus tests for receiving U.S. support; the exercise of democratic procedures is often incidental.

SOCIO-ECONOMIC SYSTEMS AND DEVELOPMENT: SOCIALISM

We now take up the question of socialism as a societal-level strategy for development. We shall proceed in the same manner as in the discussion of capitalism. First we outline the standard theoretical arguments for socialism as a socio-economic system facilitating growth. Second, we review the usual criticisms against socialism. Third, and of greatest importance, we consider some of the developmental problems that emerge within this type of system.

Socialism in Theory and Practice

Under the socio-economic system of socialism, the means of production are owned and controlled by the state. Decisions about production and investment, rather than determined by market forces and private capitalists, are based on a central plan. The plan contains growth rate targets for the national economy and the means to achieve these targets. The state, in designing and implementing the plan, considers the needs of the entire society, and in this sense directs resources on the basis of collective rather than private interest. Planning is viewed as an advantageous developmental tool because it eliminates the uncertainty inherent in market systems. Supply and demand can be written into the plan, and therefore the society does not experience the vagaries of the business cycle that result when supply exceeds demand or demand exceeds supply. The twin evils of capitalism—inflation and unemployment—presumably are eliminated by socialist planning, and development proceeds at a smoother pace. It is also argued that state control of productive property ensures that society's resources are fully utilized and devoted to national developmental goals.

In addition to the economic advantages, arguments for socialism are based on a number of other values. For example, because private productive property is controlled by the state, there is no exploitation of workers by capitalists nor windfall megaprofits concentrated in the hands of a small elite. This ensures that the distribution of income will be more equal and that the state will not be controlled by a small group of capitalists. The provision of basic human needs is also more structurally feasible under socialism because production is not undertaken solely for the purpose of private profit. Development under socialism, then, is smoother, more rational, based on national needs and priorities, more equitable, and less wasteful than under capitalism.

These compelling theoretical arguments for the superiority of socialism can be countered by a number of equally convincing criticisms against socialism (Zimbalist and Sherman 1984). First, under socialism power and control of the economy are placed in the hands of state bureaucrats who may be totally unresponsive to the needs of the people yet are in a position to decide, arbitrarily, what is best for the society, what goods should be produced, who gets what, and so on. In short, the replacement of capitalists with bureaucrats may result in greater economic inefficiencies and inequalities. Second, placing the entrepreneurial role in the public sector reduces the important private profit motive and incentive to invest, innovate, take risks, develop new products, and respond to new markets. If private individuals are unable to gain materially from their economic actions, the incentives required for dynamic efficiency are precluded. Third, socialism, by placing control of the means of production in the hands of the state, concentrates political power in the hands of those who are appointed as state managers or party bureaucrats. Finally, the absence of markets means that the central planning board is faced with the enormous task of determining supply, demand, consumer preferences, and prices. Without market-based prices the state is faced with an impossibly complex task that may result in the inefficient use and allocation of resources.

All of these charges against socialism, like those against capitalism, have a real-life basis. Some of these will be discussed in the next few sections. For the moment it is worth considering the last point: the absence of market-based prices under socialism and the resulting difficulties in efficiently allocating productive resources. There has been considerable debate over this issue (Lange and Taylor 1964; Hayek 1935; Elliott 1976).

A resolution to the pricing difficulty under centralized socialism is the system of *market socialism*. Some market mechanisms operate in all socialist economies. In Eastern Europe, Yugoslavia and Hungary rely heavily on the market, while in the Soviet Union there is greater reliance on centralized planning. Under market socialism there is an effort both to set prices in a rational way, ensuring the efficient use of resources, and to allow greater autonomy for and competition among firms as an incentive to reduce costs. On the important question of prices, Oskar Lange, the founder of market socialist principles, argued that socialist economies could establish meaningful prices just as easily as market capitalism, through the actions of a central planning board. The central planning board would keep track of the supply of and demand for any good and adjust the price accordingly, so that the good is consumed in greater quantities when it is in excess and in smaller quantities when it is in shortage (Lange and Taylor 1964). The other element of market socialism involves competition between publicly owned firms. Within a set of general guidelines managers of state firms are granted decision-making autonomy over how they use the factors of production, where they secure the inputs for production, how much they should charge for their products, and to whom they send their output.

It is worth asking, at this point, why one would opt for socialism if efforts designed to enhance efficiency require the incorporation of market capitalist principles. One of Lange's major contributions was to show how, at least theoretically, a socialist economy could carry out market-oriented forms of production in a manner superior to capitalism. Lange believed that a central planning board would be able to establish the correct prices for products with greater ease and fewer trials than in a competitive market system because it would have greater information about the entire economy.

Further, Lange argued that a market socialist economy would have the capacity to consider the needs of all segments of society, and the social costs of actions that are often ignored by private firms under capitalism. In this way the central planning board could raise costs to firms that produce negative externalities. "Internalizing the externalities" results in a net reduction in aggregate waste and a more efficient use of all of society's resources. In theory these are important and compelling arguments. In practice, of course, the mix of plan and market has created some difficulties but overall, in comparison with the centralized model, the economic performance of market socialist societies has been quite positive (see Zimbalist and Sherman 1984:chs. 14–16).

The Two Marxisms and the Transition to Socialism

According to many Marxist theorists (e.g., Brus 1975), the establishment of socialism requires two conditions. The first is that the means of production are collectively controlled, meaning that the processes of production, distribution, investment, and development are directed by public institutions. A second condition for the realization of socialism involves democratic control over these economic processes. To those who have studied the historical record of socialist practice in various nation-states, it is painfully clear that the second condition has not typically been instituted, and so one finds that the capitalist appropriators are appropriated but the masses have little democratic control over the centralized means of production. It is often for this reason that self-proclaimed socialists are hard pressed to identify a real-life example of the socialist ideal.

Under capitalism the organization of the economic sphere—private control of productive property—precludes democratic control over economic processes; under socialism the lack of political democracy precludes converting formal public control into real social control over the means of production (Brus 1975). Capitalist societies separate the economic and political spheres, therefore, at least partially, preventing the principles of democracy from encroaching on the property rights of private capitalists (but see Bowles and Gintis 1982).

The term *bureaucratic centralism* is the most apt description for the kind of regime that faces the greatest difficulty in instituting the democratic condition (see Arato 1978; Luke and Boggs 1982). Most often associated with Soviet-style socialism, the bureaucratic centralist regime is characterized by extreme centralization and concentration of all basic economic decisions, a rigid bureaucratic structure, and a top-down hierarchical planning apparatus. This bureaucratically centralized structure undermines the basis for the self-management or participation of workers. A further result is the emergence of a socio-political system of stratification in which power and influence are based on one's position in the bureaucratic hierarchy.

While bureaucratic centralism is often regarded as a betrayal of socialism, the institutionalization of this system finds a basis of legitimacy in the writings of Marx. There are two closely related elements of Marxist theory that provide a justification for the employment of a bureaucratic centralized model. First, Marx's scientific socialist scheme posited the evolution of societies from feudalism to capitalism to socialism to communism. As a part of this model Marx focused the greatest attention on the capitalist phase, the laws of this system, and, most important for this discussion, its contribution to the realization of socialism. Socialism was to be built on a foundation of material abundance. The post-scarcity socialist society envisioned by Marx stems from the historic mission of capitalism—to revolutionize the forces of production, amass and concentrate wealth, and create the capacity for material abundance. Marx describes the capitalist thus:

> . . . frantically bent upon the expansion of value, he relentlessly drives human beings to production for production's sake, thus bringing about a development of social productivity and the creation of those material conditions of production which can alone form the real basis of a higher type of society, whose fundamental principle is the full and free development of every individual. (Marx 1930:650)

For the Soviet Union, as well as most other socialist societies, the revolution preceded the consolidation of industrial capitalism. Because the capitalist phase and the associated development of the productive forces are regarded as material prerequisites for the realization of socialism, *bureaucratic centralism is a necessary substitute* for the absence of the capitalist phase. In the Soviet Union the legacy of the strong tsarist state was extended under Stalin. He employed a state centralized model in order to modernize the economy and develop the forces of production by postponing production of consumer goods in favor of investment in heavy industry. The forced collectivization of agriculture, subordinated to the industrial sector, was an integral part of this strategy. All of this was required in order to develop the material forces of production to the point that they can support the conditions for the emergence of socialism.

A fundamental problem emerges with the bureaucratic centralized strategy—the bureaucratic centralist means to achieve socialist ends become an end in themselves. The party-state apparatchiks are unlikely to relinquish power when the objective material conditions finally come to fruition because they have an objective interest in preserving the bureaucratic system on which their power and privilege are based. In short, developing mechanisms for popular control over the economy, the second necessary condition for the social control of the means of production, is thwarted by the institutionalization of the first condition.

The bureaucratic centralist road can be contrasted with the socialist *mobilization regime*, which is often seen as a direct challenge to the Soviet-style development strategy. Prime examples of the mobilization model are found in the immediate post-revolutionary periods in China and

Cuba. Based on the leadership of Mao Zedong and Fidel Castro, the mobilization strategy entailed extending the political ideology and social relations of the revolutionary struggle into the post-revolutionary period (see Dumont 1973). The essential foundation of socialism in this model is not the construction of an economic base or the development of the forces of production but an infrastructure of political and social consciousness (Petras 1983). Socialist ideas and practice are able to create socialist men and women whose actions advance the society toward higher stages of socialism.

Mao spoke of "politics in command" and "reds not experts"; Castro advocated "creating wealth with political awareness, not creating political awareness with wealth and money" (quoted in Petras 1983:140). The clear object was to offer an alternative to the bureaucratic centralist emphasis on developing the forces of production *prior* to the realization of true socialist consciousness. Instead, Third World socialism, maybe out of a sense of frustration and impatience, was to build the forces of production on the basis of socialist consciousness and commitment. In the early stages this strategy registered major economic gains, but it contained many inherent limits (see Petras 1983:ch. 6). Some of the most significant constraints on socialist strategy are imposed by the world economy (see Chapter 6).

It is interesting to note that the mobilization road to socialism also claims fidelity to Marx. The fact that bureaucratic centralist and mobilization strategies can both claim loyalty to the writings of Marx points to the dual character of Marxist theory, identified most forcefully and systematically by Alvin Gouldner in *The Two Marxisms* (1980). Gouldner argues that much of the tension in Marxist theory, as well as among contemporary Marxist theorists, is the product of conflicting strains of voluntarism and determinism in the young and the old Marx, respectively. Third World socialism borrows its theoretical inspiration from the young Marx, as seen in its emphasis on the role of revolutionary will and consciousness as the driving force for the construction of socialism. In the mobilization model the subjective sentiments of socialist men and women are able to lay the basis for the socialist transformation. This voluntarist component of Marxist theory shares some of the assumptions of individual modernization theory, which also posits the causal priority of beliefs and ideas in the development process.

The bureaucratic centralist strategy, on the other hand, fits squarely into the deterministic Marxist mode, which views social development as evolving through a number of specific stages, with the economic base assuming causal priority. Thus, objective conditions such as the development of the forces of production must be present in order for subjective socialist consciousness to emerge. On this basis, efforts to build the objective conditions through state bureaucratic planning mechanisms are justified as part of the evolutionary process.

All of this indicates the critical role of theory, in this case Marxist theory, for the understanding of socialist strategy and economic policy. A major difficulty arises when socialist societies, once the revolution is complete, are faced with the tasks of economic planning, production, coordination, and distribution under new arrangements. There is little in the corpus of Marxist writing that provides guidance for those confronting this economic challenge.

Feasible Socialism

Alec Nove, in *The Economics of Feasible Socialism* (1983), makes a significant contribution to the diagnosis of development problems under socialism. He advances a variety of compelling explanations for the economic failure of Societ-style socialism and raises many issues of central importance for development economics.

Nove believes that efforts to implement socialism are worthwhile, but that a reliance on the writings of Marx for this purpose is futile and self-defeating. According to Nove, Marx made numerous assumptions about socialist society that, unfortunately, either trivialized the economic difficulties facing socialist regimes or encouraged the view that economic problems would automatically disappear the moment the capitalist class had been overthrown. The most damaging assumption among these, for Nove, is that socialism would emerge in an economic context of post-scarcity material abundance. If a society actually possesses unlimited resources, and therefore transcends scarcity, then economic decisions are significantly simplified, trade-offs are a thing of the past, and basic conflicts and choices concerning resource allocation are transcended.[2] Marx's faith in the productive potential and accumulative power of capitalism, which was to precede socialism, contributed to his optimistic prognosis about the economic foundations of socialism. As we have already noted, socialist revolutions have not erupted in the most advanced capitalist societies; but even if they had, the post-scarcity assumption would still not hold because resource allocation remains a major source of conflict in all advanced economies.

In place of the assumption of material abundance, Nove prefers the more sobering concept of *opportunity cost*, which refers to the fact that allocating resources to one area means that other, possibly more profitable, avenues of activity are forgone. This is one version of the *zero-sum game*. Resources are finite, and thus each and every need cannot be satisfied simultaneously—some gain and some lose. This has been a fundamental fact of life in most times and places, and Nove believes there is no reason to assume otherwise, at least for present generations.

Because resources are relatively scarce, it is equally unrealistic to assume that humans, socialist or otherwise, will be nonacquisitive, unselfish, or nonmaterialistic. Nove's notion of "feasible socialism" requires accepting that resources are relatively scarce and that humans are frequently driven and motivated by self-interest. To imagine otherwise is to condemn oneself to perpetual disappointment and create an economy that will be unable to anticipate the most fundamental economic problems, dilemmas, and conflicts.

One of the basic problems facing a socialist state is the effective coordination of production and distribution through a centralized planning mechanism. Eliminating the capitalist market means that the state now assumes responsibility for ensuring that what is needed is produced, that what is needed to produce is produced, that goods are allocated and distributed where they are required, that human energy is expended in sufficient quantities, and so on. Nove's point is well taken—the task of state socialism is immense and complex. It requires, in his view, information, motivation, and means. The use of bureaucratic organizations with multilevel hierarchies is the unavoidable mechanism for the provision of these essential elements of economic production. Resources, orders, authority, incentives, and decisions are distributed through hierarchical structures and, Nove emphasizes, each of these microeconomic decisions cannot be voted on democratically, or else "next year's plan will be ready in several million years." These basic organizational problems are, for Nove, never adequately confronted by most socialists, and it is on this count that he is most critical of Marx, who, he states:

> . . . never considered the organisational implications of his ideas. By this I do not mean a blueprint or an organisational diagram, but basic principles such as: the necessary coexistence of centralisation and decentralisation, the need to reconcile the inevitable differences of view about what needs to be done; the importance of responsibility and of implementation of decisions taken, including the provision of the means of implementation. (1983:59)

Nove also is critical of Marx for suggesting that the division of labor is somehow unique to capitalism and will be overcome under socialism. This view, common among many contemporary Marxists, is a further consequence of the assumption that socialism will spring up in an environment of material abundance. In the more deterministic Marxist accounts, as we have seen, the development of the forces of production and the accumulation of wealth in the capitalist stage result from an intensified division of labor. It may be imagined that these social relations of production are no longer required under socialism because the problems of scarcity have been solved or because they are in contradiction with the highly developed forces and socialized nature of production. On the contrary, Nove believes that a division of labor is required under socialism, as under capitalism, and that it takes three basic forms: specialization between productive units, horizontal specialization between people, and vertical hierarchy.

A division of labor between productive units is generally assumed to be a requirement of all economic systems. Specialization between persons—different occupations and jobs—also is generally acknowledged as a requirement for most economies. The vertical dimension, involving hierarchy, is where the greatest debate is centered, since here one finds the generation of inequalities in income, authority, and power. There are obviously state socialist-sanctioned means that can reduce income differences, protect workers from managerial abuse, increase the bargaining power of labor, and so forth. All of these theoretical possibilities are arguments for socialism. On the question of authority, however, Nove's position is quite consistent with Dahrendorf's (1959) familiar concept of *imperative coordination*—all organizations, regardless of political ideology, require coordination and planning. This inevitably involves an authority structure for the purpose of issuing orders and supervising results.

This raises the question of incentives. Nove rejects the claim that somehow under socialism "what workers wish to do will correspond to what needs doing." Rather, there are many jobs that have to be carried out, and workers usually require some inducement (moral as well as material) in order to exert their energies. Nove suggests that under socialism the extreme disparities in income common in capitalism can be reduced. He also indicates that incomes should be based on the *principle of compensating differentials*. This refers to the fact that there are significant qualitative variations among jobs and occupations; that is, some are very pleasant, safe, and intrinsically rewarding, while others involve great physical exertion, are dirty and menial, involve significant risk, and so forth. Under capitalism it is typically the case that these differentials are not compensated. Rather, the most onerous tasks are often the most poorly compensated while the most desirable tasks, already providing considerable nonmaterial rewards, are the most highly compensated. While such sources of cumulative inequality can be dealt with under a socialist system of income distribution, which should in turn serve to equalize wages, differences in income will nonetheless persist because they are required as incentives to allocate labor where and in the amounts needed.

It is important to emphasize that Nove is aiming his critique at the "legacy of Marx." In many ways he is referring to the doctrine of Marx as represented by contemporary neo-Marxists who advance a utopian version of socialism devoid of any vestiges of capitalist ideology or inequality. As for Marx himself, while it is true that he provided little practical wisdom on matters of socialist administration, he certainly recognized that the early stages of socialism would involve a division of labor, income inequality, and incentive systems in order to move the society to a higher stage of development and affluence (Marx 1930).

To this point we have considered some of Nove's arguments relating to the deficiencies of Marxist writing as a guide to the actual implementation of a socialist economy. Nove also devotes a great deal of space to outlining some of the practical problems that inevitably arise in a centralized planned economy and how certain reforms may be required in order to attain the desired results. He clearly favors, instead of a totally planned system, the introduction of some level of market competition for the production and sale of consumer goods. He notes that all economies are interested in matching the quantity of the production of commodities with a corresponding level of demand—that the commodities produced are also consumed. One of the greatest economic uncertainties is predicting at time A what consumers will need and want at time B. In a planned economy the costs of this uncertainty can be handled, such that all that is produced is consumed, by letting the *producers determine consumption*.

> This highlights the importance of *choice*. The more choice there is, the less predictability for obvious reasons. It is therefore tempting for planners to limit or even eliminate choice, in the interests of good forecasting and the avoidance of the waste which is the inevitable consequence of getting a forecast wrong. . . . An aspect of choice is competition . . . if customers are free to seek their sources of supply, then the converse is that producers will seek customers. (1983:41)

Nove is well aware that competition for consumers and the inevitable mismatch in ex ante production and ex post consumption will result in some waste of resources. In response to this obvious drawback of competition, he makes a very simple argument, repeated throughout the book, that is often unappreciated by the tireless partisans of socialism and capitalism:

> ... *no* perfect system exists or can exist, that in general all institutional arrangements carry with them advantages *and* disadvantages. One can seldom get something for nothing. . . . The best solution is bound to be a compromise. (1983:42)

Many economic problems presumably inherent to one system or the other tend to emerge in different ways in both systems. A case in point is the negative externality or diseconomy. As indicated in our discussion of capitalism, private rationality does not always yield socially rational outcomes. It is often assumed that in a socialist economy all externalities are internalized in a single state bureaucracy. Yet, as Nove demonstrates, diseconomies are not necessarily the result of private ownership of productive property but, rather, of the *separation of decision-making units*. Under state socialism there are many different departments and agencies that are evaluated on their ability to fulfill parts of the larger plan. Successful fulfillment of the plan requires both a realistic production target and access to the supplies required to produce the particular good or service. Thus, there is a built-in incentive for enterprise managers to desire and set planning targets that can easily be met, to overapply for inputs, and to hoard labor and materials. This is rational from the standpoint of the manager who is driven by the plan fulfillment (rather than the profit) motive. But collectively the effect is to create shortages and bottlenecks, and reduce the potential surplus that would be generated if managers were willing to take greater risks and required to pay for redundant labor and supplies. Thus, external diseconomies arise out of the organization of state socialism just as they do under systems of private capitalism.

Organizational Constraints Under Socialism and Capitalism

Chapter 3 considered the role of organizations in the development process. Much of the discussion was confined to organizations operating within capitalist economies and the various strategies designed to maximize profit. It is important to demonstrate that variations at the socioeconomic system level (e.g., socialism vs. capitalism) impose different constraints on enterprises operating within these systems. A truly comparative multilevel analysis of development requires identifying how enterprises under different systems are faced with different problems.

In capitalist economies we have already noted how markets, and market exchange, may increase costs to firms. This "transaction cost approach" (Williamson 1975) has prompted advocating the use of hierarchical organizational structures as a means to control the uncertainties that prevail in markets. Exchanges should take place within a single entity, rather than between separate organizational entities so that greater information is obtained, costs are controlled, and production can be planned more adequately. In spite of all the lip service paid to the sanctity of free markets and competition, the hierarchical strategy, reflected in the contemporary behavior of major capitalist firms, shows a decided preference for non-market solutions. In short, the uncertainties inherent in market transactions lead producers to erect larger hierarchical corporate structures that more closely follow the logic of a planned socialist *nonmarket* economy. Large capitalist firms resemble mini socialist economies.

This "cost-cutting" strategy applies not only to goods but also to the human resource. Transaction cost theory argues against the use of "external" labor markets for the securing of the labor input because it contains unknown human quantities who, being reflective and conscious, may behave opportunistically and make false claims about their credentials and abilities. This prompts the use of "internal labor markets," which are hierarchical structures extended to the labor market that contain job and career ladders. Labor is recruited for advanced positions from *within* the firm, where it has been subjected to evaluation, training, and socialization. Again this reduces the uncertainties of a market-based labor recruitment strategy.

Stark's (1986) comparative analysis of labor markets in capitalist and socialist societies points to the way the distinct operating rules of the two systems impose different constraints on economic enterprises, thus forcing managers to pursue very different policies. In a market environment the capitalist firm avoids uncertainty by constructing internal labor markets that are, in fact, characterized by bureaucratic rules, job classifications, narrowly defined responsibilities, and formal operating procedures. Such rigid bureaucratic hierarchical structures are usually associated with state socialism, not market capitalism.

Stark compares the bureaucratic hierarchical labor market tendencies of capitalist firms with the labor market relations of socialist enterprises. It is important first to note that the economic environment of the socialist enterprise is characterized not by market uncertainties but by bureaucratic planning and regulation. Firms are part of a larger plan and are therefore told from whom they will receive their inputs and to whom they will send their outputs. While the planning of supply and demand is designed to eliminate uncertainties, it in fact, as Stark argues, creates a different set of uncertainties that must be faced by enterprise managers. The complex nature of coordinating an entire economy results in inevitable errors in prediction and so, in mid-plan, enterprise targets are often revised, shortages may occur, and supplies may be insufficient. Bottlenecks and shortages are the standard symptoms of a "supply-constrained" socialist economy. These planning errors result in periods of extended downtime in which production cannot proceed due to a shortage of required inputs. When these problems are finally alleviated, firms face periods of "rush work" and "storming" to meet the output target of the enterprise.

These bureaucratic planning-based uncertainties affect the internal structural arrangements for allocating and rewarding labor. First, Stark describes the way these uncertainties encourage firms to hoard labor so that a sufficient number of workers is available when materials arrive or the plans are changed. This enterprise-level behavior creates external diseconomies due to the resulting shortage of labor for the larger economy. Second, the fluctuating and uneven use of labor resulting from unpredictability, alternating between "downtime" and "rush work," requires managerial flexibility in the allocation of labor within the firm. Workers are shifted from place to place, depending upon the particular needs at the moment. When production is halted while waiting for supplies, workers may be shifted to maintenance and repair tasks. When "rush work" hits, all workers may have to participate in production tasks.

The required cooperation of workers under these kinds of conditions is not automatic or based on coercion. Because of the aggregate labor shortage, workers are often in a relatively strong bargaining position, and thus coercive bureaucratic regulations must be sidestepped in favor of a more informal negotiating system. What emerges, according to Stark, is a system of market-like transactions *within* the firm—informal bargaining with individuals and work groups. In return for managerial flexibility in reallocating labor, workers are promised extra compensation and fringe benefits. The comparative irony is described by Stark (1986:493):

Analyses of the systemic uncertainties and the organizational response of workers and managers yields a comparative model of mirrored opposition: in economies in which the firm operates in a *market environment*, systemic uncertainties regarding labor are reduced through internal *bureaucratic rules*. In the socialist economy, by contrast, where systemic uncertainties are produced by a *bureaucratic environment*, the firm responds through internal labor *market transactions*.

A similar logic operates when we consider the way the two systems seek to overcome their inherent economic difficulties. As noted by Burawoy and Lukács (1985), centrally planned economies tend to be characterized by shortages; that is, they are "supply-constrained" or plagued by under-supply. Capitalism, on the other hand, tends to produce beyond the ability of the system to consume; that is, the system is "demand-constrained" or plagued by oversupply. In order to alleviate the problem of shortage, socialist systems turn to capitalist mechanisms, most notably the market. Deficiencies in the plan are alleviated through a "second economy" existing outside the plan that allows enterprises to supply firms and consumers with what they need, using basic forms of market competition. Capitalist societies, in order to overcome the tendency toward oversupply, expand the role of the state to stimulate demand and directly consume goods and services. In short, "functional gaps in the market are filled by state intervention . . . dysfunctions of the plan in state socialist societies are countered by the opening up of the market" (Burawoy and Lukács 1985:726). Each system is forced to adopt the central mechanism of its political-economic antithesis in order to cope with its own inherent deficiencies.

CONTEMPORARY SOCIETAL-LEVEL DEVELOPMENT STRATEGIES

Corporatism in the Advanced Capitalist Nations

In this section we consider one of the most widely employed and advocated societal-level strategies for dealing with the contemporary political-economic crises of advanced capitalist societies. *Corporatism* is the term often used to describe this political arrangement, which is defined by Katzenstein as "the voluntary, cooperative regulation of conflicts over economic and social issues through highly structured and interpenetrating political relationships between business, trade unions, and the state, augmented by political parties" (1985:32). Grant sees it as

[a] process of interest intermediation which involves the negotiation of policy between the state agencies and interest organizations arising from the division of labor in society, where the policy agreements are implemented through the collaboration of the interest organizations

and their willingness and ability to secure the compliance of their members. (1985:3–4)

This two-part definition touches on the essential elements of corporatism for our purposes, though it should be noted that there is a great deal of debate over the precise meaning of the term (see Panitch 1980). As has been pointed out, political arrangements cannot be separated from economic strategies. This holds true for corporatism. It is a political arrangement with significant economic implications and, more directly in the current context, it is regarded as a political solution to potential economic stagnation and decline in advanced capitalist societies.

One way to understand the rationale for the corporatist arrangement is to consider the theory of comparative economic growth outlined by Mancur Olson (1982). Olson is best known for his analysis of the logic of collective action (1965), in which he argues that rational individuals have little incentive to contribute their energies to the provision of public goods or to participate in organizations that provide collective benefits. This is because the net gain to the individual of his/her action will be less than the effort expended; costs will exceed benefits. If all are motivated by this form of rational calculation, it is unlikely that any public goods will be provided (but see Coleman 1988a).

Individuals driven by this logic are likely to become "free riders" when public goods are distributed—they gain the benefits of the actions of others without paying any costs. An example of the free rider is the worker who realizes higher wages through union organization and bargaining but does not pay union dues. As a member of the bargaining unit or enterprise the worker receives the material benefit regardless of whether he/she contributes. This is yet another case of the externality problem. In this case the action of an organization or group of individuals has *positive externalities* because it *benefits* others who did not contribute to the original action. When benefits accrue to members of an organization, efforts are made to internalize the externalities by inducing or coercing affected parties and individuals to incur some cost for the benefits they receive. In the case of a labor union, for example, mandatory union dues are levied on all workers affected by union negotiations.

The various propositions offered by Olson have implications for the type and scope of organizations that will emerge and proliferate in a society. The basic conclusion is that narrowly based common-interests are more easily organized than broadly based interests because it is more difficult for broadly based organizations to overcome the free rider problem, that is, to internalize the externalities. And so, in a modern society with structural differentiation and an increasingly complex division of labor, narrowly based common-interest organizations accumulate and, where political channels exist, act to protect the interests of their members.

According to Olson, societies permeated by these types of interest groups are destined to suffer slow but certain economic decline. The economic health of societies is threatened by the "institutional sclerosis" that results from the power of these organizations. While this argument shows some similarities to those advanced by other theorists (e.g., Huntington 1968), that too much participation is a bad thing, it is actually much more complex. Olson applies the logic used to explain the individual propensity to join and contribute to collective organizations to explain the behavior and, ultimately, growth-retarding effects of interest groups. He believes that organizations are faced with a choice as to the best way to advance the interests of their members. Interest organizations can act in such a way that they increase the total quantity of social wealth. As the social pie expands, the size of the slice accruing to each of its members increases along with those slices going to all other members of the society. Alternatively, it can act to obtain larger shares for its members only. Olson is convinced that most rational organizations will opt for the latter strategy.

Thus there is a parallel between the individual in a group that would gain from provision of a collective good and the organization for collective action within the society. The organization that acts to provide some benefit for the society as a whole is, in effect, providing a public good for the whole society, and it is accordingly in the same position as an individual who contributes to the provision of a collective good for a group of which he or she is a part. In each case the actor gets only a part (and often only a tiny part) of the benefits of its action, yet bears the whole cost of that action. . . . Exactly the same logic we have used all along suggests that the typical organization for collective action will do nothing to eliminate the social loss or "public bad" its effort to get a larger share of the social output brings about . . . the organizations for collective action within societies that we are considering are therefore overwhelmingly oriented to struggles over the distribution of income and wealth rather than to the production of additional output—they are "distributional coalitions." (1982: 43–44)

The net effect of the self-interested behavior of distributional coalitions is to reduce the efficiency and aggregate income of the societies in which they operate, hinder the ability of society to adopt new technology and reallocate resources in response to changing circumstances, facilitate the proliferation of government regulations and intervention, and make political life less publicly legitimate and more politically divisive. All of these effects reduce the aggregate rate of economic growth.

Olson makes an important distinction between the actions of the narrowly based interest organization described above and what he calls "encompassing organizations." Encompassing organizations are organizations that represent a substantial portion of societies' members, say 20–30 percent. They therefore have a greater incentive to pursue actions that are most consistent with the interests and productivity of the whole society, because these gains accrue in larger proportion to their members. This means that while encompassing organizations are still primarily interested in advancing the material interests of their members, they are more likely to consider the effects of their actions on the larger productivity and prosperity of society. This is part of the argument for a corporatist political arrangement.

As the definition of corporatism implies, a corporatist political-economic structure involves relations, bargaining, and compromise between encompassing interest organizations. The contribution of this form of interest articulation to economic success is the subject of a number of studies, primarily of European political-economic systems (Esping-Anderson 1984; Katzenstein 1984, 1985; Schmitter 1981; and see Hicks 1988 for a review of some of this literature).

Katzenstein's (1985) detailed analysis of the "small states" of Europe (Austria, Belgium, Denmark, the Netherlands, Norway, Sweden, and Switzerland) and their success in dealing with the rapidly changing international economic conditions is a direct endorsement of the democratic corporatist system. According to Katzenstein, these systems have been able to respond in a flexible manner to changing economic demands. This can be contrasted with the social rigidity characteristic of societies that are composed of narrowly based interest organizations. In fact, the criteria selected by Katzenstein for evaluating the performance of a political economic system and determining the superiority of corporatism conforms closely to the conditions cited by Olson for sustained economic growth:

> . . . the extent to which social coalitions, political institutions, and public policies facilitate or impede *shifts in the factors of production that increase economic efficiency* with due regard to the requirements of political legitimacy. (Katzenstein 1985:29; emphasis added)

Olson's theory of economic decline is based on the rigidity and inflexibility in the factors of production that result when each self-interested organization seeks to defend the narrow interests of its members. Under corporatism interest groups are often described as "peak associations" that are "broadly based and organize a very large proportion of producers and workers" (Katzenstein 1985:33). According to Olson's thesis, this system of association would give rise to one of the distinguishing traits of corporatism identified by Katzenstein: an ideology of social partnership that "mitigates class conflict" and facilitates "notions of public interest." Representatives of peak associations meet to bargain over and set broad parameters on wages, investment strategies, employment targets, social spending, economic regulations, and so on. Once a certain set of national economic policies has been established, the members of each association are expected to abide by the agreement in the name of the general collective good, with compliance enforced on members from the top down within each encompassing organization.

It should be clear that corporatism is, for all practical purposes, a political mechanism designed to elicit consent and maintain social order in the name of economic growth and prosperity. It differs from the more authoritarian forms of political control in that social order and compliance are based not on terror and coercion but on negotiation and legitimacy. Like the lower-level work organizations discussed in Chapter 3, economic production requires cooperation and consent at the national level as well.

One of the central questions, of course, is who benefits most from this arrangement. The capitalist class? The working class? Political authorities? There is considerable debate over this issue. Some observers believe corporatism is a means to restrain and control the working class and strengthen the position of the capitalist class and the capitalist system (Panitch 1979, 1980). While it is true that corporatism is most often employed in the context of a capitalist economy, and is therefore "structurally constrained" to support the imperative of private capital accumulation, it is equally true that many of the economic policies stemming from corporatist negotiation allocate resources on a nonmarket basis. In this sense the economic policies often involve considerable government intervention and therefore convert the system away from a pure market capitalist model.

A number of empirical studies of the macroeconomic effects of corporatist practice suggest that this political arrangement supports higher levels of employment and lower levels of inflation (Cameron 1978; Schmidt 1982). Corporatism also may appear attractive in the face of alternative capitalist policies designed to stimulate capital accumulation, such as the anti-inflationary monetarist policies that, as a condition for subsequent economic expansion, subject the economy to a recessionary phase that clearly cripples the working class and undermines wage levels. Such policies have been the recent experience of the United States and Great Britain. There remains widespread skepticism over the long-term efficacy of such policies and a general recognition that some form of social contract and state planning is inevitable. Some version of corporatism, taking into account national differences, is the most frequently mentioned policy aimed at alleviating the current political-economic stalemate and market uncertainty.

Export-Oriented Industrialization in the Less-Developed Nations

Just as many advanced capitalist states have turned to some form of corporatism as a way out of economic crisis, so many less-developed nations are contemplating an export-oriented growth strategy as the key to industrial success (see Kaplinsky 1984). For the present purpose we are most concerned with the internal societal-level arrangements supporting this accumulation model. In Chapter 6 we shall consider some of the international forces that might serve to limit the economic viability of export-led development.

Much of the current enthusiasm for the export-oriented industrialization strategy is based on the recent experience of a handful of less-developed nations, most notably Hong Kong, Singapore, South Korea, and Taiwan. Since about 1960 each of these nations has pursued a concerted trade strategy that emphasizes the industrial production of goods for export markets. This represents a departure from the alternative strategy—import-substitution industrialization (ISI)—which emphasizes the internal production of manufactured products for domestic markets. ISI has, over time, created significant socio-political pressures. It has had the effect of strengthening the bargaining power of the domestic working class, which discourages foreign investment, and the import requirements of this policy have tended to increase the growing debt burden. The shift from ISI to export-oriented industrialization (EOI) is a means to reduce foreign exchange pressures and pursue an industrialization strategy that is less dependent on the buying power of domestic workers. Thus, there is a contemporary movement from inward-oriented (ISI) to outward-oriented (EOI) accumulation strategies.

The comparative economic performance of the inward- versus outward-oriented nations supports arguments for an export-led industrialization strategy. Examining a variety of macroeconomic indicators, from the growth in GNP to the share of the labor force in industry, a World Bank (1987:85) report concludes: "The figures suggest that the economic performance of the outward-oriented economies has been broadly superior to that of the inward-oriented economies in almost all respects."

The World Bank is by no means a totally unbiased, nonpartisan agency. It tends to associate the outward-oriented export strategy with its preference for an "open economy." The outward-oriented economy is regarded as more "open" to the extent that it "does not discriminate between production for the domestic market and exports, nor between purchases of domestic goods and foreign goods" (World Bank 1987:78). Again, this is in contrast with inward-oriented policies that tend to discourage production for export and place restrictions on the importation of foreign goods. In short, at least in theory, the outward-oriented strategy is more in line with the tenets of free trade and liberal economic policy that allow the free flow of goods and foreign capital investment across national borders. This free market philosophy tends to be favored by the World Bank and the International Monetary Fund not only for the economic benefits presumably accruing to the less developed nations that follow the outward-oriented strategy, but also for the opportunities this policy affords financial and industrial capital in the developed industrial nations. In reality, however, the terms "open," "free," and "unrestricted" are not wholly applicable to the regimes that exercise the outward-oriented strategy.

A particular case helps to illustrate the point. By any measure South Korea exemplifies the export-oriented industrialization model and is included in virtually every discussion of this development strategy. Yet the internal political economic arrangements supporting this policy can hardly be described as "laissez-faire," "free market," or "unregulated." The terms used to describe the South Korean model—*bureaucratic authoritarian corporatism* (Deyo 1981) and *bureaucratic authoritarian industrializing regime* (Cumings 1984)—suggest a different reality. As was noted in the earlier discussion of bureaucratic authoritarianism, such a system tends to be instituted as a means to control and deactivate the population in the name of modernization and economic growth. The term *neo-fascist* has also been applied to the South Korean regime.

The important implication of these various caricatures is that the export-oriented strategy is accompanied by a political arrangement that involves tight controls over the actions of labor and the working classes. The purpose is to discourage unionization, collective bargaining, and higher wages for industrial workers. These political actions are a direct product of a strategy that hinges on attracting foreign capital investment in manufacturing and producing competitive world-market commodities. Foreign capital is attracted to Korea because the labor force is relatively cheap and effectively controlled; export goods are internationally competitive for the same reason. The relationship between internal political arrangements and the global forces of international capital can hardly be any clearer.

The South Korean state is heavily involved in directing and planning the economy and regulating investment overall. There is a very close relationship between the state and the dominant economic actors in South Korea, the *chaebol*. They are similar to the large Japanese enterprises described in Chapter 3, and they dominate the industrial landscape of South Korea. These huge industrial enterprises account for a huge share of the GNP in manufacturing. In 1985 the four largest *chaebol* accounted for 45 percent of the GNP of South Korea (Business Week 1985:48). These enterprises are nurtured by the government through state control over banking and credit. Access to credit, and under favorable terms, is contingent on the ability of firms to penetrate foreign markets and devote a significant portion of their output to export trade. Exporting is further encouraged through currency devaluations that cheapen exports, the lowering of tariff barriers and tax holidays, and exemptions and redemptions for exporting firms (Cumings 1984). In order to relieve the state of an inordinate role in providing capital for export activities, the export-oriented strategy includes incentives to attract foreign investment in export production. The free-export-processing-zones, a common component of the overall strategy, involve setting up areas of the nation that allow unrestricted flows of capital, stringent labor controls, and other business climate incentives for foreign investors.

South Korea represents only one example of the export-oriented model of development (see Deyo 1981; Haggard and Cheng 1986; and Hamilton and Biggart 1988 for a comparative analysis of other cases). Yet it reflects many fundamental features of the general strategy, and its economic success has placed it as a role model for other less-developed nations. The ability of other nations to employ this accumulation strategy is contingent on the ability to control the domestic labor force, coordinate economic enterprises, and attract foreign investment. These factors strike at a variety of levels of analysis and, ultimately, given the "open" nature of this development policy, the international level of analysis must be considered.

Chapter 6 shifts to this global level of theorizing and addresses many of the issues relating to international trade and foreign investment, and how these external constraints and forces shape the developmental trajectory of nations.

NOTES

1. The relationship between socio-economic systems and development is part of the larger field of comparative economics. Useful texts in this area are Zimbalist and Sherman (1984), Kohler (1989), and Elliott (1973).

2. Assumptions about unlimited wealth, post-scarcity, and abundance are also a part of the "post-industrial society" literature. See Hamilton and Wright (1986) for a review of this work.

6

THE INTERNATIONAL SYSTEM AND THE WORLD ECONOMY

The modern world comprises a single capitalist world-economy. . . . nation-states are *not* societies that have separate, parallel histories, but parts of a whole reflecting that whole. To be sure, since different parts of the world play and have played differing roles in the capitalist world-economy, they have dramatically different internal socio-economic profiles and hence distinctive politics. But to understand the internal class contradictions and political struggles of a particular state, we must first situate it in the world-economy. (Wallerstein 1984:122–23)

In this chapter we turn to the broadest macro level of analysis, the international level. Theories of development operating at the international level view nations as part of a global system. The features and dynamics of this global system—imperialism, colonialism, the world market, foreign trade, flows of capital investment, MNC investment—are viewed as forces influencing the socio-economic development of nations. The international system shapes and constrains national development strategies.

DEPENDENCY/WORLD-ECONOMY THEORY

A consideration of the international level of analysis brings us to one of the most influential paradigms in the contemporary study of social change, dependency/world-economy theory. As we shall see, this theory (and there is some debate over whether it can be called a theory; see Lall 1975) contains a wide assortment of hypotheses and propositions advanced by a variety of theorists.

There are, however, three basic premises that inform all versions of dependency/world-economy theory. First, the socio-economic structure and development of less-developed nations are best understood by examining the historical pattern of integration into, and interaction with, the capitalist world economy. Second, as the first premise implies, the theoretical framework must extend beyond the societal level of analysis and consider the role of broader world-economic structures and forces in shaping national development. Dependency/world-economy theory emerged in reaction, and as an alternative, to sociological modernization and economic growth models that emphasized internal national, rather than external international, effects on development. Third, the global system, highly interconnected and interdependent, is characterized by an unequal distribution of power and influence. This results in some nations being more vulnerable, more dependent, and subjected to greater exploitation than others. Unequal and asymmetric interaction between rich and poor nations is a central theme in this model. The emphasis is on international relations within a world economic system. The major explanatory variables in this model of social change are those which define the nature of international exchange and interaction.

This chapter will review the arguments of some of the major theorists associated with dependency/world-economy theory.[1] This is followed by a consideration of the emerging and mounting attacks on this thesis and some recent revisions.

Dependency Theory: Some Early Arguments

International-level models tend to focus on the interaction between nation-states and the political-economic forces that regulate these interactions. Trade relations lie at the center of these models because the exchange of goods raises questions about international specialization, different methods of production, export vulnerability, the balance of payments, and the terms of trade. Positions in the international trade network also influence rates of socio-economic development and growth.

In the late 1940s standard models of international trade and economic development were beginning to come under attack. The most concerted effort came from the U.N. Economic Commission for Latin America (ECLA), headed by Raul Prebisch (1950). Up to this point theories of international trade had been heavily influenced by the work of David Ricardo (1933) and his "law of comparative advantage." This so-called law stipulated that each nation should specialize in the production of goods it could produce most cheaply in comparison with other goods. In his example, if Portugal could produce wine more cheaply than textiles, and England could produce textiles more cheaply than wine, then Portugal should specialize in the production of wine and England in the production of textiles. In turn, England's demand for wine, and Portugal's demand for textiles, could be met through trade. Under this system, it was claimed, nations would use their resources most efficiently and the net cost of producing various goods would be minimized. If followed faithfully, a logical outcome of this law (and one advocated by numerous development agencies) would be *specialization* in the production and export of a narrow range of goods. One of the major tasks of Prebisch and his ECLA colleagues was to examine the impact of specialization on economic development.

One of the questions raised by the ECLA group was whether the "terms of trade" were equitable for nations specializing in the production of different commodities. *Terms of trade* refers to the relationship between the world market price of a nation's imports and exports. Optimally, a nation wants the world market price of its exports to exceed the world market price of its imports. If less-developed nations specialize in the production and export of primary agro-mineral products, such as coffee, bananas, and copper, given their comparative advantage in this line of goods, how does this affect the terms of trade and, ultimately, growth and development? Under the comparative advantage arrangement, specialization in the production of agro-mineral primary products would obviously necessitate the importation of manufactured and industrial goods. The terms of trade between these different commodities therefore emerges as a significant issue.

A major contention of the ECLA group was that a serious bias existed against primary agro-mineral product exporters because the world market price of most primary products had experienced a steady decline, while manufactured products had become more expensive. Under the system of international specialization, less-developed nations experienced a decline in their per unit export revenue, while the cost of imported manufactured products remained stable or increased. This trend had created, according to ECLA, a chronic balance of payments crisis for Latin American nations. The *balance of payments*—the relationship between the total cost of imports and the total income derived from exports—would be in a state of chronic deficit so long as less-developed nations pursued a primary product specialization strategy. It was further contended that this specialization strategy, instead of being beneficial to all parties involved, worked to the advantage of the industrial nations and to the detriment of less-developed nations.

The work of the ECLA group on the issue of international trade laid the groundwork for a critical and global analysis of development problems. One important implication of their work was that the international trade structure, based on specialization and a division of labor between nations, contributed to economic decline and stagnation among less-developed nations. This shifted the level of analysis from internal national characteristics to the mechanisms of world market exchange.

Second, the claim that the terms of trade worked to the benefit of the industrialized nations of the "center" at the expense of the "periphery" suggested unequal and exploitative political-economic relations between regions of the world. This came to be a basic tenet of dependency theory.

The divergent payoffs from international specialization raised a third critical point about the *source* of comparative advantage. Why does one nation have a comparative advantage in producing nutmeg, while another nation has a comparative advantage in the production of automobiles? The conventional response was that nations possessed different "factor endowments"—that is, different quantities and qualities of natural resources, labor, and capital. These factor endowments were taken as given, as a part of the natural order rather than something that required explanation. The ECLA school called into question the origin of comparative advantage and economic specialization. They pointed to the legacy of colonialism and the external implantation of primary product export systems by the colonial powers as the source of contemporary specialization patterns.

Finally, the ECLA arguments raised the question of whether *imbalanced growth models* were a viable basis for sustained economic expansion. Imbalanced growth models argue that, rather than developing a broad number of industries simultaneously, a nation should develop or specialize in a single line of production. Through international trade other necessary products can be imported. It is assumed that, over time, other industries and sectors will emerge to produce products for, and consume the output of, the original sector. The relationship of this model to the arguments of comparative advantage should be apparent. In response and opposition to the logic of this model, ECLA prescribed a national policy of *import substitution industrialization* (ISI) that would facilitate the domestic production of previously imported industrial goods. This strategy was proposed in order to create a more balanced economic structure and reduce dependence on external sources.

Shortly after ECLA made its recommendations, reservations were raised about the ability of import substitution to resolve the developmental difficulties of Latin American nations. One of the major figures in this revision, Celso Furtado, was a member of ECLA and heavily involved in development policy in Brazil. Furtado's work (1965; 1970; 1973) is significant in its emphasis on the inherent limits of import substitution, formulations on the role of colonialism and multinational capital, the discussion of consumption patterns and the distribution of income, and the use of the concept of peripheral capitalism.

Furtado was less sanguine about the prospects for long-term development under import substitution. Like Prebisch, he felt that the international division of labor based on the law of comparative advantage had served to concentrate the benefits of technical progress among the advanced industrial societies. Obviously some effort had to be made to shift into other areas of production. However, Furtado regarded the ISI strategy as unsatisfactory. Initial stages of import substitution would inevitably involve domestic production for existing and dynamic internal markets. In Latin America many of the most dynamic markets were those for Western-style luxury goods demanded by a narrow elite segment of landowners and capitalists. For Furtado, the application of the import substitution principle to an already distorted social structure meant extending the discontinuities imposed by Western culture to the domestic economy. That is, the traditional pattern of elite importation of luxury consumer goods would simply be replaced by the domestic production of these same types of products. Furtado believed this strategy would only reinforce the concentration of income in the hands of a small elite and restrict the prospects for long-term, balanced industrial growth.

Furtado introduced the concept of *peripheral capitalism* to describe the unique pattern of Third World development characterized by import substitution based on Western consumption patterns, an inability to generate productive innovations, and phases of socio-economic development shaped by the decisions of outsiders. This latter feature of peripheral capitalism, labeled "external dependence," remains a central part of contemporary dependency theory. The outside forces to which Furtado referred were the industrialized nations of Europe and North America and their multinational corporation (MNC) appendages. According to Furtado, MNCs extend the cultural domination of the West, introduce inappropriate consumption patterns, and distort the economic structures of less-developed nations. The vilification of the MNC is another component of Furtado's analysis that is echoed in almost every subsequent rendition of dependency theory. The idea of external dependence also stands as a defining characteristic of the dependency condition and has been incorporated into what is one of the most widely used definitions of dependence:

By dependence we mean a situation in which the economy of certain countries is conditioned by the development and expansion of another economy to which the former is subjected. The relation . . . assumes the form of dependence when some countries (the dominant ones) can expand and be self sustaining, while other countries (the dependent ones) can do this only as a reflection of that expansion. (Dos Santos 1970:231)

A third major influence on dependency theory comes from the writings of Paul Baran. In Baran's seminal work, *The Political Economy of Growth* (1957), he formulated a model of underdevelopment that pointed to the distinct developmental condition of less-developed nations arising out of colonialism and imperialism. As discussed in Chapter 4, the concept of surplus played a major role in Baran's theory of economic growth. Baran tried to identify the reasons why nations did not realize their potential surplus, which was much larger than the actual surplus. Operating at the international level of analysis, Baran pointed to the forces of colonialism, imperialist penetration, and the extraction of surplus from the less-developed periphery to the advanced center states.

It is interesting to note that, in contrast with some later dependency theorists, Baran regarded competitive capitalism as a relatively progressive force (in the sense of moving societies toward socialism) that had not completely penetrated the Third World (see especially Baran 1952). He implied that the problem in backward nations was the partial or incomplete incorporation of capitalism, and its combination with feudal patterns of organization and social relations. The external imposition of capitalism on pre-capitalist societies created a distinct socio-economic structure that contained many obstacles to sustained economic growth. According to Baran, the international spread of capitalism was instigated by the needs and demands of monopoly capitalism in the advanced countries for new sources of profit. Thus capitalism did not emerge organically in the Third World but was imposed from the outside; and the capitalism that was introduced was of a monopoly rather than a competitive form. Baran regarded these two factors—capitalism from without and its monopoly form—as largely responsible for the retrogressive effects of capitalism on underdeveloped nations.

Baran's elaboration of the relationship between underdeveloped societies and the imperialist forces of the world economy has had an enormous influence on contemporary versions of dependency theory. According to Baran, the crisis of monopoly capitalism among the advanced Western nations—fully elaborated in Baran and Sweezy's *Monopoly Capital* (1966)— resulted not only in the expansion of government spending within advanced capitalist states but also the international expansion of MNCs. The monopoly stage of capitalism further required new locations and sources for investment, production, and raw materials.

Baran cited two major flow mechanisms of imperialist expansion and exploitation. First, like the ECLA group, he pointed to the *trade flows* between developed and underdeveloped states. MNCs extracted required primary products from less-developed nations at low cost. Less-developed economies imported more expensive industrial goods from the advanced capitalist states. This exchange of primary products for manufactured goods is still regarded as a defining characteristic of the dependent and unequal relations between rich and poor nations.

Second, and equally critical from Baran's perspective, was the *flow of surplus* from the underdeveloped to the advanced nations. Profits from multinational enterprises located in less-developed nations tended to be sent abroad rather than reinvested, thus undermining the prospects for sustained economic expansion. As we shall see, the international exploitation of underdeveloped by developed states, through the mechanisms of unequal trade and "surplus drainage," remains a consistent theme in the arguments of contemporary dependency theorists.

Metropolis and Satellite: Andre Gunder Frank

The single most important figure in the development of dependency theory is Andre Gunder Frank. His writings in the mid and late 1960s, based on his study of Latin America, mark the beginning of an explicit dependency theory. Though the theory has been modified since these initial formulations, numerous elements have been retained.

One of these central elements is the rejection of economic and sociological models of development based on the experience of Western Europe and North America. For Frank, the issue is whether what now constitutes the Third World is, or ever was, in a position comparable with that of preindustrial Europe and North America. If one believes that there is only one path to socio-economic development, then conventional theories and prescriptions based on Western historical experience might be relevant for understanding the currently underdeveloped nations and their economic problems. However, according to Frank, the historical experiences are so different as to make the Western-based models obsolete and useless.

The now developed countries were never *under*developed, though they may have been *un*developed. It is also widely believed that the contemporary underdevelopment of a country can be understood as the product or reflection solely of its own economic, political, social, and cultural characteristics or structure. Yet historical research demonstrates that contemporary underdevelopment is in large part the historical product of past and continuing economic and other relations between the satellite underdeveloped and the now developed metropolitan countries. (1969:54)

In pointing to the distinct socio-economic histories of developed and underdeveloped societies, Frank is also reiterating some basic dependency premises. First, that contemporary underdevelopment is the product of external rather than internal structures and forces. Second, that the legacy of colonial relations between developed and underdeveloped nations places the underdeveloped world in a qualitatively different position than was the case for preindustrial Europe and North America.

Describing the nature and the effect of the relationship between what Frank calls the *satellite* and *metropolitan* nations is a central analytic focus of dependency theory. This international perspective points to an often overlooked aspect of the development of the West—involving superordinate and exploitative relations with Asia, Africa, and Latin America—as well as the influence of these historical forces on the socio-economic structures of the now underdeveloped countries. In short, Frank argues that the development of Western Europe and North America was enhanced by the exploitation and underdevelopment of the world's hinterlands—the now underdeveloped nations. In this model, development and underdevelopment are two sides of the same coin in an international capitalist economy.

A second integral component of the dependency model involves the rejection of the *dual-society thesis*. This thesis posits the existence of a dual economic structure in less-developed economies that contains a modern, dynamic capitalist sector and a backward, feudal subsistence sector. The model attributes underdevelopment to the fact that a large part of the economy remains under the sway of feudal practices. The solution is to expose the presumably isolated feudal sectors to the forces of capitalism existing in modern sectors and industrialized nations. In sharp contrast with this view, Frank (as well as most other dependency and world economy theorists) argues that all territories of the world have been penetrated by the forces of world capitalism and that the diffusion of world capitalism is responsible for the contemporary underdevelopment of Third World regions and nations.

Therefore, the economic, political, social, and cultural institutions and relations we now observe there are the products of the historical development of the capitalist system no less than are the seemingly more modern or capitalist features of the national metropoles of these underdeveloped countries. (Frank 1969:5)

The two general themes reviewed above—the historical development of underdevelopment and the rejection of dual-society logic—laid the groundwork for a set of dependency propositions or hypotheses regarding the development process. Frank's first hypothesis states "that in contrast to the development of the world metropolis which is no one's satellite, the development of the national and other subordinate metropoles is limited by their satellite status" (1969:9). Again, Frank emphasizes the distinct historical position of the contemporary underdeveloped world. Further, the status of satellite implies weakness, vulnerability, and subordination. Nations in this position may produce a significant economic surplus, but a large portion is said to be drained off by the metropolitan nations that control production, trade, and exchange in satellite nations. This economic surplus is used to advance the fortunes and interests of the capitalist class in the metropolis.

The second hypothesis advanced by Frank is in direct contrast with the assertions of the dual-society thesis: "Satellites experience their greatest economic development and especially their most classically capitalist industrial development if and when their ties to their metropolis are weakest" (1969:9–10). According to the dual-society theory, we would expect contact with the capitalist nations of the metropolis to break down feudal barriers and to stimulate capitalist expansion. However, if, as Frank contends, satellite-metropolis relations are exploitative and asymmetrical, then the greatest potential exists when these ties are broken and nations can engage in autonomous, indigenous-based development programs.

A notable historical period is often used in support of this thesis: the period between World War I and World War II, during which the metropolitan nations were preoccupied with the two wars and economic depression and, therefore, unable to maintain their presence in and domination over the less-developed satellite states. A number of Latin American nations, previously bound by the ties of dependency, experienced a significant phase of industrial development during this period. In Brazil in the early 1930s, a political alliance hostile to the feudal oligarchy, and led by the domestic industrial capitalist class, came to power and established the Estado Novo under the Vargas regime. Policies were instituted to advance national industry, include the political participation of the working class, create a rational state bureaucracy, and usher in some form of democracy.

Similar developments occurred during the same period in Argentina, where a policy of import-substitution industrialization was initiated. This process involved the extensive internal production of formerly imported goods. In many ways this policy was necessitated by the depression in Europe and North America, which curtailed trade and capital flows. However, out of this transformation emerged a strengthened national industrial capitalist class and a politically active working class, which laid the basis for the populist Peronist movement in the mid 1940s. Neither of these movements, however, led to sustained, long-term autonomous in-dustrial development because of the reestablishment after World War II of metropolitan expansion, especially by the United States, that renewed the structure of dependence. The phase, however, is often used as evidence in support of Frank's thesis.

The transitory nature of the autonomous development phase leads us to Frank's corollary of the second hypothesis:

> When the metropolis recovers from its crisis and reestablishes the trade and investment ties which fully re-incorporate the satellites into the system, or when the metropolis expands to incorporate previously isolated regions into the world-wide system, the previous develop-ment and industrialization of these regions is choked off or chan-nelled into directions which are not self-perpetuating and promising. (1969:11)

Frank's third hypothesis argues that "the regions which are the most underdeveloped and feudal-seeming today are the ones which had the closest ties to the metropolis in the past" (1969:13). Frank uses as examples to support this claim those regions which historically served as a major source of agro-mineral primary products for the industrial development of the metropolis. Because the wealth and surplus derived from this primary product sector accrued to the world metropolis, and demand for the products or the mineral wealth eventually evaporated, these areas were abandoned to become some of the most destitute regions in the world. This argument stands as a further challenge to the view that poor regions and countries are those which have not benefited from the diffusion of world capitalist forces.

Stephen Bunker's (1984) research on the historical experience of the Brazilian Amazon provides a relevant case study lending support and much greater detail to this general thesis. Advancing what he describes as a "commodity-based model of underdevelopment," Bunker points to the "extractive commodities" that are exported to the metropolis, where they are refined, finished, and processed. These include petroleum, minerals, lumber and nuts from natural forests and undomesticated trees, and fish. Bunker traces the historical role of the Amazon Basin in providing commodities to Europe and America from the sixteenth to the twentieth century. This region exported spices, animal oils, rubber, and light metals, yet "despite its long history of supplying valued commodities for world trade, the Amazon Basin is one of the poorest areas in the world, and the economic and social systems on which many of its inhabitants depend are seriously threatened by disruption or extinction" (Bunker 1984:1022).

The reason for this result is that particular demographic, organizational, and environmental structures that were created for the purpose of exporting a particular extractive commodity—and eventually abandoned when the demand for the product waned or was replaced by a synthetic substitute—restricted subsequent forms of economic production and expansion. In the specific case of the Brazilian Amazon, the intense colonial extraction of native spices slowly destroyed the fragile human settlements and ecosystem on which the productive system depended. In the second, nineteenth-century, expansionary phase rubber was the export commodity extracted and the extraction process required a large labor force. Because of the prior destruction of the human population, labor was scarce locally and had to be recruited through the migration of peasant populations from other regions, who then developed a relationship of debt servitude with the commercial landowners. The Brazilian rubber boom ended when Asian rubber plantations outcompeted the Amazon producers. Thus, "the rubber boom repeated the pattern of original colonization—rapid enrichment of a small group followed by a sudden collapse and enduring poverty" (Bunker 1984:1032).

Frank advances two final and related hypotheses that further elaborate a general and very important point. The fourth and fifth hypotheses are directed to the issue of the development of the latifundium, the large-scale commercial agricultural enterprise.[2] For Frank, the common distinction made between hacienda and plantation agriculture—that they represent systems of feudalism and capitalism, respectively—is false. Instead, the latifundium—often characterized by feudal social relationships (the hacienda) and described as a precapitalist system—has historically been an agricultural enterprise heavily penetrated by the forces of international capitalism. However, in contrast with the expectations of the dual-society thesis, the seemingly feudal institutions employed for the production of export crops do not disappear; rather, they intensify under the influence of commercial agriculture. Again Frank is rejecting the dual-society contention that feudal contact with capitalist markets transforms the relations and forces of economic production toward rational, efficient capitalism.

This paradox—market forces reinforcing rather than transforming feudal institutions—is explained by Chilcote and Edelstein (1986:24):

> Commerce provides an incentive for the lord to extract a greater surplus from his serfs so that he can sell it to purchase luxury goods. But this change can be accomplished *within* the manorial system, using the position accorded the lord in the feudal society to make possible the increased demands on the serf. Ironically, instead of breaking feudal bonds in favor of a system of free labor, traditional relationships and agricultural methods are preserved, and the only change is a greater extraction of surplus from the serfs.

The reference to commerce raises an important issue that is central to much of the debate among dependency and Marxist theorists. This involves the distinction between merchant and industrial capitalism. *Merchant capitalism* refers to the process by which commodities are bought for one price and sold for another or, as the saying goes, "buying cheap and selling dear." When Frank (and, as we shall see, Wallerstein) refers to the worldwide expansion of capitalism, or the global dominance of market forces as early as the sixteenth century, he is referring to mercantile or merchant capitalism. Merchants were interested in gaining low-cost access to agricultural and mineral commodities in the less-developed world that could then be sold for a profit in European markets. Feudal landowners, in turn, were interested in selling these agricultural commodities to merchants and using the proceeds for the purchase of luxury goods produced primarily in Europe. Both parties were able to satisfy their needs under the feudal arrangements.

What is significant in the merchant form of capitalism is that the merchants did not have any interest in reorganizing the methods and system of agricultural production. As long as the primary commodities could be acquired cheaply, merchants were indifferent to the means used by the landowners to extract labor and a surplus from peasants. This led Frank to reject the dual-society argument that feudal structures persist because of a lack of contact with market forces, or that the hacienda is a feudal remnant and the plantation a capitalist institution. It should also be noted, at this point, that Frank defines capitalist institutions as those which have contact with and produce for a market. In this way Frank could contend that the international expansion of capitalism interacted with, supported, and reinforced these backward feudal productive structures and, therefore, contributed to the underdevelopment of the Third World.

In contrast with merchant capital, which primarily involves the *exchange* of commodities, *industrial capitalism* involves the *production* of commodities under a particular set of conditions. In this system, a capitalist or entrepreneur who owns productive property brings together wage labor, capital, and raw materials for the purpose of producing a commodity at the lowest possible cost in order to secure a profit through sale in the market. The critical part of this process, however, is the use of labor in as productive a way as possible so that goods can be produced cheaply and efficiently. Some of the methods for organizing the labor process have already been discussed. This form of capitalist profit obviously differs from that obtained under merchant capitalism, in that these capitalists have a direct interest in the methods, organization, and social relations of production.

The Capitalist World Economy: Immanuel Wallerstein

The world-economy theory developed by Wallerstein (1974, 1979) is often associated with dependency theory. Both approaches reject the view that national development can be explained by examining the internal characteristics of nation-states. Instead, nations are seen as open systems that are heavily influenced by economic forces and patterns of exchange at the international level. Like Frank, Wallerstein dismisses the dual-society thesis that attributes economic backwardness to feudal conditions of production and lack of exposure to market forces. In fact, for Wallerstein, the whole notion of stages of development or socio-economic systems, such as feudalism and capitalism, is misleading since, in his view, there is only world development and a world system. In order to understand Wallerstein's argument one must grasp his definition of a social system:

We take . . . the defining characteristic of a social system to be the existence within it of a division of labor, such that the various sectors or areas within it are dependent upon economic exchange with others for the smooth and continuous provisioning of the needs of the area. (1979:5)

Wallerstein is clearly working at a *world level of analysis* where nation-states are the interacting parts of a larger system. The parts carry out particular functions dictated by an international division of labor. The essence of this world social system is the "production for sale in a market in which the object is to realize the maximum profit" (1979:15). Where this defines the purpose of national production and exchange, the international system can be described as a capitalist world economy. Thus Wallerstein regards the sixteenth-century international economy as a capitalist world economy and, for the same period, any agricultural production for the world market as capitalist agriculture. In short, he does not believe there is any useful purpose in distinguishing between various systems of agriculture or forms of capitalism. There is one social system— the capitalist world economy—and those nations which participate in this system (produce and exchange commodities) are capitalist.

The somewhat extreme and unorthodox nature of Wallerstein's position with respect to the universal categorization of all forms of national production as capitalist is difficult to sustain. This contention is qualified to a considerable extent with the concept *modes of labor control* (Wallerstein 1974), which refers to those socio-economic relations and political structures that are instituted in order to ensure effective control over workers for the purpose of profitable world economic production. There is a great deal of value in this concept. It provides a useful way to link the myriad societal and industrial organizational arrangements throughout the world with the requirement for cost-effective world market production. All nations are under pressure to produce competitively for international trade, and this influences the national organizational strategies of labor control. In Wallerstein's model these different modes of labor control are the effects of world market pressures. Regardless of their specific socio-political nature (for instance, slave, feudal, fascist, socialist), they are considered parts of a larger capitalist world system and, therefore, capitalist.

Another element of Wallerstein's model involves describing the international system as a type of social class system. The language and imagery of social stratification and class relations are pervasive in Wallerstein's description of world-system dynamics. Like individuals in a stratified society who occupy social class positions, nations occupy classlike structural positions in the world economy. The three major positions are the core, the semi-periphery, and the periphery.

The *core* is composed of the advanced capitalist states of North America and Western Europe. Core states are politically and militarily powerful, have a high per capita GNP, and specialize in the production of manufactured and high-tech commodities. At the bottom of the international division of labor are the nations of the *periphery*. Peripheral nations are militarily weak, have a low per capita GNP, and tend to specialize in the export of agro-mineral primary products. The *semi-periphery* is composed of those nations somewhere between the core and periphery. Semi-peripheral states have relatively strong governmental structures and moderate levels of GNP, and are moving toward greater levels of industrial production. They are sometimes referred to as the "newly industrialized countries."

The relationship between the core and the periphery, in Wallerstein's account, is very similar to Frank's description of the interaction between metropolis and satellite, but the social class analogy to unequal resources, power, and exploitation is much more apparent in the writings of Wallerstein. While his critics may accuse him of ignoring social class relations within nations, Wallerstein does not ignore this dynamic at the international level. For example, he states that "capitalism involves not only appropriation of the surplus value by an owner from a laborer, but an appropriation of surplus of the whole world economy by core areas" (1979:18–19). The core, in this view, is equivalent to a world-level capitalist class, the periphery is the highly exploited working class, and the semi-periphery is the middle class.

The function of the semi-periphery is also conceptualized by Wallerstein in class structure terms: "the world economy as an economy would function every bit as well without a semi-periphery. But it would be far less *politically* stable for it would mean a polarized world-system. . . . The *middle* stratum is both exploited and exploiter . . ." (1979:23). Like a national middle class, the semi-periphery serves as the buffer zone between the antagonistic nations of core and periphery. It is a co-opted stratum that supports world capitalism because it is made up of nations that have experienced some upward mobility. That experience also serves as a concrete example for peripheral nations—that international mobility is possible within the existing structure of the capitalist world economy. With the appropriate mode of labor control the periphery also can achieve international status and power.

Wallerstein points to the competitive strategies that are employed by peripheral and semi-peripheral nations for the purpose of international upward mobility. Most notable is the emergence of "statist" and "mercantile" political structures. Consistent with his larger model, Wallerstein does not regard these kinds of state systems as anything but capitalist.

> The fact that all enterprises are nationalized in these countries does not make the participation of these enterprises in the world-economy one that does not conform to the mode of operation of a capitalist market system: seeking increased efficiency of production in order

to realize a maximum price on sales, thus achieving more favorable allocation of the surplus of the world economy. (1979:34)

Wallerstein's position on this matter leads him to characterize socialist and/or Communist states as capitalist because they, too, are parts of a capitalist whole that participate in world market production and trade. Not surprisingly this argument has generated some heated debate. It has also raised some intriguing theoretical issues. Wallerstein's theoretical model and its application to state socialist societies is the subject of a lucid review and critique by Gorin (1985). One of the many points that Gorin elaborates is Wallerstein's ambiguous and inconsistent description of the actual role played by socialist states in the world division of labor. They are at different times considered functional for the survival of the world system; anti-systemic forces capable of transforming the world economy toward socialism; and/or somewhere between co-opted technocratic producers and politically insurgent states.

The fundamental thrust of Wallerstein's position, and that which generates the most controversy, is his argument that internal organizational arrangements and social class relations are irrelevant in determining the socialist or capitalist nature of societies. The acceptance of this proposition has resulted in the even more provocative assertion that the centralization of capital and the planned coordination of production found in socialist states is the superior organizational form for world capitalist production. Or, in bolder form: "State socialism is the highest stage of world capitalism" (Bergesen 1982:100). This represents an extreme extension of the Wallersteinian logic. It is also an interesting application of the principles of transaction-cost theory (see Chapter 3), which advocates the nonmarket hierarchical coordination of productive activity as the superior organizational strategy in a market system. In this case the market system is international and the organizations are nations participating in this market system. In short, the claim is that an internally nonmarket state socialist society is best able to compete in a market-based world system. One might reasonably ask at what point the internal socio-political arrangements of nations affect the nature of the international economic system. In the Wallersteinian model, however, this would be a case of having things backward or confusing cause and effect, because it is the world-economy that determines the nature of national economic systems.

In spite of the many critical assessments that have been made in recent years, many important lessons can be learned from this world-system perspective. One of the most important is that all nations, be they capitalist or socialist, are structurally constrained by their need to produce and exchange products in a world market. What this means is that nations often pursue foreign and trade policies that seem to contradict the public pronouncements of official state ideology. In short, the imperative of economic accumulation overrides political ideology.

Andre Gunder Frank (1980) has aptly described this arrangement as "transideological enterprise." Requirements for modern technology, finance capital, and export markets—all for the purpose of capital accumulation and growth—bind nations with vastly different socio-political systems and ideologies. Like many individuals, nations are also guilty of "selling out" to, or becoming "cogs in the wheel" of, capitalism. Petras remarks upon this phenomenon in his study of the international behavior of Third World socialist states:

> Over the medium run, the underdevelopment of the productive forces within revolutionary Third World countries has forced increasingly compromised relations with imperial countries. The objective constraints imposed by the uneven distribution of productive forces on a world scale has been and will continue to be a much more important factor shaping regime behavior than the "betrayal" of this or that revolutionary group or leadership. No nation, whatever its revolutionary credentials, can escape these constraints so long as all must participate in the world economy, accumulate capital, and apply advanced technology. (1983:148)

All of these positions and statements suggest something akin to a "convergence theory," but through the logic of participation in international production and exchange. All nations that seek to modernize through world market exchange must "toe the line," conform to the macro logic of world capitalism, and repress egalitarian instincts. Chase-Dunn (1982), in an important essay on socialism and world-system theory, acknowledges the obvious parallel between the arguments of convergence and world-system theory. However, he is careful to make the distinction, noting that the converging pattern of nation-state behavior

> is a consequence of the continued operation of the capitalist mode of production at the world level. The accumulation process has continually promoted the centralization and concentration of capital such that modern states and multinational corporations are the dominant and most competitive producers competing for shares of the world product. . . . Although some see this kind of "convergence" as a consequence of the immanent logic of "modern industrial society," I

will argue that it is, rather, the result of the logic of the capitalist world economy. (1982:39)

The issue of structural convergence in world-system theory is actually somewhat more complex than the discussion of socialist states implies. Labeling all nation-states as capitalist subsystems by virtue of their participation in the world capitalist system does not necessarily mean that all states will become internally and developmentally equivalent. One must remember that the class imagery of and, more generally, the view of capitalist development in the world-system model suggest different developmental features, depending upon a nation's global class location.

Peacock et al. (1988) note that world-system theory contains arguments supporting expectations for both convergence and divergence. These seemingly contradictory expectations, however, pertain to different levels of the global system. First there are the trends *within* each of the global class positions or "zones"—the core, semi-periphery, and periphery. According to Peacock et al., the structural constraints associated with a nation's position in the international division of labor should produce convergence among nations within each of the three zones. At a second, broader level there is the question of trends *between* zones. On this count it is usually assumed that the gaps between the core and the semi-periphery and periphery will grow.

These two world-system expectations are empirically examined by Peacock et al. (1988), using data on trends in real gross domestic product over the 1950–1980 time span. Socialist states are excluded from their analysis, so the focus is on those nations which are clearly integrated into the capitalist world system. Their findings provide only partial support for the world-system hypotheses. On the one hand, the global trends are consistent with the general expectations—that is, inequality *between* the world system zones increased, while overall inequality *within* the zones decreased from 1950 to 1980. On the other hand, a large part of the increase in between-zone inequality is due to the higher rates of population growth in the periphery and semi-periphery. And, as it turns out, the overall trend toward decreasing inequality within the three zones is the result of the disproportionate influence of the core zone on the global measure. An analysis of the trends in inequality *within each zone separately* indicates that within-zone inequality actually increased over the 1950–1980 period for the periphery and semi-periphery. Only for the core was there the expected trend toward convergence. The results of this study suggest that the global polarization between the core and the subordinate zones is not growing at a very fast rate and that there is considerable mobility within each of the global class locations. This study also indicates of the kinds of empirical analysis that are informed by the global level of analysis.

It is important to emphasize that the various arguments made by Wallerstein and other world-system theorists stem directly from the level of analysis at which they operate—the world systemic level. J. David Singer (1961), in an influential essay on the level-of-analysis problem in the study of international relations, identifies a number of difficulties that result from the choice of a *systemic* framework. First, "it tends to lead the observer into a position which exaggerates the impact of the system upon the national actors and, conversely, discounts the impact of the actors on the system" (1961:80). This is clearly true of world-system theory. It is the systemic logic of world capitalism that determines the behavior of nation-states, and their motives for action. Nation-states do not, and cannot, transform or influence the operation of the system; rather, they conform to its requirements and logic.

Second, according to Singer, the systemic level of analysis "almost inevitably requires that we postulate a high degree of uniformity . . . we allow little room for divergence in the behavior of our parts when we focus on the whole" (1961:81). As already noted, in world-system theory the nature of the whole determines the substance of the parts. This ensures a uniformity such that all the parts of the system are capitalist regardless of internal national social and economic relations. The seemingly significant variations in socio-economic forms of organization and ideology are regarded as secondary epiphenomena of the broader logic of world capitalism. The bottom-line motive of all world-system participants is the maximization of profit through the exchange of commodities in the world market.

Singer's final point is that "though the systemic model does not necessarily preclude comparison and contrast among the national subsystems, it usually eventuates in rather gross comparisons based on relatively crude dimensions and characteristics" (1961:83). The broad division of nations into core, periphery, and semi-periphery is indicative of this tendency. These broad structural categories, used to define the classes and relationships at the world system level, often serve to obscure the significant variation among nations occupying common positions.

Variations on a Dependency Theme: Samir Amin

The work of Samir Amin represents a systematic attempt to combine and integrate the various insights of dependency and world-system theory. He raises many critical issues and introduces a number of valuable concepts that contribute to a clearer understanding of global capitalism and underdevelopment in the periphery.

One of the key issues for Amin (1976) is the way in which the laws of the capitalist economic system contribute to the tendency toward worldwide expansion and imperialism. In order to demonstrate that the capitalist system is characterized by a tendency toward international expansion—that this is an integral part of the process of capital accumulation—Amin must differentiate the capitalism that exists in the imperialist center states (advanced capitalist societies) from that which exists in the periphery (the underdeveloped world).

He describes capitalism in the center states as *autocentric capitalism.* Autocentric capitalism requires the existence of a "capacity to produce" and a "capacity to consume." These terms, used frequently by Amin, refer to the more familiar concepts of supply (produce) and demand (consume). For capital accumulation to take place, conditions must exist that encourage private investment by capitalists in the production and supply of commodities. This is what is meant by the capacity to produce—the existence of a certain set of conditions that encourage private investment. Capitalists are more likely to invest and produce where production costs are low enough that each commodity produced can be sold for a reasonable profit. The ability to realize a profit requires that the second condition—the capacity to consume—also be met. This refers to the existence of adequate levels of effective demand for the product. If products are produced cheaply but cannot be sold, profit is not realized. For these reasons capital accumulation requires a combination of favorable supply-side (capacity to produce) and demand-side (capacity to consume) conditions. These are the dual requirements for capitalist expansion.

One of the fundamental contradictions of a capitalist economy can be found in the relationship between these two requirements. One of the most obvious examples of this contradiction can be seen if one considers wage levels. On the one hand, low wage levels support the capacity to produce because they contribute to low production costs and, thus, the potential for enlarged profits. On the other hand, low wages will restrict the size of the market and, therefore, the capacity to consume. The opposite case—high wage levels that enhance the capacity to consume commodities—discourages the capacity to produce. Attempts to resolve this contradiction, and the associated economic crises, result in the global expansion of capitalism. For Amin, imperialism and the emergence of monopolies are responses to the crises of autocentric accumulation. Peripheral nations are used as a base for low-cost production and as an outlet or market for certain commodities. Thus, the international mobility of productive capital and commodities is seen as an inevitable outcome of the laws of autocentric capitalism. These efforts, aimed at resolving crises in the center, shape the nature of capitalist development in the periphery.

In contrast with autocentric accumulation, peripheral capitalist economies are characterized by *extraverted accumulation*. This term is meant to describe the export-oriented or "outward-looking" nature of underdeveloped economies. Extraversion is the product of the historical legacy of exploitation by external forces. As with Frank and Wallerstein, these external forces originate in the center states (metropolis, core). From the early stages of colonial expansion, where colonies provided agro-mineral products to the center states, to the contemporary incursion of foreign investment, the socio-economic structure of the periphery has been shaped by export activities. According to Amin, extraverted accumulation creates a number of structural distortions that prevent sustained and autonomous economic expansion.

The concept of *disarticulation* plays a central role in Amin's theory of peripheral capitalism and underdevelopment. Disarticulation refers to missing or nonexistent links between segments of the economy. DeJanvry (1981) makes a useful distinction, implied by Amin, between "social disarticulation" and "sectoral disarticulation." *Sectoral disarticulation* refers to an economic structure that lacks forward and backward linkages between productive sectors. An example is an economy that is involved in the extraction of a mineral resource. Under the system of sectoral disarticulation, the machines used to extract the minerals are imported from industrialized nations. Therefore, there is no national or internal *backward linkage* from the mineral sector to a capital goods sector that provides machines and equipment for mineral extraction. Suppose also that the mineral resource is exported in its raw form and processed or refined in the industrialized nations. Thus, there is also no internal *forward linkage* from the mineral extractive sector to a mineral processing sector that would manufacture the raw material into some other commodity within the peripheral nation. This type of disarticulation has negative economic consequences because the relatively dynamic economic activity in the mineral sector does not spill over and stimulate economic activity in other domestic sectors. This is because the sectors that supply the inputs and receive the output from the extractive sector do not exist within the peripheral economy but, rather, in the industrialized center states.

Social disarticulation refers to the situation where the relationship between the capacity to produce and the capacity to consume is weak and tenuous—commodities can be produced and sold profitably in spite of the absence of a capacity to consume in the national economy. This form of disarticulation is best illustrated if we consider a consumer goods industry. Where an economy is characterized by *social articulation*, the profitability of this industry depends on the buying power of the national working classes. Under an extraverted economy, where the consumer goods are exported to working-class consumers in the industrialized nations, profitability is maintained independent of the wage levels of the domestic population. Thus extraverted accumulation and development can proceed where wages are extremely low because productive sectors of extraverted peripheral economies are not dependent on the internal market. Amin notes: "Wages appear not as both a cost and an income that creates a demand essential for the working of the model, but merely as a cost, with demand originating elsewhere—either externally, or in the income of the privileged categories of society" (Amin 1976:194).

The concept of social disarticulation is a useful tool for understanding the relationship between the world-economy orientation and the political practices of peripheral nations. Where wages are a pure cost, there is little incentive for elites to promote redistibutive income policies, tolerate union organization, or allow wages to rise. Instead, there is pressure against redistribution of income, unions are often outlawed or repressed, and the standard of living in many vibrant export economies can experience significant decline. The prevalence of authoritarianism and mass repression in peripheral nations can be understood as a partial product of the fact that internal demand is not the driving force for capital accumulation. Further, in order for exports to remain competitive, and for nations to attract foreign investment, supply-side (capacity to produce) conditions tend to take precedence over the demand side (capacity to consume) in extraverted economies.

The condition of disarticulation in peripheral economies results, according to Amin, in crises that can be distinguished from those which emerge in center states. Most notable is the manifestation of economic crisis at the level of the balance of payments. Because of sectoral disarticulation, the capacity to produce in peripheral economies depends on the foreign exchange revenue derived from export trade. This foreign exchange is used to purchase capital inputs needed for production. Because of social disarticulation, foreign exchange levels depend on the level of demand in the world economy. When, for whatever reason, export revenues decline, this affects the balance of payments and the ability to import required capital goods. The balance of payments crisis, then, signals a larger economic crisis. Extraverted economies feel economic hard times when the trade ledger falls into disequilibrium—import costs exceed export receipts. Amin continually emphasizes: "Since the underdeveloped economies are extraverted, all their problems emerge in the balance of payments. Every considerable economic change that occurs in the course of development has an effect on the various elements in the balance of payments" (1976:252).

These problems are aggravated further if we consider what Amin calls the *balance of real payments*. By this he means the balance between exports and the inflow of capital investment (the credit side) versus imports and the backflow of profits (the debit side). Amin's basic argument is that, historically, nations first penetrated by colonial expansion experienced a period of surplus in their balance of payments. This slowly began to deteriorate as unfavorable terms of trade evolved to the advantage of manufactured goods and to the detriment of peripheral exports. Amin cites Prebisch on this issue, but he also points to an additional factor that can serve either to offset or to accentuate the unfavorable terms of trade—the movement of foreign capital investment. With foreign investment there is the inflow of capital and, inevitably, the backflow of profits:

It is the backflow of profits, growing bigger and bigger, that in the end becomes responsible, together with the movement of the trade balance already analyzed, for the chronic deficit in the balance of the underdeveloped countries in our time. During the nineteenth century the increasing flow of capital, exceeding the backflow of profits, made up for the progressive worsening in the trade balance. In the twentieth century the increasing backflow of profits, exceeding the inflow of new capital, is added to the progressive worsening of the trade balance, and so makes the overall balance of payments even less favorable. (1976:257)

Under the system of extraverted and disarticulated accumulation we also find that the potentially dynamic "multiplier" and "accelerator" effects are severely restricted. Conventional economic theory posits a certain number of economic forces that contribute to sustained economic expansion. The *multiplier effect* is the expansion of total income that results from changes in investment. Investment spending initiates a chain reaction that produces proportionately greater increases in the total income. This distributes income throughout the economy, which gives rise to the accelerator effect. The *accelerator effect* refers to the impact of a rise in consumer demand that, in turn, creates a proportionately greater demand for producer goods (e.g., equipment and machines). Both concepts describe the momentum and cumulative effects that are created by expansion in different segments of the economy. In order for these effects to operate, it is assumed that national economic sectors are connected and articulated so that changes in one sphere are felt in other spheres. The peripheral conditions of disarticulation described above weaken or remove the effects of these economic forces.

According to Amin, the multiplier effects are stifled for two reasons. First, owing to the backflow of profits, much of the investment capital necessary for the initiation of the multiplier process is unavailable. Second, while high profits may be realized through production in peripheral societies, the low wage levels and narrow internal market preclude continual investment of profits into new avenues of production.

Accelerator effects also go unrealized. This is directly attributable to sectoral disarticulation. With the accelerator, changes in consumer demand are said to stimulate an even larger demand for capital goods. However, because these capital goods tend to be imported—produced in the center states—it is at the center that the stimulative effects will be greatest. Again, Amin is pointing out the qualitatively different forms of capitalism that exist in the world economy and the consequences for economic development.

> This means that the advanced economy is an integrated whole, a feature of which is a very dense flow of internal exchanges, the flow of external exchanges of the atoms that make up this whole being, by and large, marginal as compared with the internal exchanges. In contrast to this, the underdeveloped economy is made up of atoms that are relatively juxtaposed and not integrated, the density of the flow of external exchanges of these atoms being much greater, and that of the flow of the internal exchanges very much less.
>
> The consequences that follow from this disarticulation are crucial. In a structured autocentric economy, any progress that begins at any point is spread throughout the entire organism by many convergent mechanisms. . . . If the economy is extraverted, all the effects are limited, being largely transferred abroad. (1976:237–38)

TWO DIMENSIONS OF DEPENDENCY: INVESTMENT AND TRADE DEPENDENCE

There are two basic forms of dependence most often emphasized by dependency theorists and represented in cross-national studies claiming to test this theory: investment dependence and trade dependence. The international flow of capital and commodities is seen as the central mechanism by which the advanced capitalist states dominate, exploit, and retard the development of less-developed nations. In this section we consider these different forms of dependence and the arguments that have been made regarding their impact on economic development.

Investment Dependence

Of the two types of dependence, investment dependence is by far the more widely analyzed. The interest in investment dependence stems from the pivotal role of multinational corporations in dependency formulations. Multinational corporations (MNCs) are the organizational embodiment of imperialism, the metropolis, monopoly capital, and the core of the world system. Their investment behavior in the periphery is regarded by dependency theorists as largely exploitative. In many dependency formulations MNC investment is said to promote underdevelopment, stagnation, and economic backwardness.

This view of MNCs, as having a retrogressive effect on the development of regions and nations, runs counter to the standard neoclassical interpretation found in dual-society theories (see Singer 1979) as well as to the orthodox Marxist position that the expansion of capitalism is ultimately a progressive force (Warren 1980). How is it that MNCs retard the development of less developed nations or reinforce backward economic structures?

The most common argument about the direct effects of foreign investment is that MNCs actually drain surplus from the less developed nations. This *surplus drainage thesis* is based on data that indicate, consistent with the claims of Amin, a net outflow of corporate profits from a number of less-developed nations. MNCs, through direct foreign investment, own and control enterprises and industries in other nations. The profits derived from these ventures do not remain as capital resources for these countries, nor are they used to expand production in other sectors. Rather, profits are typically exported back to the core and/or placed in more profitable investment outlets. This is referred to as the *repatriation of profits* and is a standard operating procedure of international capital. It retards development because the surplus, produced in the less-developed economy, is unavailable to fuel further economic expansion and other spin-offs. It is through this mechanism that the analogy to class exploitation is most apparent, since value produced by the natural, human, and capital resources in less-developed nations is appropriated by MNCs. In Frank's words, "the satellites remain underdeveloped for lack of access to their own surplus . . ." (1969:15).

A second reason that multinational investment is considered a negative force is its impact on the autonomy of less-developed nations. If multinational corporations control and decide upon the major investments in the countries they penetrate, to what extent does this undermine the ability of nations to direct their own development? Is the pace of growth and distribution of investment determined by the host nation, or has it lost control of the process to multinational capital? It is clearly implied by dependency theorists that the resources possessed by MNCs permit them to dominate the economies and governments of less-developed nations. Further, this means that the development process is shaped by the interests of external forces and may run counter to national goals. For example, it is often argued that MNCs introduce inappropriate technology for production in less-developed economies. They may utilize highly capital-intensive production techniques even though the nation is plagued by high rates of unemployment and a labor surplus. These techniques may be profitable from the perspective of the investing MNC, but they do not address the economic and employment needs of the nation.

The extent to which nation-states are actually deprived of autonomy and dominated by foreign capital is often said to depend upon the strength of the state or governmental apparatus in less-developed nations. Where less-developed nations have a strong state, they may be able to counteract and mediate the power of MNCs. There are a number of obvious problems with this claim. First, the description of national economies dominated by the investment decisions of large corporate firms can just as easily be applied to the "strong" nation-states of the United States and Western Europe. There is no reason to assume that governments, be they strong or weak, wish to oppose the power and discretion of private capital. Second, all this raises a rather curious contradiction in dependency/world-economy treatments of the role of the state. On the one hand, strong states have the potential to wrestle autonomy from large corporate actors. On the other hand, it is usually taken for granted by dependency theorists that the political elite who presumably control the state have sold out to and/or profit from MNC activity. It would therefore run counter to their interests to oppose these corporations. Finally, to add further confusion to this issue, there is the world-economy premise that nation-states are essentially powerless in the face of world-system imperatives and forces. All of this reflects the more general debate over the precise role of the state in capitalist society.[3]

A third dependency-related claim about the negative role of MNC foreign investment concerns its effects on the structure of the economy. It is often argued that foreign investment distorts the allocation of the labor force and the distribution of economic activity. The first form of distortion created by foreign investment is the *enclave economy* (Cardoso and Faletto 1979). Enclave economies are isolated economic sectors that employ relatively modern and efficient methods for the purpose of export production. These economies emerge as foreign capital, attracted to certain regions that possess agricultural and mineral resources demanded by markets in the core, gain access to natural resources, and invest heavily in the capital and technology required to extract the resource. Enclave economies are typically the most dynamic sectors of the national economy, and they can generate considerable foreign exchange through their export-oriented activities.

The distortions that result from enclave economies can best be understood by using Amin's concepts of "extraversion" and "sectoral disarticulation." Enclave sectors are a basic component of the broader system of extraversion, given the export-oriented nature of enclave production. Because production is dictated by and oriented toward external markets, the enclave sector is poorly articulated with the rest of the national economy. Capital inputs tend to be imported, and the extracted primary products, exported; thus few internal backward and forward linkages or spin-offs are generated. This enclave sector, then, is very much an appendage of the advanced capitalist economy from which the capital investment originates.

As Cardoso and Faletto (1979:71) note for Latin America:

Incorporation of the Latin American export system into the world market through the creation of enclaves required Latin American countries to form a "modern sector" that was a kind of technological and financial extension of central economies. Thus, the relative success of the export system was based on a highly specialized enclave economy with large surpluses. Growth of the export sector did not always create an internal market. It led to concentration of income in the enclave sector.

The latter point suggests, again as indicated by Amin, that accelerator effects tend to be negligible where production is sectorally concentrated and disarticulated.

A second form of distortion noted by dependency theorists is the movement of the population from rural to urban areas. Foreign investment in agriculture replaces workers with machines and tends to force small independent producers out of rural areas. This results in a rural labor surplus. Foreign investment in urban manufacturing, on the other hand, creates an industrial labor force, and potential employment opportunities draw the rural population into the cities. As discussed in Chapter 3, the supply of labor through rural-to-urban migration typically exceeds demand, and the urban population is forced into informal and service sector activities. In this way large segments of the population are unemployed or underemployed, concentrated in relatively unproductive activities, and likely to demand services that place a drain on government resources.

The effects of foreign investment on the productive structure of less-developed economies also serve to shape the class structure and distribution of income. Dependency theorists tend to emphasize the close links between foreign capital and certain elite segments. The native *comprador elite* aligns itself with foreign capital and tends to support free trade and other policies that facilitate the import and export requirements of MNCs. The comprador class bases its privilege on and benefits from service to these external interests and is usually involved in some export- or import-related activity. This native but subservient elite often opposes efforts by domestic capitalists to establish indigenous industries or policies that raise working-class wages. These would create competition with and raise the labor costs of the MNCs operating in these nations. Thus a small elite forms an alliance with MNC interests and together they direct economic and government policies in ways that are said to retard independent and autonomous economic growth.

Severe income inequality is also expected to result from foreign investment and the associated structural distortions. The distribution of income becomes highly unequal, given the nature of foreign investment in a number of restricted sectors and activities, the relatively small number of workers who benefit from this investment, and, as identified by Amin, the downward pressure on wages in export-oriented economies that restricts both the size and the scope of income.

For the above reasons—and there are many more that have been advanced (see Bornschier and Chase-Dunn 1985)—a dependency proposition has emerged suggesting that those nations most extensively penetrated by multinational capital will be the most exploited and distorted and will, therefore, have the lowest rates of economic growth. The number of studies that have investigated this hypothesis is far too great to review. The one word that best describes the accumulated results is "mixed." A large number of cross-national studies have supported the dependency proposition, and an equally significant number have rejected it. As with many empirical ventures in social science, the data did not speak for themselves, nor did they have the final word. Instead, the positive or negative effect of foreign investment has depended upon the sample, the type of foreign investment measure, the years analyzed, the number and type of control variables, the estimation procedure, and so on.

Apart from the actual statistical results it is surprising that so much effort has gone (and continues to go) into examining the effect of foreign investment on economic growth. What is even more perplexing is the belief that these statistical exercises somehow "test," "prove," or "disprove" dependency or world-economy theory. It is absurd to argue that the empirical validity of the historically rich and theoretically complex dependency/world-economy literature hinges on the strength and statistical significance of the relationship between imperfect measures of foreign capital penetration and the change in gross national product.

Some of the blame for the reduction of sophisticated theoretical relationships to statistical equations lies with dependency theorists themselves, who have frequently advanced an oversimplified *stagnation thesis*—that foreign capital has a universally retrogressive impact on the growth rates of less-developed economies. Although there is an abundance of empirical literature reporting negative effects of foreign investment on the economic growth of peripheral nations, its effects on economic production and international inequality are much more complex. It is not enough to say that the current world system benefits the core at the expense of the periphery and, therefore, the central mechanism of imperialism—foreign investment—serves to reinforce this stratified system. This static conception belies the accumulated evidence on the changing international division of labor (Froebel et al. 1980) and the critical role played by capital from the advance core states in facilitating this worldwide transformation.

The general dependency/world-economy model is sound in its emphasis on the internationalization of capital and its structuring influence on production at the periphery. The problem is the expected net effect of foreign capital penetration. Though it is not unreasonable to hypothesize a general economic effect for the presence of foreign capital, many of the dependency/world-economy theories suggest effects that are likely contingent on the sector in which the capital is invested (see Jaffee and Stokes 1986). In terms of the effects on trade dependence, foreign investment is not placed exclusively into productive sectors that reinforce traditional patterns of Third World production, such as agro-mining sectors. A significant portion is placed in manufacturing and heavy industrial sectors, and thus can be seen as a critical factor responsible for modifying traditional patterns of specialization and serving as a potential source of growth and dynamism, albeit uneven and imbalanced.

Such a trend does not undermine the validity of dependency/world-economy theory. To make such a claim only points to a second and rather striking deficiency of many empirical tests of the theory: the exclusive use of economic growth to measure the effects of dependence. It is a methodologically irresistible variable because of its metric properties and cross-national availability, yet as an indicator of the consequences of dependency relations it obscures the many structural effects of dependent world-market participation that are outlined in the vast number of theoretical works on dependence. It is paradoxical that the same theorists and researchers who point to the inability of growth in GNP to lay the foundation for sustained, balanced, and equitable economic expansion often rely on this very same measure to assess the empirical validity of dependency theory. A careful reading of the literature should make it abundantly clear that dependency does not preclude growth, nor vice versa.

This fact is acknowledged by the concept of *dependent development*, associated with Cardoso and Faletta (1979:xxiii–xxiv), which defines a particular form of growth and underdevelopment that is simultaneously economically dynamic and structurally distorting:

By development, in this context, we mean "capitalist development." This form of development, in the periphery as well as in the center, produces as it evolves, in a cyclical way, wealth and poverty, accumulation and shortage of capital, employment for some and unemployment for others. So we do not mean by the notion of "development" the achievement of a more egalitarian or more just society. These are not consequences expected from capitalist development, especially in peripheral economies.

By pointing to the existence of a process of capitalistic expansion in the periphery, we make a double criticism. We criticize those who expect permanent stagnation in underdeveloped dependent countries because of a constant decline in the rate of profit or the "narrowness of internal markets," which supposedly function as an insurpassable obstacle to capitalistic advancement. But we also criticize those who expect capitalistic development of peripheral economies to solve problems such as distribution of property, full employment, better income distribution, and better living conditions for people. . . . Development, in this context, means the progress of productive forces, mainly through the import of technology, capital accumulation, penetration of local economies by foreign enterprises, increasing numbers of wage-earning groups, and intensification of social division labor.

Support for the basic arguments of the dependent-development position is provided both by case studies (Evans 1979) and by time-series analyses of single countries (Bradshaw 1988). The findings of this research point to the important role of the state as an ally of foreign capital in directing the process of economic growth. It appears that foreign investment can facilitate growth in less-developed economies, particularly in the modern manufacturing sectors and often at the expense of agriculture (Bradshaw 1988). The net results may be highly uneven growth, increasing income inequality, and balance of payments crises. The fact that such counterproductive patterns accompany economic growth should be sufficient to indicate the problem with evaluating the efficacy of development theories using only economic growth measures.

Trade Dependence

Trade dependence represents a second general form of dependence cited as an obstacle to economic development. We have already discussed the critique of the international trade system advanced by the ECLA as well as Amin's concept of "extraversion." In this section we consider some additional arguments about the role of trade in the development process and the way the contemporary trade structures of less-developed nations serve to retard economic growth. The presentation of arguments can be organized around a set of characteristics used to define the trade structure of less-developed countries. These are export dependence, primary product specialization, commodity concentration, and partner concentration.

Export dependence, in its simplest formulation, exists when a large share of the gross product of an economy is generated by exports. Many less-developed nations rely on export trade for well over 50 percent of their gross domestic product. With the financial health of the economy heavily dependent on the external market, deterioration in the terms of trade, as well as fluctuations in world market prices for a nation's exports, can wreak havoc on the long-term planning capacity of a nation state (Prebisch 1950; Barratt-Brown 1974). This *vulnerability thesis* points to the way in which common vagaries of the world economy—dramatic shifts in supply and demand, monopoly pricing policies, the use of synthetic substitutes for primary products—have the potential to undermine the economies of heavily trade-reliant nations. The development of synthetic rubber in the 1960s and the drop in world petroleum prices have exacted a heavy economic toll on nations that are dependent on these export commodities for their foreign exchange.

Even if sufficient revenue can be generated from export trade, and there is considerable evidence to suggest that it can, there is no reason to assume that this income will be invested in new industries and, therefore, that it will have the expected accelerating effects on economic growth. This judgment is informed by the enclave economy theory. In an enclave economy there are both political and economic disincentives for using export revenues for diversified investment. Since export-oriented enclave sectors tend to be dominated by MNCs, a large proportion of the generated capital and profits is controlled and repatriated by foreign firms, leaving little capital for national economic investment. Further, a typical pattern in such economies is for an elite to emerge whose fortunes are directly tied to the export sector. Many of the policy decisions essential for the development of domestic industry—such as protective tax and tariff regulations and an expansion of the internal market—tend to be fiercely resisted by this elite.

A second common feature of the trade structure of less-developed countries is *primary product specialization*. It is widely accepted that specialization in the export of raw materials and unprocessed goods will impede economic growth and development (Hirschman 1958), make nations vulnerable to downward pressure on their terms of trade (Prebisch 1950), create instabilities in export revenues as world commodity prices fluctuate (Barratt-Brown 1974), and, in sum, hamper sustained economic growth (Galtung 1971). Most underdeveloped countries are characterized by such an export structure and plagued by these very difficulties. Many of the negative economic effects discussed for export dependence are applicable here because the exports on which most less-developed nations depend are commonly primary products. Independent of this connection, it remains the case that specialization in the production of raw materials and basic products generally reduces the likelihood of balanced economic growth and development because this type of production is able to generate neither substantial spin-off effects in other areas of production nor job and income opportunities (Beckford 1972). The low level of productivity also curtails its ability to serve as an engine for growth.

Theoretically and empirically associated with primary product specialization is the third trade structure characteristic, *commodity concentration* or *monoculture*. Under this condition a nation relies on a small, restricted number of export commodities, usually a few primary products. Again, where a nation's production is concentrated in a narrow range of commodities, the negative effects that result from being dependent on the external world market are amplified to an extreme degree. The economy is dependent on exports and on the viability of a narrow range of products in the world market. A decline in the terms of trade, or fluctuations in the price of these pivotal goods, can leave dependent economies reeling in their wake.

Commodity concentration also affects the distribution of industry and income. The production of a narrow range of primary products for export precludes the likelihood of balanced economic growth, instead engendering a single dynamic economic sector or enclave with most spin-offs having a restricted effect. Thus monocultural economies are likely to have high levels of sectoral disarticulation and sectoral inequality. This affects the distribution of income opportunities, the size of the internal market, and the prospects for balanced, diversified growth.

The final trade structure characteristic concerns a nation's trade network and is often referred to as *trade partner concentration*—the confining of trade to relatively few partners or countries. In general it is argued that partner concentration reduces the bargaining power of a country because there are fewer established buyers for its products (Galtung 1971). Under this condition of monopsony—a single or few buyers for the product—the potentially profitable effects of demand competition are minimized. Instead, the supplier (exporter) is dependent on what the few buyers are willing to pay. This can, consequently, limit the total revenue gained from export trade and thus hamper economic growth.

Within the broad framework of the world economy, partner concentration has been conceptualized as a "feudal" form of global interaction (Galtung 1971). The nations of the periphery, rather than having multilateral exchanges with each other, are tightly integrated as satellites of the economies of the core. In most discussions of partner concentration it is assumed that the bulk of the trade of less-developed nations is with developed nations of the core, and that negative consequences are based on unequal forms of international exchange between these groups of nations (see Emmanuel 1972; Amin 1976; Mandel 1976).

It is further contended that in any system where there exists an unequal distribution of power, those with the greatest resources will structure interaction patterns to their advantage (Baumgartner et al. 1979). Arguments about declining terms of trade for peripheral nation exports emphasize that this distortion takes place within the context of core-periphery trade interaction (Prebisch 1950). Finally, Kay (1975) argues that the core, through its monopoly position, organizes international trade in such a way that exchange favors the core at the expense of the periphery. The primary mechanisms of unequal exchange, in this thesis, involve tariffs, quotas, and monopoly and transfer pricing. The core states, through their domination of world trade, are in a position to manipulate supply and demand, and thus distort the market prices that prevail for the goods produced by the periphery. For all these reasons there may be a discrepancy between the costs of production and the revenue gained from exports such that peripheral nations derive less income than expected from export trade.

It should be clear that the dynamics of international trade play a central role in theories operating at the global level of analysis. At this level foreign trade assumes major importance by virtue of its being both a key point of entry in defining membership in the capitalist world economy and a leading mechanism by which economic resources are transferred from the underdeveloped to developed states. The key determinants of integration and structural position in the world economy are the level of participation in international trade, the degree of penetration by foreign investment, and the types of commodities exchanged in the world market. In the capitalist world-economy model, where the world is a system with a division of labor among nations, and where positions in the system are based on the nature of world market production and exchange, the process of foreign trade is especially significant. Current standing and patterns of mobility in the world economy are a function of a nation's production for and exchange with the larger world economic system. Thus, trade structure characteristics are indispensable to a global level of analysis.

BRINGING SOCIAL RELATIONS AND MODES OF PRODUCTION BACK IN

The accumulated critiques of dependency/world-economy theory are too numerous to review here.[4] There are, however, a number of early statements that identify the basic problems and raise the fundamental issues. Robert Brenner's (1977) essay on the origins of capitalist development is the most notable of the Marxist critiques. Brenner views the underdevelopment theories of Frank and others as a logical reaction to the inadequacies of orthodox Marxist theory, which predicts that the international expansion of capitalism will stimulate industrial capitalist development in all nations of the world. Given the existing disparities between rich and poor nations, some revision was obviously required.

According to Brenner, dependency theorists have come to accept only half of the Marxist proposition—that capitalism has expanded worldwide. However, since this has not had a universally progressive impact, dependency theorists formulate a theory of international capitalist development that assumes the impoverishment and exploitation of some regions as a condition for the enrichment and affluence of others. Thus, we have the metropolis exploiting the satellites and the core exploiting the periphery. For Brenner, the assumption that capitalism has expanded worldwide and penetrated all socities is problematic because it is not based on the existence of what he sees as the defining characteristic of capitalism: the emergence of a particular set of social class relationships. Dependency theory, in contrast, attributes the development of the core, and the under-development of the periphery, to the exploitative relationship between regions rather than social classes.

Brenner believes the fundamental flaws in dependency theory are reproduced and extended in Wallerstein's world-economy model. This model, according to Brenner, defines the growth and development of capitalism in *quantitative* terms through the expansion of the system, international specialization, and the transfer of surplus from the periphery to the core. In contrast, Brenner views capitalist development as *qualitatively* distinct from previous productive arrangements in that it requires innovation, the constant revolution of productive forces, and the efficient use of wage labor. This qualitative change serves to increase the size of the surplus and stimulate the rate of economic growth.

Brenner repeatedly emphasizes the concepts of wage labor and relative surplus value. His point is that a system of wage labor signifies *capitalist social relations*—laborers are hired by capitalists for a wage and brought together with capital goods and raw materials for the purpose of commodity production. Under these social relations, in comparison with pre-capitalist or feudal arrangements, owners are compelled to utilize production techniques that allow them to produce the greatest amount of output in a given amount of labor time. The wage labor "constraint" and the forces of competition drive capitalists to increase the productivity of labor. *Relative surplus value* is created by using superior organizational and productive techniques that reduce the unit cost of production. Higher levels of output are achieved with constant inputs of labor. This is compared with *absolute surplus value*, which rises because of greater inputs of labor or an extended working day. The essence of capitalism, for Brenner, is the wage–labor social relationship and the production of relative, as opposed to absolute, surplus value.

Wallerstein defines capitalism as production for profit in a market. Brenner rejects this view because production for profit in a market can, and did, take place without the wage–labor relationship and without the production of relative surplus value. Merchant capitalism and production for trade represent only one form of capitalism and, at least for Brenner, an insufficient one.

This point can be further understood if we consider what is referred to as the *circuit of capitalism*. In Marxist political economy there are three basic components of the circuit. In the first phase a capitalist uses money to purchase the factors of production: land (or raw materials), labor, and capital. A wage labor relationship has already been established. Workers are hired by capitalists and are paid a wage. The second phase, the production process, entails bringing the three factors together, using organizational techniques for the purpose of producing a commodity. The third phase involves selling the commodity in a market with the hope that the money gained through the sale of the commodity will be greater than the costs of producing it.

The critical difference between Wallerstein and Brenner is their focus on different phases of the circuit of capitalism. Wallerstein identifies the essence of capitalism in the third phase: the "sphere of exchange," where goods are sold for a profit. Brenner defines capitalism on the basis of the first phase: the purchase of labor power and the establishment of the wage–labor relationship. Thus they see the essence of capitalism at different points of the circuit.

It is important to emphasize that the debate between Wallerstein and other Marxists, such as Brenner, is basically an argument over the appropriate level of analysis (see Denemark and Thomas 1988). As Wallerstein's inclusion in this chapter indicates, he is operating at a world-system level of analysis. The properties and laws of the system determine the nature and developmental trajectory of the parts. For Brenner and other Marxist critics, the appropriate level of analysis is the nation-state, and the focal unit is class relations/class struggle. Again we see a fundamental division in the explanation of socio-economic development hinging on the dispute over the appropriate level of analysis. What is particularly ironic in this case is that the various theorists on both sides of the debate regard themselves as Marxists. Further, the early neo-Marxist arguments, in reaction to conventional neoclassical and modernization models, advocated expanding the level of analysis to include the role of imperialist exploitation and the pernicious effects of world market forces. This is now regarded by those like Brenner as antithetical to orthodox Marxist doctrine. A return to internal social class processes is urged as the more correct way to understand underdevelopment.

This is the central point of Brenner's critique; he contends that underdevelopment results not from exchange relations between core and periphery but from social class relations that exist within the different nations. Production in the core is carried out under social relations that create greater rates of relative surplus value while production in the periphery is hampered by pre-capitalist social relations that are less productive. In short, the major thrust of the critique by Brenner, and many other critical Marxists, is that dependency and world-economy theorists have thrown out a critical internal characteristic. Class relations need to be brought back into the analysis.

A second Marxist critique of dependency theory comes from a diverse group of scholars who advocate a *modes-of-production approach* to the study of development (see Ruccio and Simon 1988 for an outstanding and in-depth review of this and other radical perspectives). The modes-of-production approach, like Brenner's critique, rejects the dependency/world economy claim that there is a single economic system and that all nations and forms of social organization participating in and producing for this system are capitalist. Instead, it contends that the international economy and national economies can contain different modes of production simultaneously and that the relationship between different modes should lie at the center of any analysis of development and underdevelopment. The critical implications are that not all societies and forms of production are entirely capitalist, and that the absence of the capitalist mode of production may be the cause of underdevelopment.

Some of the key concepts and definitions used in the modes-of-production perspective were first elaborated by Ernesto Laclau (1977). Most central is the concept of *mode of production*, which Laclau defined as "an integrated complex of social productive forces and relations linked to a determinate type of ownership of the means of production" (1977:34). More specifically, different modes of production are determined by the forms of labor control responsible for the production of surplus, the system of surplus appropriation, and the ownership/control of productive resources. Thus, a capitalist mode of production is characterized by a wage labor system of control, appropriation of the surplus by the nonproducing class (capitalists), and ownership and control of the means of production by the nonproducer class. As with Brenner, it is the conditions under which commodities are produced, not exchanged, that determine the mode of production as capitalist, feudal, and so on.

Laclau introduced a second distinct concept, *economic system*, which he defined as "the mutual relations between the different sectors of the economy, or between different production units, whether on a regional, national, or world scale" (1977:35). An economic system can contain more than one mode of production. The economic system does not, in this model, determine the nature of its parts. The coexistence of different modes of production within an economic system has implications for the socio-economic development of the larger society. In this sense, as described by dual-society theory, two modes of production may exist side by side, but the important difference is that in the mode-of-production approach they interact. The coexistence of different modes is usually assumed to be a temporary transitional phase on the road to the dominance of a single mode of production.

The mode-of-production theorists attempt to show the ways in which different modes of production coexist, reinforce each other, and/or stand as obstacles to development. In most of the formulations on underdevelopment and backwardness, capitalist and noncapitalist modes of production coexist within a single national economy. The persistence of the noncapitalist mode in less-developed nations, even in the face of world capitalist expansion, is attributed to its functional relationship with merchant capitalism or the capitalist mode of production. These possibilities were illustrated in the earlier discussion of the commercial hacienda and the systems of "functional dualism." It is usually argued that noncapitalist modes of production stand as obstacles to sustained capitalist development. In short, only with the complete victory of the capitalist mode of production, and the elimination of noncapitalist modes, can full-scale capitalist industrialization occur.

A final Marxist-based attack on dependency theory is presented by Bill Warren in his book *Imperialism: Pioneer of Capitalism* (1980). Warren returns to what might be regarded as the orthodox Marxist position—that the world expansion of capitalism is a progressive force that serves to initiate capitalist industrialization, revolutionize the forces of production, and lay the groundwork for world capitalism and, ultimately, world socialism. He believes that this fundamental Marxist tenet regarding the expansion of capital was subverted by Lenin's (1948) writings on the role of imperialism as a stage of core capitalist development that involves the rise of monopoly enterprises, the export of capital to less-developed regions, and the "parasitic" and "retrogressive" effect of this "monopoly capital" stage. Warren rejects all of these characterizations of imperialism as presented by Lenin and later incorporated into dependency theory. He goes on to argue that:

> Direct colonialism, far from having retarded or distorted indigenous capitalist development that might otherwise have occurred, acted as a powerful engine of progressive social change, advancing capitalist development far more rapidly than was conceivable in any other way, both by its destructive effects on pre-capitalist social systems and by

its implantation of elements of capitalism. Indeed, although introduced into the Third World externally, capitalism has struck deep roots there and developed its own increasingly vigorous internal dynamic.

. . . Within a context of growing economic interdependence, the ties of "dependence" (or subordination) binding the Third World and the imperialist world have been and are being markedly loosened with the rise of indigenous capitalisms; the distribution of political-economic power within the capitalist world is thereby growing less uneven. Consequently, although one dimension of imperialism is the domination and exploitation of the non-communist world by a handful of major advanced capitalist countries (the United States, West Germany, Britain, France, Japan, etc.), we are nevertheless in an era of declining imperialism and advancing capitalism. (Warren 1980:9–10)

Warren's position on the role of colonialism and imperialism stands in sharp contrast to the claims of dependency and world-economy theory (see Amin 1984 for a response to Warren's thesis). For Warren, colonialism and imperialism are mechanisms that serve to destroy inefficient and backward pre-capitalist modes of production, and form the basis for the establishment of industrial capitalism and indigenous development.

A similar thesis is advanced in the case studies of African nations by Sender and Smith (1986). In their theoretical and empirical account they attempt to show how the period of colonialism promoted the beginnings of a wage labor system and the potential for dynamic capitalist development. During the post-independence period there have been significant variations in the economic performance of African nations, which they attribute not to the exploitative forces of the world economy or MNCs but, rather, to the internal macroeconomic policies pursued by African elites. In this sense their analysis reinterprets the historical role of capitalist expansion and proposes a return to an examination of internal societal-level economic policies as the appropriate explanatory framework for the study of socio-economic development.

THE INTERNATIONAL DIVISION OF LABOR: CHANGE OR STABILITY?

The notion of an "international division of labor" is a fundamental element of international-level theories of development (see Caporaso 1987 on the many meanings of the term). The term implies that there is an international system of production and a global system of specialization and functional interdependence. According to most dependency/world-economy formulations, a nation's position in the international division of labor—for example, whether it is at the core or the periphery—determines its prospects for socio-economic development. The international division of labor is viewed as a historically evolving structure based on the legacy of imperialism, colonialism, and the investment patterns of MNCs. Most accounts of it distinguish nations of the core, specializing in the production and export of manufactured products, from the less developed periphery, specializing in the cultivation, extraction, and export of agro-mineral primary products. This rigid division of labor between rich and poor nations has contributed to the dependency/world-economy expectation of perpetual divisions between core and periphery and growing inequality. However, this description of the division of labor is in need of revision because the international system has undergone significant changes since 1970. The question now emerges whether there is a *new* international division of labor and, if so, what the effect of this world-system transformation is on the prospects for development of less-developed nations.

The *new international division of labor* (NIDL) refers to a set of developments in the global organization of production (see Froebel et al. 1980). Most notable is the international dispersion of manufacturing production. A number of less-developed nations now engage in various forms of manufacturing production for export. The manufacturing processes located in less-developed nations tend to be labor intensive and are primarily confined to textiles, clothing, electrical machinery, and consumer electronics. The bulk of the output is destined for export as inputs into other production processes or as consumer goods for external markets. All of this is part of the "global assembly line" model, in which MNCs spatially disperse integrated production processes through various subsidiaries and joint ventures (Cohen 1988).

National policies encouraging export-oriented industrialization obviously complement the NIDL, and newly industrialized countries, such as Korea and Taiwan, are prime examples of the changing global system of production. At the international level of analysis, however, the emphasis is less on deliberate government policy than on the logic of capital accumulation on a world scale. One of the major developments facilitating the NIDL has been the increasing mobility of capital investment. The shifting of capital resources out of industrial regions and nations and the wholesale relocation of manufacturing facilities has contributed greatly to the NIDL trend. This general process of deindustrialization in the core has been attributed to declining profits and increased international competition, which encourage the restructuring of manufacturing production (Bluestone and Harrison 1982). With technological advances in transportation and communication, spatial restructuring becomes an increasingly viable strategy of capitalist firms. It allows various aspects of the production process to be carried out in the most cost-effective geographic location. For relatively labor-intensive forms of manufacturing, wage costs are a significant portion of total production cost and are therefore shifted to low-wage, less-developed nations.

This general logic has given rise to the proliferation of manufacturing throughout the less-developed world, particularly in those nations which are able to contain wage costs, suppress labor movements, and offer attractive business climate incentives (see Chapter 4). The NIDL also depends heavily upon the role of women workers, who, denied access to other forms of economic livelihood, work for as little as 17 cents an hour (see Ward 1984, 1987). Women workers make up a large portion of the labor surplus available in *export processing zones* (or free trade zones) (Takeo 1978). These enclave zones are set up for the explicit purpose of attracting multinational capital by providing all the required physical infrastructure (energy, roads, docks), industrial facilities (buildings and warehouses), financial incentives (low or no taxes, import duties, or export restriction), and social infrastructure (a labor surplus of unorganized workers).

In spite of these significant changes in the world economy, there is considerable and well-founded skepticism over the actual depth of global industrialization and whether such a trend signals the emergence of a qualitatively new international division of labor (Chase-Dunn 1987; Petras 1983; Landsberg 1979). These reservations center on two basic questions. First, how widespread is the shift from traditional primary to manufactured export production? Second, how does the industrialization process in less-developed nations differ from the pattern experienced in the advanced capitalist states?

On the first count—the actual international scope of industrial export manufacturing—it is clear that the arguments about NIDL are based on the experience of a small handful of countries. The nations of East Asia—Hong Kong, South Korea, Singapore, and Taiwan ("the gang of four")—are the most frequently cited cases of both the productive transformation and the positive socio-economic effects. Yet if one looks beyond these selected cases, the shift to export manufacturing is rather limited. Petras (1983) examined the percent of exports accounted for by primary commodities versus manufactured products in 1976 for a selected number of low- and middle-income countries. He reported that for 80 percent of the countries, primary products still accounted for 70 percent or more of their exports. Data for 1985, for the same set of countries, indicate a slight change in the direction predicted by NIDL advocates. In 1985, for 70 percent of the low- and middle-income countries, primary commodities accounted for at least 70 percent of their exports (World Bank 1987). While there is some movement toward manufacturing, the traditional pattern of international specialization remains dominant. The vast majority of the world's national economies revolve around the production and export of primary products.

Questions have also been raised about the nature of the industrialization process in less-developed nations, particularly the export-oriented variety emphasized in NIDL accounts. The issue is whether this form of industrial manufacturing is qualitatively different from that experienced by the West and whether it can serve as a viable strategy for long-term development.

It is clear that much of the manufactured output of less-developed nations is concentrated in "light manufacturing," textiles, clothing, and consumer goods, rather than producer goods—machines, rubber, steel, iron, chemicals—which are inputs into further manufacturing processes. Western industrialization was built on a foundation of producer goods manufacturing. Consumer goods production followed the establishment of this heavy industrial base. For the less-developed economies the pattern tends to be reversed. Manufacturing begins with the production of consumer goods or components. These sectors of manufacturing in the less-developed economies obviously require producer goods of some sort; these tend to be imported from developed capitalist nations. Thus, industry is predominantly light rather than heavy, and internal linkages between economic sectors are weak because producer goods industries are either poorly developed or nonexistent and, therefore, required inputs must be imported. This is another case of the sectoral disarticulation problem, described by Amin, pointing to the shallow nature of the industrial push, and the distinction between industrial development in the core and the periphery.

Further evidence of the tenuous foundation of Third World manufacturing is seen if one considers the factors facilitating foreign capital investment in manufacturing production. The economic viability of many newly industrialized countries with regard to the attraction of foreign capital and the expansion of manufacturing hinges on the maintenance of a satisfactory business climate (see Chapter 4). As Petras (1983:128–131) explains:

[I]n many countries the location of industries is contingent on a specific set of social factors—low wages, no taxes, no strikes—

which, on the one hand, limit the "spread effects" of industrial development and, secondly, could lead industry to pack up and abandon a country if their conditions changed . . . an eruption of class conflict or nationalist movements could increase labor costs and cause corporations to pack up their screwdrivers and hop to another island. The industrial transformation is in these cases superficial and *subject to reversal*.

The effects of the changing business climate are already being felt as indicated in this telling report in *Business Week*:

When Tandy Corp. set up an electronics manufacturing facility in South Korea in 1972, the lure of low-cost, docile Korean labor was an obvious attraction. But this past March, Tandy closed its factory in the face of an angry anti-American labor confrontation, leaving 1,400 workers without jobs. In addition to the strife, Korea's labor costs have exploded, and it no longer made economic sense to make low-end computer components there. . . .

Radical labor leaders have taken charge of many unions, and about 50 labor disputes have broken out at foreign plants so far this year. Besides Tandy the disruptions have hit IBM, Motorola, Pico Products, American Life Insurance, and Fairchild Semiconductor. . . . Pico Products shut down a plant, and on May 3, Fairchild announced that it, too, would close its plant and negotiate a severance package for 271 workers.

The strife is taking on an increasingly political hue. U.S. companies "came here for cheap labor, and that means exploitation of Korean workers," says a leaflet distributed by the Tandy union. The result: Many U.S. executives are rethinking their decisions. "You should not come to Korea unless you have to," says one American executive. (May 15, 1989:45–46)

A final criticism of the NIDL is its reliance on low-skill and unskilled labor. The production of components is primarily labor intensive, and there is little investment in work force training. Thus there is little direct human capital investment by firms and no significant demand for technically trained native labor. As noted, the more technically sophisticated elements of the production process tend to be carried out in the advanced capitalist nations. This simply facilitates the brain drain from the less-developed nations.

In sum, the NIDL points to one of the most visible changes in the international system, specialization in the export of manufactures by a certain set of nations. There is no doubt that this development has had significant effects on the nations in question. Yet these effects may not conform to the expectations of those who view the NIDL as the beginning of Western-style industrialization in the less-developed world. The character of Third World industrialization—its light, fragile, export-oriented, and investment-dependent nature—distinguishes it from earlier Western forms. Furthermore, the socio-political effects—rising labor costs, worker militance, the emergence of labor movements, and anti-imperialist nationalism—may serve to undermine the entire development strategy. The international diffusion of Western capitalism has unleashed effects that are not necessarily conducive to independent, indigenous socio-economic development. Rather, the emerging struggles against these world-economic forces may be the most important force shaping the future of the less-developed economies.

NOTES

1. For an extensive review of the origins of, and theorists associated with, the dependency/world-economy perspective, see Chilcote (1984) and, for a more critical assessment, Brewer (1980).

2. The fourth and fifth hypotheses are, specifically:

[The fourth hypothesis] is that the latifundium, irrespective of whether it appears as a plantation or a hacienda today, was typically born as a commercial enterprise which created for itself the institutions which permitted it to respond to increased demand in the world or national market by expanding the amount of its land, capital, and labor and to increase the supply of its products. The fifth hypothesis is that the latifundia which appear isolated, subsistence-based, and semi-feudal today saw the demand for their products or their productive capacity decline and that they are to be found principally in the above-named former agricultural and mining export regions whose economic activity declined in general. (Frank 1969:14)

3. For a systematic review of competing theories of the state, see Alford and Friedland (1985).

4. Critical appraisals of dependency/world-economy theory are offered by Lall (1975), Brewer (1980), Cypher (1979), Palma (1978), Warren (1980), and Skocpol (1977).

7

CONCLUSION

This book has reviewed theories of socio-economic development and their relationship to the different levels of analysis. Explanations for socio-economic development center on the individual, work organizations, the prevailing social institutions, and the dynamics of the international system. Each of these focal points has its own built-in strengths and weaknesses. Ultimately, different levels of analysis must be integrated in order to gain a complete picture of the opportunities for and constraints on development. One must avoid a psychological or structural determinism that takes cultural beliefs or structural arrangements as independent forces beyond the influence of other levels of analysis.

This chapter summarizes some of the observations and arguments advanced in previous chapters about the explanatory logic of the different levels of analysis and associated theories. It concludes with some practical suggestions for studying socio-economic development.

1. *Individual-level* theories of development place the greatest emphasis on the causal role of individual characteristics. Particular cultural beliefs, attitudes, motives, and forms of human capital are believed to be required in quantities sufficient for industrial development to take place.

One of the difficulties with this model is the tendency to engage in simple forms of psychological reductionism. The cultural values and beliefs of a nation's population are inferred from the level of economic development. It is assumed that modernization requires a certain psychocultural mind-set. If a nation is poor, then the population is assumed to lack the necessary set of values and beliefs. Rich nations, conversely, are assumed to possess a population with the "appropriate" consciousness.

A second shortcoming of the individual-level model is the tendency to view individuals in isolation from social, economic, and political structures. An important question concerning subjective sentiments and individual attributes is the origin of these characteristics and their possible effect on the larger society. Neither question can be answered without extending the theoretical framework to include other levels of analysis. Individual motives, behavior, and consciousness are a direct result of the organization of property and power in a society. The developmental effect of human capital expansion or achievement motivation will be contingent on the level of industrial/technological development and existing opportunity structures. It is purely asociological to view these individual-level characteristics, and their effects, in isolation from organizational and institutional structures.

2. *Organizational-level* theories of development focus on the structure of work organizations. A consideration of the organizational level is necessary in order to understand the economic behavior and incentives of individual actors. The "backward," "traditional," and "irrational" economic beliefs and behaviors, assumed to be the cause of underdevelopment in individual-level theses, often find their source in the organizational arrangements of production. These arrangements also affect the level of productivity and efficiency and, in turn, contribute to or restrict a nation's potential economic output. In this sense the organizational level of analysis provides a theoretical basis for explaining individual-level sentiments and behavior as well as the broader process of national development.

Political movements and revolts frequently stem from the reaction to particular forms of work organization and the associated patterns of economic distribution. An important component of development is the transition from agricultural to industrial forms of organization. Labor process studies of industrial capitalist economies link the evolution of organizational arrangements to the pace and rate of capital accumulation and growth. More recently, comparative studies have delineated the most appropriate organizational strategies, based largely on the Japanese industrial relations system, for success in the modern world economy.

3. The *societal-level* of analysis gives rise to the widest assortment of explanations for development. Generally, societal-level theories emphasize the role of national institutions in promoting development. As noted, much of this literature—the structural modernization and political development variants—is influenced by structural functionalism. This results in institutional prescriptions for developmental success that advocate abstract operating principles related to an ideal-type bureaucratic model. The political and sociological modernization literature is also permeated by a distinct pro-order bias that produces a defensive and politically conservative model of development.

Conventional economic theories of development also operate at the societal level and attempt to determine the mechanisms promoting economic growth. Growth models assume that development stems from a set of macroeconomic conditions subject to manipulation by national governments. It is important to recognize the political economy of growth models and the fact that the conditions presumed necessary for growth exact greater costs on certain segments of the population, particularly workers. The inegalitarian results of standard economic growth policies have fueled the proliferation of alternative models that emphasize equity over growth.

The comparative analysis of socio-economic systems also falls within the societal level of analysis. Models of capitalism and socialism contain arguments about their relative superiority as engines of growth and development. One must always be aware of the divergence between theory and practice for each type of system and the fact that each contains its own irrationalities and contradictions. There are inevitably trade-offs when choosing any kind of development strategy, and these usually raise issues that fall beyond the realm of economic calculation: equality, justice, freedom, autonomy, quality of life, fairness, public welfare, and the collective good.

At present nations of the world are attempting to devise development strategies that take into account the changing nature of world capitalism. Forms of corporatism have been suggested for the advanced capitalist nations. This strategy seeks to expand the role of public planning through industrial policies, "managed trade," or "neo-mercantilism" while gaining the cooperation of business and labor. For less-developed nations the contemporary trend is toward building an export-oriented niche in the world economy.

4. *International-level* theories have dominated the study of development since the mid 1970s. The most influential approach has been the dependency/world economy perspective. Its popularity is associated with the trend in social science toward structural explanations that emphasize the environment, external forces, and structural constraints. Ultimately this requires including broader levels of analysis. In the case of dependency/world economy theory this means that nations are not "free to choose" or autonomous, self-determined units but parts of a global system whose logic affects national outcomes and determines national policies. This is an invaluable contribution to development theory, and there are few scholars today who confine their study of national development exclusively to internal national factors.

More recent assessments of dependency/world-economy theory have criticized its tendency toward structural determinism. These critiques have come from Marxists and non-Marxists alike, and essentially advocate a less deterministic and more dialectical approach toward national/world-economy interaction. In short, social class relations, national policies, and internal national struggles have significant effects on development that cannot be reduced to epiphenomena of the logic of world capitalism.

The work by MacEwan and Tabb (1989a) is representative of the current trend to integrate and synthesize national and international levels of analysis. They use the concept of *combined and uneven development* to describe the dynamic relationship between the national/societal and international levels of analysis.[1] They go on to explain that:

> While developments in many regions of the international economy are unified or "combined" by the international operation of capitalism, they nonetheless proceed in an "uneven" manner because of multiple national foundations of capitalist activity. Distinct national foundations embody separate social structures, styles of political organization, and historical experiences, and these yield different responses to economic interdependence. The difference [sic] between the unevenly developing parts of the system matter, but those differences always exist within the interconnections of the entire system. (1989a:69)

MacEwan and Tabb offer a useful theoretical strategy for the analysis of socio-economic development. The notion of combined and uneven development is an explicit recognition of two fundamental facts: (1) that capitalism is a global system of economic organization affecting all nations that participate in the world economy, and (2) that there are important national variations within the global system related to internal class relations and the political economic policies of national governments. MacEwan and Tabb argue that the current era of international instability is the product of the interaction between these two levels of analysis.[2] Thus they reject a deterministic, one-way analysis in favor of an integrative approach:

> In the current period of crisis, economic affairs would appear to be moving us toward a global system. . . . In short, it would appear that the international economy is becoming more and more "combined."
> Yet the extreme globalist interpretation of these occurrences can be sustained only by a thorough separation of economics and politics,

a separation which would be damaging to reality. . . . Politics, and
other aspects of national-specific social organization, maintain
capitalism's "unevenness." (1989a:69–70)

Students of development are well advised to follow the type of analytic
scheme advanced by MacEwan and Tabb. Their arguments reflect the
emerging theoretical effort to bring class, politics, and national policy back
into the development equation while retaining a global perspective. In
addition to the national and international factors emphasized in MacEwan
and Tabb's analysis, one should not lose sight of the lower levels of
analysis involving organizational and individual dynamics. Understanding contemporary international events requires a full-scale integration of the theoretical levels.

In conclusion, as emphasized repeatedly in these pages, there is no one
best level of theory for the study of development. The issue is not which
level of analysis should be employed, but how the levels are linked and
causally related. The notion of combined and uneven development helps
avoid the pitfalls of global determinism and national voluntarism. By
grasping the multiple levels of socio-economic development theory and
social reality, it is hoped that readers will approach the literature with a
more critical eye and construct an explanatory theoretical framework that
is integrative rather than exclusionary.

NOTES

1. This term was first used by Leon Trotsky (1959) to describe the different paths
to socialism in the world economy. It has also been used by dependency theorists (e.g.,
Sunkel and Paz 1970).

2. See MacEwan and Tabb (1989b) for a collection of essays that applies the
"combined and uneven development" model to specific contemporary development
issues.

BIBLIOGRAPHY

Abercrombie, Nicholas, Stephen Hill, and Bryan Turner. 1986. *Sovereign Individuals of Capitalism*. London: Allen and Unwin.

Adelman, Irma, and Cynthia Morris. 1973. *Economic Growth and Social Equity in Developing Countries*. Stanford, CA: Stanford University Press.

Aglietta, Michel. 1979. *A Theory of Capitalist Regulation: The US Experience*. London: NLB.

Alford, Robert, and Roger Friedland. 1985. *Powers of Theory: Capitalism, the State and Democracy*. New York: Cambridge University Press.

Almond, Gabriel. 1960. "Introduction." In Gabriel Almond (ed.), *The Politics of Developing Areas*. Princeton, NJ: Princeton University Press.

———. 1965. "A Developmental Approach to Political Systems." *World Politics* 17:183–214.

Almond, Gabriel, and G. Bingham Powell. 1978. *Comparative Politics: System, Process and Policy*. 2d ed. Boston: Little, Brown.

Amin, Samir. 1976. *Unequal Development*. New York: Monthly Review Press.

———. 1984. "Expansion or Crisis of Capitalism?" *Contemporary Marxism* Fall: 3–17.

Andrisani, Paul L., and Herbert S. Parnes. 1983. "Commitment to the Work Ethic and Success in the Labor Market: A Review of Research Findings." Pp. 101–20 in Jack Barbash, Robert J. Lampman, Sar A. Levitan, and Gus Tyler (eds.), *The Work Ethic: A Critical Analysis*. Madison, WI: Industrial Relations Research Association.

Apple, N. 1983. "The Historical Transformation of Class Struggle in Late Capitalist Liberal Democracies." Pp. 72–128 in Stewart Clegg, Geoff Dow and Paul Boreham (eds.) *The State, Class and Recession*. London: Croom Helm.

Arato, Andrew. 1978. "Understanding Bureaucratic Centralism." *Telos* 35: 73–87.

Averitt, Robert T. 1968. *The Dual Economy: The Dynamics of American Industry Structure*. New York: Norton.

Baran, Paul. 1952. "On the Political Economy of Backwardness." *The Manchester School*, 20:66–84.

———. 1957. *The Political Economy of Growth*. New York: Monthly Review Press.

Baran, Paul, and E. J. Hobsbawm. 1961. "The Stages of Growth." *Kyklos* 14:234–42.

Baran, Paul, and Paul Sweezy. 1966. *Monopoly Capital*. New York: Monthly Review Press.

Barbash, Jack, Robert J. Lampman, Sar A. Levitan, and Gus Tyler (eds.). 1983. *The Work Ethic: A Critical Analysis*. Madison, WI: Industrial Relations Research Association.

Barratt-Brown, Michael. 1974. *The Economics of Imperialism*. Harmondsworth, England: Penguin.

Baster, Nancy. 1972. *Measuring Development: The Role and Adequacy of Development Indicators*. London: Frank Cass.

Bauer, P. T. 1984. "The Vicious Circle of Poverty." Pp. 321–37 in Mitchell A. Seligson (ed.), *The Gap Between Rich and Poor*. Boulder, CO: Westview.

Baumgartner, Tom, W. Buckley, and Tom Burns. 1979. "Unequal Exchange and Uneven Developments: The Structuring of Exchange Patterns." *Studies in Comparative International Development* 11:51–72.

Becker, Gary. 1964. *Human Capital*. New York: National Bureau of Economic Research.

Beckford, G. 1972. *Persistent Poverty: Underdevelopment in Plantation Economies in the Third World*. New York: Oxford University Press.

Bergesen, Albert. 1982. "Rethinking the Role of Socialist States." Pp. 97–100 in Christopher K. Chase-Dunn (ed.), *Socialist States in the World-System*. Beverly Hills, CA: Sage.

Block, Fred. 1977. "The Ruling Class Does Not Rule: Notes on the Marxist Theory of the State." *Socialist Revolution* 33:6–28.

Bluestone, Barry, and Bennett Harrison. 1982. *The Deindustrialization of America*. New York: Basic Books.

Bornschier, Volker, and Christopher Chase-Dunn. 1985. *Transnational Corporations and Underdevelopment*. New York: Praeger.

Boswell, Terry. 1987. "Accumulation Innovations in the American Economy: The Affinity for Japanese Solutions to the Current Crisis." In Terry Boswell and Albert Bergesen (eds.), *America's Changing Role in the World-System*. New York: Praeger.

Bowles, Samuel, and Richard Edwards. 1985. *Understanding Capitalism: Competition, Command, and Change in the U.S. Economy*. New York: Harper and Row.

Bowles, Samuel, and Herb Gintis. 1982. "The Crisis of Liberal Democratic Capitalism: The Case of the United States." *Politics and Society* 11 (1):51–93.

Bradshaw, York W. 1988. "Reassessing Economic Dependency and Uneven Development: The Kenyan Experience." *American Sociological Review* 59:693–708.

Braverman, Harry. 1974. *Labor and Monopoly Capital*. New York: Monthly Review Press.

Brenner, Robert. 1977. "The Origins of Capitalist Development: A Critique of Neo-Smithian Marxism." *New Left Review* 104:25–92.

Brewer, Anthony. 1980. *Marxist Theories of Imperialism: A Critical Survey*. London: Routledge and Kegan Paul.

Brus, Wlodzimierz. 1975. *Socialist Ownership and Political Systems*. London: Routledge and Kegan Paul.

Bunker, Stephen. 1984. "Modes of Extraction, Unequal Exchange, and the Progressive Underdevelopment of an Extreme Periphery: The Brazilian Amazon, 1600–1980." *American Journal of Sociology* 84:1017–64.

Burawoy, Michael. 1983. "Between the Labor Process and the State: The Changing Face of Factory Regimes under Advanced Capitalism." *American Sociological Review* 48:587–605.

Burawoy, Michael, and János Lukács. 1985. "Mythologies of Work: A Comparison of Firms in State Socialism and Advanced Capitalism." *American Sociological Review* 50:723–737.

Burns, Tom, and George M. Stalker. 1961. *The Management of Innovation.* London: Tavistock.

Business Week. 1985. "The Koreans Are Coming." *Business Week*, no. 2926 (December): 46–53.

———. 1989. "Is the Era of Cheap Asian Labor Over?" *Business Week*, May 15: 45–46.

Calhoun, Craig. 1982. *The Question of Class Struggle.* Chicago: University of Chicago Press.

Cameron, David. 1978. "The Expansion of the Public Economy: A Comparative Analysis." *American Political Science Review* 72:1243–61.

Campbell, Tom. 1981. *Seven Theories of Human Society.* Oxford: Clarendon Press.

Caporaso, James A. 1987. "The International Division of Labor: A Theoretical Overview." Pp. 1–41 in James A. Caporaso (ed.), *A Changing International Division of Labor.* Boulder, CO: Lynne Rienner.

Cardoso, Fernando Henrique, and Enzo Faletto. 1979. *Dependency and Development in Latin America.* Berkeley: University of California Press.

Chase-Dunn, Christopher. 1982. "Socialist States in the Capitalist World-economy." Pp. 21–56 in Christopher Chase-Dunn (ed.), *Socialist States in the World-System.* Beverly Hills, CA: Sage.

———. 1987. "Cycles, Trends, or Transformation?: The World-System Since 1945." Pp. 57–83 in Terry Boswell and Albert Bergesen (eds.), *America's Changing Role in the World-System.* New York: Praeger.

Chilcote, Ronald H. 1984. *Theories of Development and Underdevelopment.* Boulder, CO: Westview.

Chilcote, Ronald H., and Joel Edelstein. 1986. *Latin America: Capitalist and Socialist Perspectives of Development and Underdevelopment.* Boulder, CO: Westview.

Chirot, Daniel. 1986. *Social Change in the Modern Era.* New York: Harcourt Brace Jovanovich.

Clark, Gordon. 1981. "The Employment Relation and Spatial Division of Labor." *Annals of the Association of American Geographers* 71:412–24.

Clawson, Dan. 1980. *Bureaucracy and the Labor Process: The Transformation of U.S. Industry, 1860–1920.* New York: Monthly Review Press.

Clegg, Stewart, Paul Boreham, and Geoff Dow. 1986. *Class, Politics and the Economy.* Boston: Routledge and Kegan Paul.

Cochran, Thomas Childs. 1985. *Challenge to American Values.* New York: Oxford University Press.

Cohen, R. B. 1988. "The New International Division of Labor and Multinational Corporations." Pp. 120–129 in Frank Hearn (ed.), *The Transformation of Industrial Organization: Management, Labor, and Society in the United States.* Belmont, CA: Wadsworth.

Coleman, James S. 1986. "Social Theory, Social Research and a Theory of Action." *American Journal of Sociology* 91:1309–35.

———. 1988a. "Free Riders and Zealots: The Role of Social Networks." *Sociological Theory* 6:52–57.

————. 1988b. "Social Capital in the Creation of Human Capital." *American Journal of Sociology* 94 (supp.):95–120.

Converse, Phillip. 1964. "The Nature of Belief Systems in Mass Publics." Pp. 206–61 in David Apter (ed.), *Ideology and Discontent*. New York: The Free Press.

Cornelius, Wayne. 1975. *Politics and the Migrant Poor in Mexico City*. Stanford, CA: Stanford University Press.

Cumings, Bruce. 1984. "The Origins and Development of the Northeast Asian Political Economy: Industrial Sectors, Product Cycles, and Political Consequences." *International Organization* 38:1–40.

Cypher, James M. 1979. "The Internationalization of Capital and the Transformation of Social Formations: A Critique of the Monthly Review School." *The Review of Radical Political Economics* 11(4):33–49.

Dahrendorf, Ralf. 1959. *Class and Class Conflict in Industrial Society*. Stanford, CA: Stanford University Press.

deJanvry, Alain. 1981. *The Agrarian Question and Reformism in Latin America*. Baltimore: Johns Hopkins University Press.

Denemark, Robert A., and Kenneth Thomas. 1988. "The Brenner-Wallerstein Debate." *International Studies Quarterly* 32:47–65.

Denison, Edward F. 1965. "Education and Economic Productivity." Pp. 327–47 in S. Harris (ed.), *Education and Public Policy*. Berkeley, CA: McCutchen.

Deutsch, Karl. 1966. "Social Mobilization and Political Development." Pp. 205–26 in Jason L. Gable and Richard W. Finkle (eds.), *Political Development and Social Change*. New York: John Wiley.

Deyo, Frederic C. 1981. *Dependent Development and Industrial Order: An Asian Case Study*. New York: Praeger.

————. 1982. "State Labor Regimes and the New Asian Industrialism." Paper presented at the American Sociological Association meetings, San Francisco.

Dohse, Knuth, Ulrich Jurgens, and Thomas Malsch. 1985. "From 'Fordism' to 'Toyotaism'? The Social Organization of the Labor Process in the Japanese Automobile Industry." *Politics and Society* 14:115–46.

Domar, Evsey. 1957. *Essays in the Theory of Economic Growth*. New York: Oxford University Press.

Domhoff, William. 1971. *Higher Circles: The Governing Class in America*. New York: Random House.

Dore, Ronald. 1973. *British Factory, Japanese Factory: The Origins of National Diversity in Industrial Relations*. Berkeley: University of California Press.

Dos Santos, Theotonio. 1970. "The Structure of Dependence." *American Economic Review* 60:231–36.

Dumont, Rene. 1973. *Socialisms and Development*. New York: Praeger.

Durkheim, Emile. 1966. *On the Division of Labor in Society*. Translated by George Simpson. New York: The Free Press.

Duvall, Raymond, and John A. Freeman. 1981. "The State and Dependent Capitalism." *International Studies Quarterly*. 25:99–118.

Edel, Abraham. 1979. *Analyzing Concepts in Social Science: Science, Ideology, and Value*. New Brunswick, NJ: Transaction Books.

Edwards, Richard. 1979. *Contested Terrain*. New York: Basic Books.

Eisenstadt, S. N. 1968a. "The Protestant Ethic Thesis in an Analytical and Comparative Framework." Pp. 3–45 in S. N. Eisenstadt (ed.), *The Protestant Ethic and Modernization*. New York: Basic Books.

———. 1968b. *The Protestant Ethic and Modernization: A Comparative View*. New York: Basic Books.

Elliott, John E. 1973. *Comparative Economic Systems*. Englewood Cliffs, NJ: Prentice-Hall.

———. 1976. "Marx and Contemporary Models of Socialist Economy." *History of Political Economy* 8:151–84.

Emmanuel, Arghiri. 1972. *Unequal Exchange*. New York: Modern Reader.

Esping-Anderson, Gosta. 1984. *Politics Versus Markets: The Social Democratic Road to Power*. Princeton, NJ: Princeton University Press.

Evan, William M. 1976. *Organization Theory: Structures, Systems, and Environments*. New York: Wiley.

Evans, Peter. 1979. *Dependent Development: The Alliance of Multinational, State, and Local Capital in Brazil*. Princeton, NJ: Princeton University Press.

———. 1982. "Reinventing the Bourgeoisie: State Entrepreneurship and Class Formation in Dependent Capitalist Development." *American Journal of Sociology* 88 (supp.):S210–47.

Evans, Peter, and Michael Timberlake. 1980. "Dependence, Inequality and the Growth of the Tertiary: A Comparative Analysis of Less Developed Countries." *American Sociological Review* 45:531–52.

Evans, Peter B., Dietrich Rueschemeyer, and Theda Skocpol. 1985. *Bringing the State Back In*. Cambridge: Cambridge University Press.

Form, William, and Kyuttan Bae. 1988. "Convergence Theory and the Korean Connection." *Social Forces* 66:618–44.

Frank, Andre Gunder. 1969. *Latin America: Underdevelopment or Revolution*. New York: Monthly Review.

———. 1980. *Crisis: in the World Economy*. New York: Holmes and Meier.

Frieden, Jeff. 1981. "Third World Indebted Industrialization: International Finance in Mexico, Brazil, Algeria and South Korea." *International Organization* 35:407–31.

Froebel, V., J. Heinrichs, and O. Kreye. 1980. *The New International Division of Labor*. Cambridge: Cambridge University Press.

Furtado, Celso. 1965. *Diagnosis of the Brazilian Crisis*. Berkeley: University of California Press.

———. 1970. *Economic Development of Latin America: Historical Background and Contemporary Problems*. Cambridge: Cambridge University Press.

———. 1973. "The Concept of External Dependence in the Study of Underdevelopment." In Charles Wilber (ed.), *The Political Economy of Development and Underdevelopment*. New York: Random House.

Galtung, Johann. 1971. "A Structural Theory of Imperialism." *Journal of Peace Research* 8:81–117.

Gerschenkron, Alexander. 1962. *Economic Backwardness in Historical Perspective*. Cambridge, MA: Harvard University Press.

Gillis, Malcolm, Dwight Perkins, Michael Roemer, and Donald Snodgrass. 1987. *Economics of Development*, 2d ed. New York: W. W. Norton.

Gold, David A., Clarence Y. Lo, and Erik Olin Wright. 1975. "Recent Developments in Marx's Theories of the Capitalist State." *Monthly Review* 27 (October): 29–51.

Gorham, Lucy. 1987. *No Longer Leading: A Scorecard on U.S. Economic Performance*. Washington, DC: Economic Policy Institute.

Gorin, Zeev. 1985. "Socialist Societies and World System Theory." *Science and Society* 59:332–66.

Gouldner, Alvin. 1970. *The Coming Crisis of Western Sociology*. New York: Basic Books.

———. 1980. *The Two Marxisms: Contradictions and Anomalies in the Development of Theory*. New York: Seabury.

Grant, Wyn. 1985. "Introduction." Pp. 1–31 in Wyn Grant (ed.), *The Political Economy of Corporatism*. New York: St. Martin's Press.

Hage, Jerald, and Kurt Finsterbusch. 1987. *Organizational Change as a Development Strategy: Models and Tactics for Improving Third World Organizations*. Boulder, CO: Lynne Rienner.

Hage, Jerald, Maurice A. Garnier, and Bruce Fuller. 1988. "The Active State, Investment in Human Capital, and Economic Growth: France 1825–1975." *American Sociological Review* 53:824–37.

Hagen, Everett E. 1962. *On the Theory of Social Change*. Homewood, IL: Dorsey Press.

Haggard, Stephen, and Tun-jen Cheng. 1986. "State and Foreign Capital in the 'Gang of Four.' " Pp. 84–135 in Frederick Deyo (ed.), *The New East Asian Industrialization*. Ithaca, NY: Cornell University Press.

Hamilton, Gary G., and Nicole Woolsey Biggart. 1988. "Market, Culture and Authority: A Comparative Analysis of Management and Organization in the Far East." *American Journal of Sociology* 94 (supp.): 52–94.

Hamilton, Richard F., and James D. Wright. 1986. *The State of the Masses*. New York: Aldine.

Harbison, Frederick. *Human Resources as the Wealth of Nations*. New York: Oxford University Press.

Harvey, David. 1982. *The Limits to Capital*. Chicago: University of Chicago Press.

Hayek, Frederick A. von. 1935. *Collectivist Economic Planning*. London: Routledge and Kegan Paul.

Hicks, Alexander. 1988. "National Collective Action and Economic Performance: A Review Article." *International Studies Quarterly* 32:131–53.

Hirschman, Albert. 1958. *The Strategy of Economic Development*. New Haven: Yale University Press.

Hoselitz, Bert. 1957. "Economic Growth and Development: Non-economic Factors in Economic Development." *American Economic Review* 47:28–41.

———. 1960. *Sociological Factors in Economic Development*. Glencoe, IL: The Free Press.

Huntington, Samuel. 1968. *Political Order in Changing Societies*. New Haven: Yale University Press.

Hymer, Stephen. 1970. "The Efficiency (Contradictions) of Multinational Corporations." *American Economic Review* 60:441–48.

———. 1972. "Multinational Corporations and the Law of Uneven Development." Pp. 113–40 in J. N. Bhagwari (ed.), *Economics and World Order: From the 1970's to the 1990's*. New York: Macmillan.

Inkeles, Alex, and David Smith. 1974. *Becoming Modern: Individual Change in Six Developing Countries*. Cambridge, MA: Harvard University Press.

Jaffee, David, and Randall Stokes. 1986. "Foreign Investment and Trade Dependence." *The Sociological Quarterly* 27: 533–46.

Kaplinsky, Raphael. 1984. *Third World Industrialization in the 1980's: Open Economies in a Closing World*. London: Frank Cass.

Katz, Claudio J., Vincent A. Mahler, and Michael G. Franz. 1983. "The Impact of Taxes on Growth and Distribution in Developed Capitalist Countries: A Cross-National Study." *American Political Science Review* 77:871–86.

Katzenstein, Peter J. 1984. *Corporatism and Change: Austria, Switzerland and the Politics of Industry*. Ithaca, NY: Cornell University Press.

———. 1985. *Small States in World Markets: Industrial Policy in Europe*. Ithaca, NY: Cornell University Press.

Kay, Geoffrey. 1975. *Development and Underdevelopment: A Marxist Analysis*. New York: St. Martin's Press.

Kerr, Clark, et al. 1964. *Industrialism and Industrial Man: The Problem of Labor and Management in Economic Growth*. New York: Oxford University Press.

Klaven, Peter. 1977. "The Social and Economic Consequences of Modernization in the Peruvian Sugar Industry, 1870–1930." Pp. 229–52 in Kenneth Duncan and Ian Rutledge (eds.), *Land and Labor in Latin America*. Cambridge: Cambridge University Press.

Kohler, Heinz. 1989. *Comparative Economic Systems*. Glenview, IL: Scott, Foresman.

Kornblum, William. 1988. *Sociology: A Changing World*. New York: Holt, Rinehart and Winston.

Kornhauser, William. 1959. *The Politics of Mass Society*. New York: The Free Press.

Laclau, Ernesto. 1977. *Politics and Ideology in Marxist Theory*. London: New Left Books.

Lall, Sanyaja. 1975. "Is 'Dependence' a Useful Concept in Analyzing Underdevelopment?" *World Development* 3:798–820.

Landsberg, Martin. 1979. "Export-Led Industrialization in the Third World: Manufacturing Imperialism." *The Review of Radical Political Economics* 11(4):50–63.

Lange, Oskar, and Fred Taylor. 1964. *On the Economic Theory of Socialism*. New York: McGraw Hill.

Lawrence, Paul R., and Jay W. Lorsch. 1967. *Organizations and Environment*. Boston: Graduate School of Business Administration, Harvard University.

Lehmann, J. P. 1982. *The Roots of Modern Japan*. London: Macmillan.

Lenin, V. I. 1948. *Imperialism: The Highest Stage of Capitalism*. London: Lawrence and Wishart.

Lerner, Daniel. 1958. *The Passing of Traditional Society*. Glencoe, IL: The Free Press.

Lewis, W. Arthur. 1958. "Economic Development with Unlimited Supplies of Labor." Pp. 400–499 in A. N. Agarwala and S. P. Singh (eds.), *The Economics of Underdevelopment*. New York: Oxford University Press.

Leys, Colin. 1982. "Samuel Huntington and the End of Classical Modernization Theory." Pp. 332–49 in Hamza Alavi and Teodor Shanin (eds.), *Introduction to the Sociology of "Developing Societies."* New York: Monthly Review Press.

Lincoln, James R., and Arne L. Kalleberg. 1985. "Work Organization and Workforce Commitment: A Study of Plants and Employees in the U.S. and Japan." *American Sociological Review* 50:738–60.

Lipset, S. M. 1960. *Political Man*. Garden City, NY: Doubleday.

Lowy, Michael. 1989. "Weber Against Marx? The Polemic with Historical Materialism in the Protestant Ethic." *Science and Society* 53:71–83.

Luke, Timothy, and Carl Boggs. 1982. "Soviet Subimperialism and the Crisis of Bureaucratic Centralism." *Studies in Comparative Communism* 15:95–124.

MacEwan, Arthur, and William K. Tabb. 1989a. "The Economy in Crisis: National Power and International Instability." *Socialist Review* 89(3):67–91.

————. 1989b. *Essays on Instability and Change in the World Economy*. New York: Monthly Review Press.

Macpherson, C. B. 1973. *Democratic Theory: Essays in Retrieval*. Oxford: Clarendon Press.

Mandel, Ernst. 1976. *Late Capitalism*. London: New Left Books.

Mandle, Jay R. 1980. "Basic Needs and Economic Systems." *Review of Social Economics* 38:179–89.

Martin, Andrew. 1979. "The Dynamics of Change in a Keynesian Political Economy." Pp. 88–121 in Colin Crouch (ed.), *State and Economy in Contemporary Capitalism*. London: Croom Helm.

Marx, Karl. 1930. *Capital: A Critique of Political Economy* Vol. 2. London: J. M. Dent and Sons.

Massey, Doreen. 1985. *Spatial Divisions of Labor*. New York: Methuen.

McClelland, David. 1961. *The Achieving Society*. New York: The Free Press.

Miliband, Ralph. 1977. *Marxism and Politics*. Oxford: Oxford University Press.

Mills, C. Wright. 1956. *The Power Elite*. New York: Oxford University Press.

Mintz, Beth, and Michael Schwartz. 1985. *The Power Structure of American Business*. Chicago: University of Chicago Press.

Moore, Barrington. 1967. *Social Origins of Dictatorship and Democracy: Lord and Peasant in the Making of the Modern World*. Boston: Beacon Press.

Morawetz, David. 1977. *Twenty-five Years of Economic Development, 1950–1975*. Baltimore: Johns Hopkins University Press.

Morishima, M. 1983. *Why Has Japan "Succeeded"?* Cambridge: Cambridge University Press.

Nove, Alec. 1983. *The Economics of Feasible Socialism*. London: Allen and Unwin.

Nurkse, Ragner. 1962. *Problems of Capital Formation in Underdeveloped Areas*. New York: Oxford University Press.

O'Connor, James. 1973. *The Fiscal Crisis of the State*. New York: St. Martin's Press.

————. 1984. *Accumulation Crisis*. New York: Basil and Blackwell.

O'Donnell, Guillermo. 1973. *Modernization and Bureaucratic-Authoritarianism: Studies in South American Politics*. Berkeley: Institute of International Studies, University of California.

————. 1978. "Reflections on the Patterns of Change in the Bureaucratic Authoritarian State." *Latin American Research Review* 13:3–38.

————. 1979. "Tensions in the Bureaucratic Authoritarian State and the Question of Democracy." Pp. 285–318 in D. Collier (ed.), *The New Authoritarianism in Latin America*. Princeton, NJ: Princeton University Press.

Offe, Claus, and Helmut Wiesenthal. 1980. "Two Logics of Collective Action: Theoretical Notes on Social Class and Organizational Form." Pp. 67–115 in Maurice Zeitlin (ed.), *Political Power and Social Theory*, Vol. 1. Greenwich, CT: JAI.

Olson, Mancur. 1965. *The Logic of Collective Action*. Cambridge, MA: Harvard University Press.

————. 1982. *The Rise and Decline of Nations: Economic Growth, Stagflation and Social Rigidities*. New Haven: Yale University Press.

Ouchi, William G. 1981. *Theory Z: How American Businesses Can Meet the Japanese Challenge*. Reading, MA: Addison-Wesley.

Paige, Jeffery M. 1975. *Agrarian Revolution: Social Movements and Export Agriculture in the Underdeveloped World*. New York: Free Press.

Palma, Gabriel. 1978. "Dependency: A Formal Theory of Underdevelopment or a Methodology for the Analysis of Concrete Situations of Underdevelopment?" *World Development* 6:881–924.

Panitch, Leon. 1979. "The Development of Corporatism in Liberal Democracies." Pp. 119–46 in P. Schmitter and G. Lehmbruch (eds.), *Trends Toward Corporatist Intermediation*. Beverly Hills, CA: Sage.

———. 1980. "Recent Theorisations of Corporatism: Reflections on a Growth Industry." *British Journal of Sociology* 31:161–87.

Parsons, Talcott. 1951. *The Social System*. Glencoe, IL: The Free Press.

Peacock, Walter Gillis, Greg A. Hoover, and Charles D. Killian. 1988. "Divergence and Convergence in International Development: A Decomposition Analysis of Inequality in the World System." *American Sociological Review* 53:838–52.

Perrow, Charles. 1986. *Complex Organizations: A Critical Perspective*. New York: Random House.

Petras, James F. 1970. *Politics and Social Structure in Latin America*. New York: Monthly Review Press.

———. 1981. *Class, State, and Power in The Third World*. Montclair, NJ: Allenheld, Osmun.

———. 1983. *Capitalist and Socialist Crises in the Late Twentieth Century*. Totowa, NJ: Rowman and Allenheld.

Piven, Frances Fox, and Richard Cloward. 1971. *Regulating the Poor*. New York: Pantheon.

———. 1982. *The New Class War*. New York: Praeger.

Portes, Alejandro. 1976. "On the Sociology of National Development: Theories and Issues." *American Journal of Sociology* 82:55–85.

Portes, Alejandro, and John Walton. 1981. *Labor, Class, and the International System*. New York: Academic Press.

Prebisch, Raul. 1950. *The Economic Development of Latin America and Its Principal Problems*. New York: United Nations.

Prosterman, Roy L., and Jeffrey M. Riedinger. 1987. *Land Reform and Democratic Development*. Baltimore: Johns Hopkins University Press.

Pye, Lucian. 1968. "The Concept of Political Development." Pp. 83–91 in Jason L. Finkle and Richard W. Gable (eds.), *Political Development and Social Change*. New York: John Wiley and Sons.

Ricardo, David. 1933. *Principles of Political Economy and Taxation*. London: Dent. (1817)

Rostow, W. W. 1956. "The Take-off into Self-sustained Growth." *The Economic Journal* 66:25–48.

———. 1960. *The Stages of Economic Growth: A Non-Communist Manifesto*. Cambridge: Cambridge University Press.

Ruccio, David F., and Lawrence H. Simon. 1988. "Radical Theories of Development: Frank, the Models of Production School, and Amin." Pp. 121–73 in Charles K. Wilber (ed.), *The Political Economy of Development and Under-Development*, 4th ed. New York: Random House.

Samater, Ibrahim M. 1984. "From 'Growth' to 'Basic Needs': The Evolution of Development Theory." *Monthly Review* 36:1–13.

Schmidt, M. 1982. "Does Corporatism Matter? Economic Crisis, Politics and Rates of Unemployment in Capitalist Democracies in the 1970's." Pp. 237–58 in G.

Lehmbruch and P. C. Schmitter (eds.), *Patterns of Corporate Policy Making*. Beverly Hills, CA: Sage.

Schmitter, Phillipe. 1981. "Interest Intermediation and Regime Governability in Contemporary Western Europe and North America." Pp. 285–327 in S. Berger (ed.), *Organizing Interests in Western Europe*. New York: Cambridge University Press.

Schumpeter, Joseph. 1949. *Change and the Entrepreneur*. Cambridge, MA: Harvard University Press.

Scott, W. Richard. 1981. *Organizations: Rational, Natural and Open Systems*. Englewood Cliffs, NJ: Prentice Hall.

Sender, John, and Sheila Smith. 1986. *The Development of Capitalism in Africa*. New York: Methuen.

Sidelsky, Robert. 1979. "The Decline of Keynesian Politics." Pp. 55–87 in Colin Crouch (ed.), *State and Economy in Contemporary Capitalism*. London: Croom Helm.

Simmons, John. 1979. "Education for Development, Reconsidered." *World Development* 11/12:1005–16.

———. 1983. "Education for Development, Reconsidered." In Michael P. Todaro (ed.), *The Struggle for Economic Development*. New York: Longman.

Singer, Hans. 1979. "Dualism Revisited: A New Approach to Problems of Dual Societies in Developing Countries." *Journal of Development Studies* 7:55–67.

Singer, J. David. 1961. "The Level of Analysis Problem in International Relations." Pp. 77–92 in Klaus Knorr and Sidney Verba (eds.), *The International System: Theoretical Essays*. Princeton, NJ: Princeton University Press.

Skocpol, Theda. 1977. "Wallerstein's World Capitalist System: A Theoretical and Historical Critique." *American Journal of Sociology* 82:1075–90.

Smelser, Neil. 1963. *The Sociology of Economic Life*. Englewood Cliffs, NJ: Prentice-Hall, Inc.

Smelser, Neil J., and Talcott Parsons. 1956. *Economy and Society*. Glencoe, IL: The Free Press.

Spencer, Martin E. 1987. "The Imperfect Empiricism of the Social Sciences." *Sociological Forum* 2:331–72.

Spengler, J. J. 1966. "Economic Development: Political Pre-conditions and Political Consequences." Pp. 253–68 in Jason L. Finkle and Richard W. Gable (eds.), *Political Development and Social Change*. New York: John Wiley.

Stark, David. 1986. "Rethinking Internal Labor Markets: New Insights from a Comparative Perspective." *American Sociological Review* 51:492–504.

Stewart, Frances, and Paul Streeten. 1976. "New Strategies for Development: Poverty, Income Distribution and Growth." *Oxford Economic Papers* 28:381–405.

Stinchcombe, Arthur. 1961. "Agricultural Enterprise and Rural Class Relations." *American Journal of Sociology* 67:165–76.

Stokes, Randall G. 1975. "How Long Is the Long Run: Race and Industrialization." *International Review of Community Development* 33–34:123–36.

Storper, M., and R. Walker. 1982. "The Theory of Labor and the Theory of Location." *International Journal of Urban and Regional Research* 7:1–41.

Streeten, Paul. 1977. "The Distinctive Features of a Basic Needs Approach to Development." *International Development Review* 19:8–16.

Sunkel, Osvaldo, and Pedro Paz. 1970. *El Subdesarrollo Latinoamericano y la Teoría del Desarrollo*. Madrid: Siglo Veintiuno de España Editores.

Takeo, Tsuchiya. 1978. "Free Trade Zones in Southeast Asia." *Monthly Review* 29:9–15.

Theodorson, George A. 1966. "Acceptance of Industrialization and Its Attendant Conse-
quences for the Social Patterns of Non-Western Societies." Pp. 297–304 in Jason
L. Finkle and Richard W. Gable (eds.), *Political Development and Social
Change*. New York: John Wiley.

Thurow, Lester. 1970. *Investment in Human Capital*. Belmont, CA: Wadsworth.

———. 1983. *Dangerous Currents: The State of Economics*. New York: Random House.

———. 1985. *The Zero-Sum Solution*. New York: Simon and Schuster.

Timberlake, Michael, and Jeffrey Kentor. 1983. "Economic Dependence, Overurbanization and Economic Growth: A Study of Less Developed Countries." *Sociological Quarterly* 24:489–507.

Tönnies, Ferdinand. 1963. *Community and Society*. Translated by C. P. Loomis. New
York: Harper and Row.

Trotsky, Leon. 1959. *The Russian Revolution*. Garden City, NY: Doubleday.

Valenzuela, J. Samuel, and Arturo Valenzuela. 1984. "Modernization and Dependency:
Alternative Perspectives in the Study of Latin American Underdevelopment."
Pp. 105–18 in Mitchell A. Seligson (ed.), *The Gap Between Rich and Poor:
Contending Perspectives on the Political Economy of Development*. Boulder,
CO: Westview.

Vanneman, Reeve, and Lynn Weber Cannon. 1987. *The American Perception of Class*.
Philadelphia: Temple University Press.

Verba, Sidney, and Norman Nie. 1972. *Democracy and Social Equality*. New York:
Harper and Row.

Vernon, Raymond. 1966. "International Investment and International Trade in the
Product Cycle." *Quarterly Journal of Economics* 80:190–207.

Wallerstein, Immanuel. 1974. *The Modern World-System: Capitalist Agriculture and the
Origins of the European World-Economy in the Sixteenth Century*. New York:
Academic Press.

———. 1979. *The Capitalist World Economy*. New York: Cambridge University Press.

———. 1984. "The Present State of the Debate on World Inequality." Pp. 119–32 in
Mitchell A. Seligson (ed.), *The Gap Between Rich and Poor: Contending
Perspectives on the Political Economy of Development*. Boulder, CO: Westview.

Ward, Kathryn. 1984. *Women in the World-System: Its Impact on Status and Fertility*.
New York: Praeger.

———. 1987. "The Impoverishment of U.S. Women and the Decline of U.S.
Hegemony." Pp. 275–90 in Terry Boswell and Albert Bergesen (eds.), *America's
Changing Role in the World System*. New York: Praeger.

Warren, Bill. 1980. *Imperialism: Pioneer of Capitalism*. London: Verso.

Weaver, James, Keith P. Jameson, and Richard N. Blue. 1978. "Growth and Equity: Can
They Be Happy Together?" *International Development Review* 20:20–27.

Weber, Max. 1930. *The Protestant Ethic and the Spirit of Capitalism*. London: Allen and
Unwin.

———. 1947. *The Theory of Social and Economic Organization*. Translated by A. M.
Henderson and Talcott Parsons. New York: Oxford University Press.

Weisskopf, Thomas E., Samuel Bowles, and David M. Gordon. 1985. "Two Views of
Capitalist Stagnation: Underconsumption and Challenges to Capitalist Control." *Science and Society* 49 (Fall): 259–86.

Wharton, Clifton. 1983. "Risk, Uncertainty and the Subsistence Farmer." Pp. 234–38 in
Michael P. Todaro (ed.), *The Struggle for Economic Development*. New York:
Longman.

Williamson, Oliver. 1975. *Markets and Hierarchies: Analysis and Antitrust Implications.* New York: The Free Press.

Wolf, Eric R., and Sidney W. Mintz. 1957. "Haciendas and Plantations in Middle America and the Antilles." *Social and Economic Studies* 6:380–412.

Woodward, Joan. 1965. *Industrial Organization: Theory and Practice.* New York: Oxford University Press.

World Bank. 1980. *World Development Report, 1980.* New York: Oxford University Press.

———. 1987. *World Development Report, 1987.* New York: Oxford University Press.

———. 1988. *World Development Report, 1988.* New York: Oxford University Press.

Wright, James D. 1976. *The Dissent of the Governed.* New York: Academic Press.

Zimbalist, Andrew, and Howard J. Sherman. 1984. *Comparing Economic Systems: A Political Economic Approach.* Orlando, FL: Academia.

INDEX

ABOUT THE AUTHOR

DAVID JAFFEE is currently an assistant professor of sociology at the State University of New York at New Paltz. He received his B.A. from the University of Florida in 1977 and his M.A. from Washington University, St. Louis, in 1980, both in political science. In 1984 he received a Ph.D. in sociology from the University of Massachusetts at Amherst.

Jaffee teaches courses in social and economic development, organization theory, social statistics, and introductory sociology.

He has published articles in *Social Forces, Social Problems, The Sociological Quarterly*, and *The Social Science Quarterly* on trade dependence and economic growth, the effects of foreign investment on less-developed economies, the political economy of deindustrialization, and gender inequality in the work place.